RATED X

THE MORAL CASE
AGAINST TV

RATED X

THE MORAL CASE AGAINST TV

MARY LEWIS COAKLEY

ARLINGTON HOUSE·PUBLISHERS
NEW ROCHELLE, NEW YORK

P 10 9 8 7 6 5 4 3 2 1

Manufactured in the United States of America

Library of Congress Cataloging in Publication Data

Coakley, Mary Lewis, 1907-
   Rated X.

   Includes index.
   1. Television broadcasting—United States—Moral and
religious aspects.   I.   Title.
PN 1992.6.C6   791.45'0973   77-25045
ISBN 0-87000-400-X

Contents

Acknowledgments

I wish to thank:

JACK EDMUND NOLAN, who gave me advice and suggestions as well as information. Mr. Nolan was for years a TV reviewer for *Films in Review*, and contributor to dozens of movie and TV magazines in this country and in Europe. Presently he is working on many projects about the Right, Left, and Center in the media.

JOHN BOLAND, who sent me clippings that were pertinent to my subject. Mr. Boland formerly wrote for the *Jefferson City* (Mo.) *News-Tribune*, and has contributed to *Human Events, Friar, National Review*, the *Wanderer, National Catholic Register*, and other organs.

OLGA GILLESPIE, a friend, who acted as a one-woman clipping service, collecting for me newspaper and magazine articles about TV.

RATED X

THE MORAL CASE
AGAINST TV

Chapter 1

What Are You Looking At?

Household God

"Why get married when you can live together?"

The god has spoken—our household god, yours and mine. He happened to speak these words on "All's Fair," but he has repeated the same thought on dozens of other shows.

This god of ours is, of course, that electronic box we call TV. We give him, or it, a place of honor in our livingroom and we enshrine duplicate deities, big and small, in a variety of places from the basement workshop to the bedrooms on the second floor.

What does this god do for us?

Well, it is great at implanting ideas. As Fred Friendly (professor of broadcast journalism at Columbia University and former president of CBS News) said on Bill Buckley's "Firing Line," "Broadcasting is going to determine what kind of people we are . . ."

But many of us plead that our god has tricked us. It slipped

11

in like a Trojan horse. Long ago, when we let the thing come into our homes and gave it a central position there, we didn't suspect that it might debase or even destroy values that we cherish. Now that our suspicions are aroused, we are criticizing it.

Oh, admittedly, we have always groused about TV to some extent, but today our criticism is different because TV itself is different.

Remember when Newton Minow, former chairman of the Federal Communications Commission, called television "a vast wasteland"? He was speaking mainly of its banalities. But that was back in the 60s, which is almost like saying it was back when dinosaurs roamed the earth; TV has changed that markedly.

Though we still have the banalities (like the poor, they are always with us), TV in recent years has brought to bloom a whole new crop of undesirables that were barely glimpsed until the 70s.

Then and Now

On November 21, 1976 NBC put on a program called "Big Event," celebrating its 50 years in radio and television. Actually, for television, it was the last 20 to 25 years, since the first national television programs were not broadcast until 1947, and television did not become a factor in American homes until the early 50s.

To see the past on parade was an amazingly nostalgic experience for those of us with long memories. It was to return to a world that, we realized with a start, has gone with the wind as surely as has the world of Scarlett O'Hara and Rhett Butler. Fifteen years ago, ten years ago, even eight years ago, so much seemed delightful, refreshing, and full of fun. Today, by contrast, nearly all TV offerings are soiled by an obsession with sex and a sneering attitude toward the traditional underpinnings of American society.

Daytime TV, 1977, by Jason Bonderoff, says of the soap opera "The Young and the Restless" that it "brought an end to the 'innocent years' . . . by introducing rape, prostitution, incest, alcoholism, and insanity."

Yes, a new era was ushered in somewhere close to 1970, and it seems to be one of reckless hedonism and hostility toward morals, religion, marriage, free enterprise, family, and country. As one viewer put it, "America is being buried alive in prime time and we're paying for the funeral."

It Adds Up

It is not so much that any one particular program is, for instance, violent, or reeking with sick sex, or oozing anti-Americanism; rather it is that almost every program is tinged or tainted to some degree. To cite a single phrase or scene that offends some viewers seems like nit-picking. Instead, we must gather them into a pile to see them. One slightly suggestive remark, one brief erotic scene, one barb thrown at an American historical hero or at a religious tenet, by itself might well seem as infinitesimally small as a snowflake; but it is the cumulative effect, the constant, ever-falling stuff that does the trick—that implants ideas and corrodes the national soul.

The ideas are fairly easy to spot once we get the hang of it, for they appear and reappear in slightly different guise in program after program. We can make a game of tracing them as we might trace the strands of red, yellow, or green wool in a length of tweed material. "All in the Family" may have an episode about homosexuality, the next week "Mary Hartman, Mary Hartman" may have one, the next week "Family," and so on until pretty soon homosexuality seems to us as normal and as natural and acceptable as heterosexuality. It might even seem more so. On "The Nancy Walker Show" of October 7, 1976, Nancy and her husband were arguing about his fidelity, and Nancy's male secretary remarked, "Oh, you 'silly heterosexuals.'"

It was good for a laugh and seemed at the moment to have an element of truth in it. A few more shows on the same theme and the innuendo would seem completely true.

So it goes with other idea-strands running through TV.

13

Everybody, Everywhere, All the Time

And none of us, it seems, can avoid watching TV. We would feel as though we had moved to Mars if we didn't know what our friends were talking about when they mentioned Archie Bunker, or Kojak, or Rhoda, or Fonzie.

Whether we like it or not, TV is an integral part of our lives. It is not just another form of entertainment, comparable to the movies, or a bridge game, or bowling, or golf. It is not something that some of us leave our homes to do once a month, or once a week, or three times a week. It is right there in the house, as much a fixture as the kitchen sink, and it runs every day, and in some families, all day long.

About 97 percent of all dwellings in America sport television sets. In his book *Children and Television* Gerald S.

"That's the trouble with TV—you find yourself taking it everywhere."

Lesser says, "More families have sets than have bathtubs, telephones, toasters, vacuum cleaners, or a regular daily newspaper."

He adds that even in the worst poverty pockets of Appalachia, where the average income is below $5,000, over 95 percent of the families have sets. After all, a person doesn't even have to know how to read to look at television.

Other experts support Mr. Lesser's figures and his statements. The dust-jacket blurb on Terry Galoney's book *Tonight!* talks about just one particular show among hundreds, "The Tonight Show," and says that it has reached "more people than all the rock-festivals, coronations, football games, white-sales, crusades, pilgrimages to Mecca, and all the people on public transportation at five o'clock everywhere. . . . [It] takes more time out of viewers' lives than their dinner, their love-making, their exercising, their reading, or other recreations."

Growing, Growing, Growing

Moreover, every year the vast army of TV viewers grows, despite a declining birth rate, because families are no longer content with one or two sets. Sets are scattered all through the house because each child now wants a set for his or her bedroom, Mom wants a portable mini-set to take with her into the kitchen while she cooks dinner, or into the laundry while she irons, and Dad wants one for his den or the office he fixed up in the room over the garage. The total number of viewing hours is rising with each passing day.

The *Report of the Surgeon General, United States Public Health Service*, which came out in 1972, stated that even then, "more than one-third of the U.S. families now own more than one television set."

Fred Friendly, quoted above, said that the average American watches TV over six hours a day.* An exaggeration, we

* During January 1977, when much of the country suffered bitter cold weather, the Bureau of Advertising reported that average daily TV viewing reached 7 hours and 12 minutes.

15

say? Actually, that's not the whole story; often people absorb subliminally more than six or seven hours' worth of TV influence since in some families the set is never turned off except for sleep at night.

Television is not like the theater or ballet; we don't have to keep our eyes on it every minute in order to follow a show. We can polish the silver or paint the wainscot and still know what's happening on the screen, because its programs are designed to have virtually continuous dialogue.

In 1972 a book entitled *The Marvin Kitman Show* appeared; author Kitman spoke of the Con Edison advertising campaign to save energy: one way "to save a watt" was to "turn off television sets . . . when you are not looking or listening." Kitman commented, "The structure of television is based on people leaving their sets on when they are not watching or listening to them." He adds, perhaps with tongue in cheek, "Actually, TV sets rank in the extreme bottom group of electricity-consuming devices, along with radios, little corner-table lamps, and electric clocks. It is just as logical for Con Edison to warn the public, 'Turn off your electric clock when not reading time.' "

Apparently, people don't know that they can live without TV. In about 95 percent of the cases of TV breakdown, a repairman is called within 24 hours.

Once a small town in North Carolina was cut off from TV for three days. Writing about the incident in *TV Guide* (November 13, 1976), Ed Williams said that everybody in the place was jittery and fidgety; they didn't know what to do with themselves. And, he added, the proprietor of "the Chadbourn Motel had something in common with a lion-tamer who was locked in the cage empty-handed at feeding-time." His guests were that restless.

They must all have been like the man the *Wall Street Journal* mentioned in an article of October 21, 1976. One summer he and his family went camping and he said, "It was so quiet I nearly went out of my mind until we got out the portable television, and I could relax. I said, 'Never again.' I'll take a motel with television any time."

16

Generation Gap

Those of us who were born before 1950 cannot really grasp how much TV means to people younger than ourselves. To us, it is just one form of entertainment; we can take it or leave it—though mostly we take it.

Not so the post-1950 generation. To them, it is *the* preeminent form of entertainment, and their primary link with the world at large. It is the biggest part of their education. They could probably give up a second or third set less easily than an alcoholic could forswear liquor, and they have no organization like Alcoholics Anonymous to help them do it.

Bigger and Bolder

In fact, everything encourages them—and us—to increase, if possible, our viewing of TV. For one thing, the technical excellence of TV constantly improves. The new sets feature an invisible color standard called the vertical interval reference (VIR) used by broadcasters to keep the colors right from the time the show is broadcast until it gets to our homes. The VIR travels along with the picture, and the new sets use it to adjust color intensity and tint at the receiving end.

Moreover, cable television is coming; indeed, is already here. About one U.S. household in seven is connected to a cable system. A cable can carry 30 TV channels into every home. Then, video cassettes will give us a wider choice of viewing fare. We will be able to build up a library of cartridges, plug in and tune in whatever program we like, when we like. Two-way interactive television will allow real exchanges between television and the audience.

So TV goes on and on, becoming, though not better, bigger and bolder all the time. It is a fact of life. At this point, we could no more stop it than we could stop the rotation of the Earth.

But who wants to?

Probably none of us wants to stop it permanently. Some of us, however, would like to make changes in it.

What changes?

Well, let's see what needs changing. It might take a whole book to do that.

Chapter 2

Anything Goes

Wanton Words

Bill Buckley once declared on "Firing Line" that Pasteur emptied a drawingroom by using one unacceptable word. Somebody asked the scientist what he was working on and he answered, "Syphilis," whereupon everybody got up and left.

Baby, we've come a long way—or have we regressed? Now, thanks to television, VD is often mentioned in the livingroom, and nobody moves unless it is to find a spot that affords a better view of the screen.

Agnes Nixon, queen of the soap-opera scripters, is the moving spirit behind ABC's "One Life to Live." In one episode she had Cathy Craig, a newspaper reporter, talk at length about the story she was writing on the VD epidemic.

Tom Hartman, Mary's husband in "Mary Hartman, Mary Hartman" (the serial so popular during the 1976-77 TV season),* spoke of his fear of having contracted the disease during his sessions with his girlfriend at the auto plant.

The girlfriend of J.J., a character in "Good Times," told him that she had VD and that he had given it to her.

But social disease is only one favorite topic of TV dialogue. As one writer remarked, "TV characters are relentlessly uninhibited conversationalists. There is nothing they will not discuss."

In the process, they often use language that is anything but delicate. Terry Galoney, in his book *Tonight!*, said, "All the four-letter words have been part of the proceedings at one time or another" on NBC's late-night television. Many actors and actresses, he noted, have had their mouths washed out with "bleep soap." But not enough.

Along with the four-letter words go a few profane ones—just for seasoning. Or maybe it is more than a few. Kay Gardella of the New York News Service wrote that "without question 'God' is one of the most abused words in television dialogue. 'Damn' and 'hell' are tossed around like confetti at a wedding."

Though some of this profanity may be excusable on the grounds of realism, much of it is not excusable on any grounds. It may not have been pleasant, but it was probably realistic to hear Pat of "Mary Hartman, Mary Hartman" say to that despicable bully, her wife-beating husband, "Take your God-damn hands off me." How different and how much worse to hear writers Henry Miller and Norman Mailer punctuate their entire conversation on "The Today Show" with the word "Christ." Christ this, Christ that. What did they gain by dragging His name in the mud?

And Actions Speak Louder

Now let's focus for a minute on the action we see on the screen. In the book just quoted, *Tonight!*, Mr. Galoney stated

---

* Although this show has been axed, it spawned two sequels, "Forever Fernwood" and "Fernwood Tonight." Both are set in Mary's hometown and feature some of the regulars, but not Louise Lasser, who played Mary.

that TV has been just about fearless in choosing guests and subjects, and he mentioned everything and everyone from bomb throwers to bigots. His list, however, did not include—though it could have—Satanists, wife-swappers, homosexuals, rapists, and other perverts. Whatever appears in the rankest scandal sheets, TV takes for its own, blowing it up until it is larger than life. In a weird, nightmarish way, TV shows us our culture at its worst. It contains elements of the true and the false, like any wild distortion, but the overall effect is almost totally false.

In August 1976, for example, NBC ran the movie *Klute*, which is the story of a callgirl and her sadistic lover. Not to be outdone, ABC in November put on the almost unbelievably bestial and brutal *Nightmare in Badham County*. In it a black girl is raped by a small-town white sheriff while her friend in another jail cell hears and partially sees what is going on. A "minor" incident in the same show concerned a white girl who is subjected to sexual molestation and, to escape more of the same, slashes her wrists. In the topsy-turvy world of television, prostitutes and perverts seem to be privileged characters.

Al Haas, writing in the *Philadelphia Inquirer*, commented that practically everything has been stricken from the old list of taboos: "Drugs and abortion came off some time ago. Prostitution and pimps are more recent." He ended by saying that about the only thing declared out of bounds was bondage—and he wasn't speaking quite accurately when he made that exception.

There are certainly plenty of dope addicts and pushers. It is not unusual to find, on the same evening, two programs built around narcotics. On October 8, 1976, both "Serpico" and "The Rockford Files" were devoted to drugs. In early January of 1977 NBC ran a film based on Thomas Thompson's *Richie*, the grisly (and true) account of a father who killed his dope-addicted son. As far back as 1968, when the soap opera "One Life to Live" was new on television, the script writers introduced dope addiction as part of the plot. Several episodes were taped on location at an actual drug rehabilitation center. No wonder some wag has remarked, "TV programs could no more get by without a drug problem than they could get by without a sponsor."

Marijuana is old hat, of course. It was treated as a joke on "The Nancy Walker Show" (October 21, 1976). When Nancy's husband demurred about trying it, wondering if it might lead to an evil habit, Nancy answered that " 'evil' spelled backwards is 'live.' " Nancy couldn't have put it better. That is exactly what most TV characters seem to believe.

In our parents' day, people used to think that fornication and adultery were evils that threatened to destroy the family; to TV characters today they are as natural as sunset over Waikiki. These fictional people wouldn't know how to go on from day to day without their favorite pastimes. In fact, there is enough adultery and fornication and kinky sex on TV to fill a separate and sexplicit chapter later. This chapter will merely disentangle and sort out the different strands that appear and reappear, with sickening regularity, on current TV.

Another recurring theme on TV is anti-Americanism: hatred for the "Establishment" and favoritism toward far-outs. That certainly needs a separate chapter, though it is enmeshed in other subjects.

Giving the Devil His Due

We hear more complaints about TV violence and gore than about anything else. There will be plenty of time to air our grievances about this as we go along. Even more objectionable, perhaps, is the antireligious or irreligious strand that runs through TV. "Give 'em hell" must be the slogan of many producers, if we may judge by the Satanism that has become fashionable on television during the past five years. In September 1973 ABC put on a feature called "Satan's School for Girls." Written by Margaret Armen, it combined devil worship with lesbianism. The same year, the networks presented "The Cat Creature," "Devil's Daughter," and "Poor Devil," every one dealing with Satanism.

Norman Lear produced and presented in the summer of 1977 a show entitled "A Year at the Top." It was about aging musicians who, like Faust, sell their souls to the devil in exchange for favors. They want a year of popularity as a young rock-music group.

In 1976 the movie *Rosemary's Baby*, shown on ABC, again portrayed Satanism. Rosemary bore a child sired by the devil.

What Happened to Rosemary's Baby? followed up the evil and the horror. Devil worship is made to appear fascinating and intriguing. No wonder we have our Charles Mansons.

And in ABC's "Sunday Night Movie" there was *Live and Let Die*, with voodooism as its motif.

Crime and Criminals

So much has been written about TV crime and violence and so many studies have been made of the subject that we are all painfully aware of it. But are we aware of the fact that some TV, with its liberal bias, glorifies, or certainly sympathizes with, real-life criminals?

David Susskind has had criminals on his talk show. Dennis Banks, the radical thug who leads the American Indian Movement (AIM), appeared on "The Today Show." "Gentleman" Dennis Banks started out his career as a burglar, and within a year managed to tote up 15 convictions.

Once out of jail, he helped found the AIM and took over the town of Wounded Knee, South Dakota. He proceeded to sack the place, expelling the Oglala Sioux and destroying property. Then he and his companions cavorted in front of the cameras that thronged the scene.

As James Bormann (director of public affairs, WCCO-TV Minneapolis) wrote, "The militant Indians had a story to tell, but so did the reservation Indians who opposed them. However, it was the militants who got most of the play in the media."

The TV reporters—some of them—admitted, according to the *Arizona Republic*, that they had been taken in, but that didn't stop NBC from having Banks on "The Today Show," along with his AIM confrere Russell Means and actor Marlon Brando.

When the Hanafi Muslims seized three Washington buildings, killed one journalist, and wounded or injured 11 other people, TV gave the event such extensive and repetitive coverage that Patrick Buchanan wrote in *TV Guide* (March 26, 1977), "American TV has become patsy, promoter, and paymaster for political terrorists."

First Prize for Depravity

One program shown during the 1976-77 season seemed to "put it all together," as they say: "Mary Hartman, Mary Hartman," known to the industry as MH2. While it was on the air, MH2 attempted to satirize the whole gamut of TV soap operas and sitcoms, so it had elements of each.

Leading characters in this grab-bag "fun" show were such half-depraved, half-pathetic creatures as Mary's grandfather, who exposed himself to little girls; Mary's sister, a promiscuous lass who didn't know which of her many boyfriends was the father of her baby; Mary's 13-year-old daughter, who complained of menstrual cramps and worried because most girls her age had larger "bazooms"; an eight-year-old preacher, the Reverend Jimmy Joe Jeeter, who was electrocuted in the bathtub when the TV set on which he was watching the evening news fell into his bath water; Ed and Howard, two homosexual "lovers"; Tippy-Toes, who confessed that when she was a little girl her stepfather sexually molested her, and who turned out to be AC-DC; Merle and Wanda, who on their wedding night went their separate ways, he to visit a prostitute, she to visit another woman with the idea of a possible lesbian attachment; a teenager who massacred a family of five people and then, to give a "comic" touch, killed two goats and eight chickens; a blackmailer, who arranged with a hooker to get Mary's father in a compromising position so that rival-union politicos could snap damaging pictures of him; Mary's friend Loretta, and her husband Charlie, who lost a testicle when he was shot with the gun that he meant to use on a man attempting to seduce his wife; Mary's friends Garth, a wife-beater, and his wife Pat, who finally fought back and ended up being accused of murdering her husband with an aluminum Christmas tree; Mary's husband, Tom, an alcoholic who at one time suffered from a "performance problem"—though not with Mona, a girl at the auto plant where he worked; and last, pathetic Mary herself, who had an affair with Dennis and whose life was more involved than the Gordian knot itself. Sometimes, looking at the show, we were tempted to say: "This isn't television. It's a sneak preview of hell."

24

The TV Lifestyle

Marriage fares badly on TV. Rarely do we see a happy couple. Furthermore, odd, far-out marital arrangements are portrayed as though they were just alternative lifestyles. MH2 had its *ménage à trois*: Merle, Lila, and Wanda. The last two had a lesbian thing between them and Merle, the man, slept on occasion with both the women. But, to repeat, more of this later, along with divorce, abortion . . . and other delights.

Just so that we at least list the various TV phenomena, we might mention suicide here. The emotional soaps frequently use it for hype effect.

In "Another World" one of the women characters, Sharlene, when she was forced to reveal her past to her husband, Russ, proceeded to gulp the contents of a bottle of sleeping pills. That made for drama, and drama is the lifeblood of soaps. Screaming sirens tore the air, as Sharlene was rushed off to the hospital.

When we tune in the set, we know we are on our way to an accident—about to happen. Crime shows have automobile crashes by the dozen. Soap operas use accidents as a standby to pep things up. In "Ryan's Hope," for instance, Jack was nearly killed driving home one stormy night. Rushed to the hospital for emergency surgery, he nearly died. His heart stopped beating for seconds as he lay on the operating table; the doctor had to massage it to start it up again. Anything to keep the characters, and hence the viewers, in a state of sustained hysteria.

Murder too makes for drama and some TV scripters lose no opportunity to kill somebody off—and that's not counting the detective and police shows. The public is getting a little sated with the whole ugly picture that so much of TV presents.

The Worm Turns

Syndicated writer Jon-Michael Reed mentioned in a newspaper article that "The Doctors" had alienated viewers. It had become, he said, "negative and indignant." And he went on to talk about the show's "lascivious spectacles" and the "nearly week-long romp in the sack" of the characters Nick and Althea; the "kidnapping of Carolee by Dr. Ann who then waylaid Carolee's husband, Dr. Steve, on the livingroom couch"; the "pubescent panting" of Steve's son; and "revenge-bent" Dr. Paul's "Svengali-like transformation of sweet young thing Stacy into a dope-and-sex fiend."

Some of the scenes between Nick and Althea he described as "steamy."

The same writer, speaking about another show, "As the World Turns," had this to say of its star, Eileen Fulton, who plays the part of Lisa Miller: "The actress was not at all enthralled with playing a 'Goodie-Two-Shoes role,' [so she] quickly peppered the part with overt seasonings of sheer bitchery . . . Lisa lied, deceived, etc. . . ."

Enough is enough. No wonder the public is getting fed up.

Grin and Bare It

There are signs that the public is finding even nudity no longer titillating, but tiresome. Yesterday's sensation is today's ho-hum. Or as Gypsy Rose Lee is supposed to have said, "After you take it all off, what do you do for an encore?"

Yet nudity is still injected into so many shows that there is no avoiding it. For instance, in "Charlie's Angels" (November 24, 1976) Jill applied as a centerfold candidate for a girlie magazine. In "All's Fair" Charley, the girl photographer, on her first visit to Richard, barged into his bathroom while he was showering, and her introduction to him was seeing him in the altogether.

In TV's dramatization of Anton Myrer's book *Once an Eagle*, Sam Elliott's girlfriend unbuttons her blouse to the waist to show him what he's running away from.

Then there are many jokes, quips, and remarks about nudity on TV, from the silly to the sickish.

Sickish was Mary Hartman's explaining "sex exercises"; to

get rid of guilt feelings, she said, one partner stands in front of a mirror nude and describes his or her body.

As we said, nudity on TV is hard to avoid. The TV moguls are so sure that there is a voyeur market that they even inject nudity into news programs.

Probably there have been nudist colonies around from Eve's time onward, but it took until September 1976 for them to make the network news. At that time, CBS had an item on its evening news about a colony in New Jersey. Men and women, completely stripped, sitting in a circle, were filmed and shown in the livingrooms of our land. Admittedly, the shots were taken from the rear, which softened the impact. Moreover, when the nudists were interviewed, the men were shown only from the waist up, the women only from the neck up. But since when is nudism a worthy subject for a national news program? The interviewer himself, to add a cutesy touch, gave the impression that he was nude too. Whether or not he actually was, we will probably never know. When the cameras caught him he was standing behind a bush, and was obviously bare to the waist.

Other nudity, or near-nudity, on TV is more suggestive. In his book *The Marvin Kitman Show* Kitman tells about an appearance Ann-Margret made on "The Johnny Carson Show." As she greeted Johnny with the customary kiss of a guest star, the shawl she was wearing (accidentally?) slid aside, showing apparently bare breasts. The camera, Kitman said, faltered and then focused elsewhere. The NBC censor who spoiled all the fun commented, "We don't care if Ann-Margret goes to parties naked, but the public is not going to the party."

Possibly more distasteful was the silly remark of Mother Dexter, the 86-year-old grandmother on the now-axed "Phyllis": "I had a beautiful dream. I was dancing with Charles Bronson stripped to the waist."

Only a few years ago when TV showed a man and woman in bed together, it showed the naked torso of the man, but the woman wore a nightgown. Who has seen a nightgown on TV lately? Usually, the camera dollies in on the woman, showing her bare shoulders protruding from the covers. A few films have shown her sitting on the side of the bed, her bare back to the camera.

Apparently, TV personnel would have us believe that most

women sleep naked and, of course, that no man has ever heard of pajamas. "Maude" says she will add a little human interest to a press interview by admitting, "I sleep in the raw."

Vulgarity

"Human interest" in TV often means vulgarity thrown in for no apparent artistic reason.

In ABC's "Block Party" one office worker said to another, "We ordered carbon paper and they sent us toilet paper instead."

The reply was, "You should be thankful it wasn't the other way around."

On the same show, a woman said to a man, in the hearing of the office employees, "We'll go to my place and (with a leer) maybe do a little fooling around."

He whispered, "Sssh!"

She said, "Why be so secretive? I like you, you like me. We're grown up people. So we're going to my place and maybe fool around a bit."

A member of the office staff commented, "That's the way it should be. A relationship out in the open."

But if TV speech is often vulgar, so are some of the gestures. In "All's Fair" the girl photographer, Charley, gave her editor the raspberry. On "Hee Haw" a girl said, "I was coming down with a cold but I shook it off." Here the girl (demonstrating that she was wearing no bra) shimmied.

Also vulgar—if not worse—is so much talk of subjects like transsexuals. One whole episode of CBS's "Medical Center" was about a famous vascular surgeon who horrified his wife, his son, and his colleagues by demanding a sex-change operation. Then Ralph Penza on CBS's "Newswatch" at 6 P.M. and 11 P.M., February 21–25, 1977 reported on "transsex realities from Christine Jorgensen to Renée Richards."

Then there was the to-do about Charlie Hagger's testicle. Charlie, a character on MH2 who was shot in the groin after a tussle with another character, consulted a doctor about a testicle transplant. The doctor turned out to be a veterinarian who wanted to use the testicle from a Great Dane dog for the transplant.

Vulgar—if not obscene—is the highlighting of transvestism. In "The Streets of San Francisco," for instance, a male night-club entertainer does his act wearing feminine garb. In "M.A.S.H." Corporal Klinger, a regular in the series, constantly dons women's clothes and poses as a transvestite to win a discharge from the army. In "Chico and the Man" a joke was told about a man who found himself engaged to a man who was a transvestite. In "One Day at a Time," on the *Christmas* show of December 28, 1976, a transvestite appeared, etc., etc., etc.

In trying for shock effect, TV too often portrays the aberrant, the catastrophic, the lurid, the unhappy, the un-American, the subversive, the ultrasexy, and the disruptive. Almost always it is vulgar.

Just about anything goes. Bawdy allusion to, jokes on, and scenes and episodes about striptease artists, harlots, degenerates, junkies, and blackmailers are commonplace, as are obscenity, perversion, seduction, cruelty, dishonesty, euthanasia, sadism, exhibitionism, artificial insemination, alcoholism, greed, treason, and just plain boorishness.

An anonymous wag once said, "Early to bed, early to rise, makes a man miss the late-late show." Small loss! When somebody on "The Johnny Carson Show" asked, "Is it EST, TM, or BM?" someone else gave an answer that was worse than the question. One could only say "Ugh," turn off the set, and go to bed.

Chapter 3

Sexsational

Who's Whose?

Says she, "All right, so I haven't let a man touch me since Dave died! Is that a sin?"

"It's a crime," says he, "a criminal waste of a pretty sensational dame."

Those few lines spoken in a soap opera sum up the attitude of many TV characters, and are as good an opening as any for this chapter about freewheeling sex.

If there is a halfway attractive woman on the scene, it would be a waste, a criminal waste, not to get her to bed quickly with the nearest man . . . or woman.

Fornication and adultery are so common that the different shows tend to merge in the mind and we forget which character belongs in which show. It is a case where the comment "if you've seen one, you've seen them all" most aptly applies.

But not only do we have a hard time keeping the different shows separate in the mind; if we look at only one show, it's a strain to keep the relationships straight. This is true even of a show like "Ryan's Hope," where the characters are not mere marionettes clothed in flesh, but distinct individuals.

In their sexcapades, men and women jump in and out of bed with one another at such a dizzying pace that we need a score pad to keep track of who is sleeping with whom this week, and who is trying to seduce whom. A singer on "Hee Haw" expressed the idea in a song about "makin' love," intoning that "nobody knows who's making love.... Nobody knows who belongs to who."

Sometimes they don't even know which child belongs to whom. Kathy in "Mary Hartman, Mary Hartman" (MH2) wasn't sure by which man she became pregnant. Jill, in "Ryan's Hope," wasn't sure, until she stopped to figure the timing, whether it was Frank or Seneca who fathered her child.

That doesn't faze the denizens of TV land. They continue to change partners as quickly and as casually as other people change coats. In the first episode of "All's Fair," when editor Richard Barrington's mistress of three years, Barbara, left him, saying with a wry smile that she couldn't buck the competition, he didn't bother to see her to the door. Instead, he remained sitting on the floor, cuddling up to girl photographer Charley, whom he had just met. In the next episode, when the new twosome threatened to break up (it didn't), somebody said, "The whole affair was shorter than summer camp."

Guilty Feelings

The notion that these sexual gymnastics might be wrong or immoral or even merely offensive to any segment of the viewing public never seems to occur to TV scripters—or does it?

Somewhere in their subconscious there must lurk a sense of guilt about the sexual license, because occasionally they try to justify it. Some faint remembrance of the commandment "Thou shalt not commit adultery" must have stuck in the hidden crannies of the mind.

In one show, girl says apologetically to boy, "But we *love*

31

one another." That much-abused word love was supposed to make going to bed together right, beautiful, and, above all, "meaningful."

Not dismayed by the contradiction, Jill, in "Ryan's Hope," had been having an affair with Frank, a married man, but then went off with Seneca to spend a few days. Frank had gone back to his wife (temporarily) and Jill explained that her action was prompted mainly by compassion for Seneca. She still loved Frank.

So you see, TV scripters want it both ways. Adultery and fornication are all right as long as you love the person; they are all right too if you don't love the person. The only thing wrong is repression; that can wreck a person's life. In "Secrets" (February 20, 1977) a mother had brought her daughter up to believe in virginity before marriage, and then after marrying Prince Charming, to expect happiness as a faithful matron. The result? When the "repressive" mother died, the victim daughter was triggered into instant nymphomania.

Yes, free love is wholesome. It is proper for the young boy who has just started to shave; it is proper for the wrinkled geezer who needs a cane to hobble across the room. The Findlays' doctor friend, Arthur, in CBS's "Maude" (October 4, 1976) spoke of having an 81-year-old patient who "still has sex three times a week."

In that same episode, Maude tried to persuade her elderly housekeeper-cook, Mrs. Naugatuk, and the woman's aged boyfriend to live together. Maude went so far as to fix up an apartment over her garage for the octogenarian lovebirds. But the old woman complained because, she said, Maude didn't really believe that old people "still get horny."

Garbage Galore

The philosophy portrayed on TV adds up to the popular "do your thing." Pleasure is equated with happiness. In one show, the girl takes the boy to task for not telling her about his mother's life. He answers, "There wasn't anything to tell."

"Well," the girl retorts, "she did leave her husband to run

32

off with another man," whereupon the boy says angrily, "My mother has as much right to happiness as anybody."

TV sex is sometimes crassly commercial. In CBS's "Love of Life" a girl needs money to pay for her mother's hospital bills. Enter a man who suggests that she have sex with him and he will take care of her bills.

Now this kind of behavior has been going on since Adam ate the forbidden fruit, but it is still a messy thing to have flaunted in the livingroom day after day. Garbage—the drippy coffee grounds, the slimy egg shells, the soggy crusts of bread, and the sloppy mashed potatoes with gravy scraped from the dinner plates—has always been a household feature. It's real. Despite disposals, it is a part of life and, yes, it would be dishonest to deny its existence. Garbage is. Still, who wants the stuff dumped into the livingroom, atop the white brocade sofa?

Where Does It Stop?

Certainly, we can turn off the set. Many people do. But that's an unsatisfactory solution. A housebound person, an invalid, or a person with eyesight too poor to read or sew would find TV a godsend if it presented better fare. Come to think of it, anybody in any situation, or in any state of health, welcomes decent and dignified entertainment.

But if we don't like one show, it is often argued, what's to prevent us from changing channels? Nothing—except that it is often like changing from arsenic to cyanide. Switch from "Search for Tomorrow," where Steve accuses Liza of sleeping with Woody, to "All My Children," where Erica is sleeping with her father-in-law . . .

And even when the sexiness is slight and consists of no more than a mildly risqué line here and there, it gets tiresome after a while; it's like trying to laugh at a thrice-told joke.

The songs are usually sexy too. On "The Peter Marshall Show" (NBC, September 18, 1976) a man sang about a girl who took him to a drive-in movie, parked in the back row, and grabbed his leg. The refrain of the song was "Turn loose of my leg. I'm not that kind of man."

When he finished the song, he suggested to the women of his audience that they grab the leg of the man next to them. Cute!

Even documentaries and interviews inject sex whenever possible. In September 1976 public television put on a two-part interview of Helen Singer Kaplan, a sex therapist. Just a few of the terms used, and problems discussed, were "hang-up about masturbation," "erection problem," "tactile stimulation," "vaginal lubrication," "inorgastic women," and "erotic zones."

And TV critic Kay Gardella in her syndicated column mentioned a weather announcer who made "a flip on-air remark about a rape involving an eight-year-old girl."

Sex Mania

In a show like NBC's "People," which zeroed in on celebrities, it was their sex lives that were the focal point. Country singer Loretta Lynn was showcased in the fall of 1976. Her old doctor was with her and he remarked, "When Loretta was 13 I told her, 'Honey, you're pregnant.' She said, 'What's that?' "

Never mind that the baby would be a bastard. Nobody seemed a bit disturbed about that, only amused that Loretta was so ignorant.

Then, on the same show, emcee Lily Tomlin said, "Every time I see a 'yield' sign on the road, I feel sexually threatened."

These people have a sex mania. They are like the legendary Frenchman who said that the Empire State Building reminded him of sex because everything did.

Suggestive one-liners and double entendres are injected into nearly every show. Example: in "All's Fair," when Richard objected to his girlfriend, Charley, having a man stay in her apartment, she answered that he would sleep on the couch and anyway, he was just "sleeping over for the weekend."

"Over whom?" snapped Richard.

Apparently some shows are *planned* as smut vehicles. In her autobiography Shirley MacLaine tells about suggesting to the producer of her short-lived show, "Shirley's Life," that the series could feature her cavorting with "friends all over the world." She would even "go to bed with one of them every once in a while."

In this case, her producer vetoed the idea. That was back in the early 70s. In 1977 a girl in "Secrets" slept with seven different men on about seven successive nights; and in MH2, Mary, who was married to Tom, made love to Dennis in his hospital bed.

MH2 had every variation of sex in it. The *New York Times* (October 3, 1976) reported that "the magazine *Sexual Medicine* sees it as a seminar on sexual dysfunction."

Obviously, it would have to feature a homosexual pair.

Queer Doings

Homosexuality, as we noted in the last chapter, carries the television seal of approval. Queers (a quaint term in this enlightened age) romp across the screen at all hours of the broadcasting span. Ironically, two shows with the word "family" in their titles each devoted whole episodes to homosexuality. In "All in the Family" son-in-law Mike brought home a long-haired friend who Archie wrongly suspected was "that way." Later, in the beer parlor with his buddies, Archie was given to understand that a husky, broad-shouldered ex-football player actually *was* "that way."

(Parenthetically, it is interesting to note that TV never seems to cast the homo as an effeminate or a milquetoast, but always as a big, strapping, manly looking person. The better to make him look attractive and normal?)

One episode of ABC's "Family" pleaded for "tolerance" and "understanding" of homosexuality. Willie, the 18-year-old son, had a friend, Zek, who turned out to be gay. When Willie, shocked and hurt, was less than cordial to Zek, Willie's mother told him he was acting "disgracefully"; he should be more sympathetic. The show ended with Willie apologizing to Zek at the airport before the latter hopped a plane back to college.

CBS's "Alice" had an episode where the widowed waitress

35

went out with a once-famous football pro. During the course of the evening he confessed to being a homo. Though at first Alice was shocked, she soon got hold of herself and tried to understand.

Almost the same plot was dusted off and put into NBC's "Practice." Here the girl fell in love with a medical student only to discover that the young man was a homo. Once she got over the initial shock, she accepted the fact with a it-happens-all-the-time shrug.

In "The Nancy Walker Show" Nancy's male secretary, Terry, was a homo who was sometimes visited by his sexual partner, Dennis.

In MH2 one of the subplots had to do with Tom Hartman's friend Ed, who remarked, "My type is six feet tall and wears a size 11 shoe."

Ed's sex partner, Howard, had a mother who clung to the belief that her son was a latent heterosexual. In one episode she asked Mary to take Howard to bed with her to test the theory.

Naturally, there are also interviews, talk shows, and documentaries about homos. On January 31, 1977, Phil Donahue spotlighted two gays on his program. One had opened a hotel for homos in Fort Lauderdale, packaged a syndicated TV show, and published a magazine for and about homos. The other man was the author of a book about the history of homosexuality in America.

During the audience-participation part of the show, somebody mentioned procreation, whereupon one fag answered that homosexuality was "God's way of controlling overpopulation." When another member of the audience pointed out that the Bible condemned homosexuality, several people in the studio answered that the Bible banned certain foods, implying that the Bible was therefore no guide. Another said that God doesn't make mistakes and God had made him gay. A minister expatiated on the beauties of love.

On another Phil Donahue show, featuring male prostitutes, one of the men boasted that he had both male and female clients.

Besides these shows that openly promote homosexuality, many other shows have occasional jokes about or casual references to homosexuality. In one episode of "Streets of San Francisco" a man on the witness stand was accused of having a homosexual relationship. In "All's Fair" the girl photographer, Charley, mentioned in passing a "married couple," Leonard and Albert, who lived in her apartment building. And there are others. The Gay Media Task Force said that it was "very pleased with the character portrayals" on TV.

If you look at enough TV, you will end up believing that among the male population, homosexuality is more frequent than the common cold.

Television characters rarely use the word "homosexual." Instead, they use the once-delightful word "gay," debasing it so much that we dare not use it in its original sense. Even Don Marquis' famous cat, Mehitabel, couldn't speak today of being "toujours gai."

And of course scripters never speak of a person who is sexually "normal" either. The term they employ is "heterosexual." They do not admit that any particular form of sexual practice is normal. Anything is normal if it satisfies anybody.

Obviously, lesbianism is accepted in TV land, and it is only slightly less prevalent than male homosexuality. Occasionally there is a whole show on the subject, and more often there are short references to lesbians. One example occurred in an episode of "All's Fair" (October 25, 1976); Richard blurted out to Charley the reason for his divorce—his ex-wife was having an affair with another woman. Richard explained, "It wasn't my inadequacy; it was her need."

"Battered with Revulsion"

Flourishing too on TV is rape—even rape of males. NBC's dramatization of Arthur Hailey's novel *The Moneychangers* depicted a male gang rape in a prison shower room. Writing in the *Chicago Tribune*, a disgusted Bob Wiedrich said that the viewers "got as explicit a portrayal of sodomy as any ever foisted on an audience." The scene, he continued, was presented in such detail as to "batter its audiences with revulsion."

As for rape of women, that is a commonplace on TV. On October 31, 1976, "Delvecchio" had an episode about a man who raped and strangled three women. On October 27, 1976, "Baretta" had an episode about a man who raped and strangled his victims. On October 21, 1976, "Streets of San Francisco" had an episode about a man who beat, raped, and murdered his victims. On October 20, 1976, "Charlie's Angels" had an episode about a man who, after kidnapping a girl, tortured, raped, and murdered her.

In less than two weeks, then, there were four rape programs. These come easily to mind. With a little digging four times that many could probably be found.

Moreover, rapes are not confined to crime shows. On the soap opera "The Young and the Restless" a girl was raped by an ex-con.

At least in these shows the rapists were treated with less sympathy than the women they raped. By exercising their extraordinary talent for muddled thinking, though, scripters of some shows make the rapist come off smelling like a rose, while they besmudge the victim and hint that she may have enjoyed the experience.

One example. In "Serpico" a policewoman, working with Serpico to catch a loanshark, was raped, and afterwards told Serpico, "It was like I wanted him to do it. Like I needed it."

Could anybody's thinking get sicker? Perhaps it could when it turns to incest. That happens too. In *Chinatown*, a theater film telecast on November 17, 1976, a father raped his daughter, and later she bore a child who, she said, was both her sister and her daughter. NBC's "Laugh-In" (October 10, 1977) featured a song about "relationships" that mentioned a sister and a brother who were dating each other.

Prostitution, Fornication, Adultery

The data about prostitution are disgusting and depressing. In "Philemon: Hollywood Television Theatre," PBS Philadelphia (October 10, 1976), the protagonist tells his lady friend that he loves her and then begs her to take to the streets to make money for them both.

38

This is a period piece, set in first-century Rome, but in show after show set in modern America, prostitution figures prominently too. "Hawaii Five-O" (October 14, 1976) had an episode defending callgirls. On the same night "Streets of San Francisco" had an episode about a boyish Pied Piper who leads teenage girls to prostitution. The night before, "The Blue Knight" had the police going after a prostitution racket. In "All My Children" a pimp called Ty added a fillip to the teleplay by slapping prostitutes around and sometimes taking their money "to keep it safe" for them. In one sequence, he stabbed a man who was trying to collect the money due one of the girls.

NBC's "Dawn: Portrait of a Teenage Runaway" was about a 15-year-old girl who left home and became a prostitute. Nothing unusual in that, for Hollywood. So the scripters added a new twist to the story: she soon fell in love with a male prostitute.

Then there was NBC's "Little Ladies of the Night," also showing teenage prostitutes. The male lead was an ex-pimp turned policeman, while a black pimp—who was not "ex" by any means—slapped around the girls in his "stable," including the 15-year-old female lead.

The same network ran "Weekend," which was a report of actual prostitution. To film it, technicians used concealed cameras focused on a block between Lexington and Park Avenues in New York at 11:30 P.M.

Within a month or so of the last-mentioned show, "The Days of Our Lives" had a smutty little episode. A young boy, Mike, upset almost to the point of hysteria, visited an older woman, Linda. While he was with her, the camera showed a flashback of a recent experience. He had gone to bed with a girl his own age, but apparently their attempt at intercourse had ended in a fiasco. He confessed to Linda, "I tried it with Trish. She was ready to be a woman for me, and I failed. I can't make love to anybody. There must be something wrong with me."

Linda tried to soothe and reassure him, telling him that he was normal, just young and inexperienced. Having no success, she finally invited him into her bedroom. Fornication therapy of course!

To make matters worse, Linda was supposedly in love with a man whom the boy called "father" (really Mike's uncle), who at the time was in a mental institution. Later, the older man learned that Mike had fallen ardently in love with Linda, his (the "father's") girlfriend. Complications, not to say fireworks, ensued—together with a rich helping of sick sex.

Jason Bonderoff, writing of this soap opera in *Daytime TV, 1977*, said it offers "four generations' worth of incest and adultery."

For Mature Audiences Only

No need to go into detail about every one of these more than slightly nauseating programs. A very brief mention is enough for the following: on ABC's "One Life to Live" Karen seduced

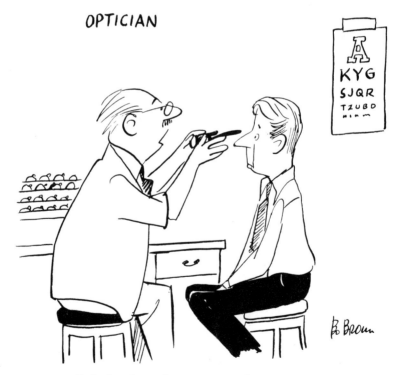

OPTICIAN

"I feel guilty making it so easy for you to see those smutty TV shows."

Larry and rented a rendezvous apartment; on "General Hospital" the same situation, only the names and locale were different: Monica and Rick, and a motel instead of an apartment. A trivial plot line? Sure. But it's repeated endlessly.

Seduction takes on added fascination when the man and woman are in different age brackets. In bygone days the older man seduced the sweet young thing. For some years now TV has reversed that formula. Back as far as September 1971 there was a two-hour pilot program, "Owen Marshall, Counselor at Law," in which a middle-aged woman lured a teenager to her bed.

That sort of thing has resurfaced regularly. Fairly recently CBS ran *The Graduate*. In this well-acted film, a middle-aged woman was again the aggressor with a mere boy, the son of her husband's business partner. On the screen before the show began flashed the familiar words, "For mature audiences."

That kind of message is often used. It appeared the night that ABC broadcast *Heartbreak Kid*, Neil Simon's movie about honeymooners. On the third day of his honeymoon, the groom falls for another girl whom he picked up in Miami Beach, and he proceeds to neglect his bride who stays in the hotel room nursing a bad case of sunburn. On the fifth day of his honeymoon, he doesn't make it back to the hotel in time for a nine o'clock dinner with his wife. Instead he dines with his new love and her family, and tells her father that he plans to get a divorce and ask for the hand of his daughter.

Before he arranges all this, he deserts his wife and follows the other girl to Minnesota, where she has gone in the meantime. Once there, he trysts with her in a cabin in the woods.

True love at last! Or is it something else?

How do *you* spell "love"? Surely most television scripters think that "mature" people spell it l-u-s-t.

Chapter 4

Home, Sweet Home?

"Just because a man yields to the temptation of lust doesn't mean he loves his wife less."

This remark, made on "The Nancy Walker Show" (October 7, 1976), sums up the reigning TV philosophy of marriage: little sexual forays outside the home are quite acceptable, even "normal."

The same show hinted that Nancy's marriage was a hitherto unimportant and uninhibiting thing in her life. Her husband, a navy captain, had been at sea for all but two months of their 29-year-old union. When he appeared one day and announced that he was retiring, she could only exclaim in consternation, "Oh, my God, I'm married!"

At least she had somehow stayed married, though separated from her spouse, for a number of years. On TV that is rare. Serial monogamy is the norm. After all (so the implicit argument runs), people outgrow one another. It would be hypocrisy to stick with one wife or one husband for long.

On the other hand (so the implicit argument continues), people's needs remain. They hunger for sex just as they hunger for bread, so they must satisfy that hunger. Since it is natural, it can't be wrong.

Quite clearly, TV people have never realized that although it is possible for husbands and wives to outgrow one another, it is also not only possible but probable that they grow closer as the years go by. Why have so few scripters taken as the theme for a scenario the obvious truth that togetherness is not just physical proximity, but reaching a deep level of understanding and probing a rich undercurrent of devotion to one another; that successful marriages don't just happen, they are a great soul-satisfying achievement that comes with years of loving effort?

Although the TV people are right about sex being a kind of hunger, they are wrong to say with a shrug, "Since it's natural, you can't control it any more than you can control your heartbeat." TV has molded our minds to the point where we have forgotten that the natural can be guided and helped by a force that is stronger than nature. The truly free person, our religious heritage declares, is the person who, by the grace of God, gains control over himself. The paradox is that free love is slavery.

Boys Will Be Boys (and Girls, Girls)

Now TV's subtle propaganda line is to the believer just as harmful as, if not more so than, the easily recognizable overt action, the torrid bedroom scenes and the rest, for some of the implied stuff sinks into the subconscious. After seeing countless television shows that tell us time after time, either explicitly or implicitly, that it is normal when married couples are scrambled up like eggs, and John Doe is sleeping with James Doe's wife, many of us come to believe it. We almost agree with what Archie's co-worker in CBS's "All in the Family" (September 22, 1976) said: "What's wrong with a married man having somebody stashed away somewhere?"

Or we are taken in by what happened on CBS's "The Jeffersons." In one episode (October 9, 1976) Louise suspected that her husband was having an affair. Her friends told her not to take it seriously. They argued: having an affair is the most natural thing in the world. It happens to most men. You shouldn't get upset. Besides, this is the sizzling '70s! Do you want to turn back the clock? So he strayed a little. Shrug, shrug. What else is new?

In this case, Louise's suspicions were actually groundless, so she was glad that she didn't get excited enough to walk out. Later, somebody said to Louise's friend, Helen, "You've saved the marriage [for Louise]," and Helen answered, "Too bad I couldn't do something nice for her instead."

The laugh track goes "Ha, Ha," and most of us do too.

Another joke at the expense of marriage occurred on the same sitcom on November 17, 1976. Tom had saved George's life and Ralph was collecting for a party in honor of the event. He went to Louise, George's wife, and said, "I know you will give what your husband is worth."

She answered, "Oh, I'll give more than that!"

In "Love of Life" a husband who was invalided made bitter jokes about marital fidelity. So far, his wife had been faithful to him, but he apparently didn't believe that state of affairs could last. The vow to cleave to one person "in sickness or in health" is like a treaty in the eyes of the Communists—pie crust to be broken.

One wonders why TV scripters bother with the marriage license and the band for the fourth finger of the left hand. These are really meaningless if the vow itself is "sound and fury, signifying nothing."

Many real-life young people today who live together without acquiring these appurtenances are more logical than those scripters who have their characters marry when the vow is mere mumbo jumbo.

The casual nature of most TV marriages was spelled out again in that show which so expertly and accurately parodied most of TV's offerings, MH2. Tom, Mary's husband, happened to walk in on Mary while she was kissing Dennis (who later, for a short time, became her paramour) and blew his top. That night, however, Tom and Mary made up, and in bed Mary comforted him. The only trouble is that she absentmindedly called him Dennis.

Ah, well, as Juliet said, "What's in a name?"

"Are you and daddy married or are you just friends
like people on TV?"

The Marriage Merry-go-round

Little wonder few people stay married on TV. And those
few people who do stay married rarely seem to be enjoying
conjugal bliss. Archie of CBS's "All in the Family" is more
happily married than most TV characters, but when he was
first tempted to go visit the waitress who was making eyes at
him, he said to a co-worker, "I'm a married man and a married
man ain't entitled to no fun."

Many other TV characters would agree with Archie that
"fun" means a girl or a boyfriend on the side; they would dis-

agree with him, however, that marriage precludes that sort of thing. They consider marriage as ephemeral as skywriting—and just about as important. This attitude is typified by the girl that Tom Hartman once picked up when he was out bowling. She mentioned, "I have a six-year-old kid from my second marriage—or was it my third? I'm so bad at numbers."

That remark, of course, was supposed to get a laugh, but even on would-be-serious soap operas, the characters divorce and remarry, divorce and remarry, more often than an ordinary person buys a car. Their behavior recalls Jackie Cooper's gag: "Nobody should be allowed to marry unless he's been married twice before."

During the brief periods that TV marriages do last, many couples apparently think of their union as a merry-go-round of sex—period. Marriage for them denotes no special spiritual or mental rapport, or exalted friendship. Though Archie (of "All in the Family") is a butt of fun, supposedly never to be taken seriously, nonetheless he summed up the thinking of these TV characters when he told Edith, "You ain't my friend, you're my wife."

From the ever-fecund MH2 came perfect examples of the marriage-offers-sex-only category. As the scripters wrote the part, Loretta loved her "baby boy," dear "ole Charlie," despite his bald head, merely because in bed he gave her "four minutes of skyrockets plus." (Actually, Mary Kay Place, who played the role, did manage to portray a deeper kind of love and loyalty.) And Mary Hartman's mother, Martha, told her husband, George, after he had strayed with a hooker, that she couldn't stand looking at him any more, but added that they could still make love in the dark where she couldn't see him. Perhaps the most degrading remark about marriage on MH2 (or on any other program) was Wanda's remark to Merle, "That's what marriage is, concentrated lust."

Even mixed-up Mary herself might repudiate that statement. Marriage to her might have meant lust up to a point, but she would have dimly sensed something more too: otherwise why should she have agonized over every matrimonial snag? Mary Hartman was typical of the kind of TV character whose marriage is beset by difficulties that, though they are often related to sex, are not *always* related to sex.

For example, Mary was concerned about Tom's drinking, as well as about his impotence and the possible "adultery cure" that the attractive blonde sex therapist might offer.

46

Mary's marriage included nearly every kind of problem known to TV marriage messes—with the exception of wife-swapping.

Changing Partners

Wifeswapping has occurred on other shows, however. One episode of CBS's "All in the Family" was built around that theme. Admittedly, it was handled very lightly and humorously (but with a cutting edge during the dance sequence). In the end, the swap was not accomplished, so only a prude would object. Right?

Certainly the first impulse is to shrug and say "So what!" However, for the very reason that it was handled lightly and humorously, the wifeswapping idea for the moment seemed a joke, instead of a weapon thrust at marriage and the family.

Wifeswapping was the subject of a "Maude" episode (November 29, 1976) too. A couple whom the Findlays had never met walked into Maude and Walter's home and almost immediately the visiting man said to Maude, "I'd like to go to bed with you." The arrangement was contingent upon his wife's desire to go to bed with Walter.

Again nothing happened, but the idea was discussed throughout the whole episode. Finally, Arthur and Vivian dropped by and were miffed because the couple had not asked *them* to swap partners in preference to Maude and Walter.

What do the scripters have against marriage and the family?

Occasionally, too, they put very bitter words into the mouths of the performers. In CBS's "The Young and the Restless" a grown son enters a room as his middle-aged mother is pouring herself a drink. "Aren't you going to congratulate your mother?" she asked. "I'm celebrating my escape from the bonds of matrimony."

TV seems to be striking at homely values as well as at homely virtues. A decade ago it wasn't like this; television soap operas then had numerous marriages that could actually be called happy.

The writer of an article that appeared in *Ms.* (April 1975) asked Agnes Nixon how she and other TV scripters "got off the

47

non-stop, pro-marriage, baby-boom go-round" that was so popular in yesteryear. The answer was that "the best way to entertain people is to make them think."

Think, and by inference question marriage and monogamy? Possibly that is what Ms. Nixon meant. You would certainly get that impression from the plot lines she has spun out.

Maternal Love, TV-Style

While the scripters are wielding their destructive weapons, they don't forget to take a swipe at maternal love, and often there is an unhealthy and unloving relationship between offspring and mother. In "Love of Life" mother and daughter were both after the same man. When the mother saw that the daughter was going to win out, she threatened to ruin the man with a five-million-dollar lawsuit.

Fairly often too the scripters take the "Ha, Ha" approach and make a big joke of maternal love. When Kathy of MH2 was discussing the need for money that was forcing her to sell her unborn baby through the black-market adoption agency, Martha's supposedly hilarious response was, "Maybe I could sell some of my plants. But no—they're too much like children."

Of course we laughed. What else? The remark was so preposterous that it was truly funny. Apparently, Martha's grandchild was less a child to her than were her plants. But a few more such laughs and we subconsciously make an association of ideas. We begin to discredit maternal love. And TV supplies the "few more such laughs."

In the first episode of "The Nancy Walker Show" Nancy said, "I'd rather boil kids than babysit them." In another episode of the same show, when Nancy's zany married daughter came to her parents' home, the two women actually whacked one another with what looked like feather dusters. In still another episode (October 21, 1976) Nancy said in an aside to her husband that she would soon send the girl home. He weakly protested and asked if that was the usual maternal attitude. Nancy answered, "All over the world there are millions of mothers who want to throw their daughters out."

The reason Nancy particularly wanted to get rid of the daughter was that she (Nancy) was about to experiment with smoking marijuana. It was her wedding anniversary and this was her idea of celebrating. Marriage and marijuana!

Incidentally, is Nancy Walker's real-life attitude about children similar? According to an article in *TV Time* (November 7, 1976), when ABC's Fred Silverman first spoke to her about starring in the show she told him, "I'd like to use the W. C. Fields approach with children. . . . I don't really care about children. . . . I say, 'Get it out in the open. Children are so boring. Throw 'em out before they hang around forever.' "

Babies: A Big Bother

Children in most TV shows are not the offspring of their mother's current sexual partner; they are children of one of the mother's former husbands or they are illegitimate.

Among the television characters who bore illegitimates were Willie's girlfriend in "Family," Kate Lawrence's lifelong friend also in "Family," and Kathy in MH2. In "Ryan's Hope" both Jill and Delia have conceived children out of wedlock, but Delia miscarried and never delivered hers.

Aborted babies are more common on TV than illegitimate babies. Fairly often some character will speak coyly of "terminating a pregnancy," and will then take that course of action without the slightest qualms of conscience. TV abortion will be discussed at greater length in another chapter.

One more word about babies—ABC presented a two-hour film on October 17, 1976 called "Having Babies." It interwove the personal drama of three couples and an unwed expectant mother, all of whom were using the Lamaze method of preparing for childbirth. (This is a form of physical conditioning, stressing total relaxation before labor and delivery.) The finale of the film was an actual delivery shown on the screen—the first time in a prime-time network TV drama that a real birth was pictured.

Though shot not from the front but from above, the scene was still dramatic. However, what struck the viewer with equal force when all was said and done was that not one of those three couples had a really happy marriage. Granted that none of the marital situations was extraordinary (a stepson in trouble with the police, financial difficulties, a husband tempted by a shady deal, in-law friction, a husband and wife bickering over the wife's professional career outside the home). Granted too that there are many marriages far more discordant than the ones described and granted, moreover, that even in the happiest of marriages there are periods of stress; still it would not have been falsely romantic to make at least *one* of the couples very obviously in love with each other and eagerly awaiting their baby.

In the end the three couples did seem to smooth out their problems for the moment, and the unwed girl went off contentedly to Colorado, so the film ended on an upbeat. But why do TV writers feel that to be realistic they have to inject disruption and discord into every marriage, even just before the birth of a baby?

Chapter 5

TV, the Privileged Polluter

The Environmental Protection Agency tries to protect us from air and water pollution. Automobile manufacturers were ordered at one time to put emission-control devices on every car that came off the assembly line, factories were told to stop dumping chemical waste into streams and rivers, and makers of pesticides had to remove certain of their products from the market.

In other words, the EPA made, and is still making, herculean efforts to keep pollution within limits.

For a short period the National Association of Broadcasters, under pressure from the FCC, set aside a two-hour Family Viewing Time, during which raw sex and extreme violence were not to appear on the screen. How much good that short interval did is a question that is useless to discuss now, after the fact. Family Viewing Time is no more. But we still have shows that are defined as "good clean shows." The trouble is that few of these shows remain completely unsullied by the pollution of filth and falsity that seeps through in small—and sometimes even fairly large—amounts.

51

Porn Pollution

Arthur Fiedler, the grand old man who for 47 seasons has conducted the Boston Pops Orchestra, has a delightful program on PBS. On August 8, 1976, however, his guest for the evening, Tony Randall (who himself has a show), added a new element. About to recite verses from Dame Edith Sitwell's "Facade," written over 50 years ago, he smirked, "If you lean on the libidinous side of your nature, you'll probably find a meaning to these verses—a dirty one."

Then he spoke of the girls who prefer each other to men, and added, "You didn't know they knew about such things back in 1923."

Yes, even a fine program like Fiedler's is not entirely immune to virulent and pervasive pollution—this time porn pollution. It pervades so much of TV that it is almost impossible for any program to escape it entirely.

Usually it is deliberately added. Alan J. Bell, vice president and general manager of KYW-TV, Philadelphia, said it is "gratuitously" dumped in purely for " 'hype' purposes."

Though "The Mary Tyler Moore Show" is now off the air, it was a pertinent example of a good show that can on occasion have a smidgen of smut.

In the episode of November 20, 1976, Mary's Aunt Flo came to town and rekindled an old romance with Mary's boss, Lou Grant. Lou told Mary he wanted to propose marriage to Flo but didn't know how to go about it. Mary suggested he use the same formula that he used with his first wife.

He answered, "I don't think that would work."

"What did you say?" Mary asked.

"I said, 'Don't worry, I'll marry you.' "

One mother, hearing this, commented, "I've preached to my kids against premarital sex, so I'm not thrilled with that line, especially in a show that everybody thinks is a paragon of morality."

Nor was she thrilled with the rest of the show. Lou told Mary about his routine as a single man, saying he went home after work, had a drink, ate dinner, showered, and went to bed. But if he got married, he said, he would go home, have a drink, go to bed, shower, and eat dinner.

Later Lou did propose to Flo and she turned him down. When he protested that he had the honeymoon all planned, Flo suggested, "Let's have the honeymoon and skip the wedding."

So the complaining mother said, "A bit of glunk trickles into nearly everything," and she wanted to know, "What can you do? It's not realistic to think we can confine our own family viewing to Disney and 'The Waltons,' yet I hate my kids to be told ten times a day that extramarital sex is the norm." She sighed and added, "TV could be such a great family unifier, if everybody from Dad to the fifth-grader would sit around looking at the same show and sharing the same laughs without fear of the least contamination."

Actually, the episode she cited was not the only MTM episode that was slightly tainted. There was, for instance, the one where Lou spent the night with the Happy Homemaker, Sue Ann Nivens, and the episode where a hard-boiled prostitute was introduced.

But TV people are quick to say, "Programs can't be geared to children, nor can sex be deleted."

Silly and Suggestive

The argument isn't quite as logical as it sounds. Actually, many so-called adult shows are geared to the intellectual level of a ten-year-old, and by that age, in today's world, the child knows something about sex. He learns the "facts of life" shortly after he learns his ABCs. The objection both for the children and for ourselves is not that TV mentions sex, but that so often it cheapens sex and makes it something silly and suggestive to be snickered at.

We saw this fairly frequently in another "good" show, CBS's "Phyllis," which, incidentally, was a MTM spinoff. Before Judith Lowry's death from a heart attack at age 86 on November 29, 1976, the series was continually being sullied around the edges by the suggestive remarks of the Mother Dexter character that Lowry played. She was a gnarled and stooped crone with white hair, spectacles, and widow's hump who looked every bit her calendar age. From her mouth came crude sexy comments and the incongruity was supposed to be uproariously funny, but usually was boring or faintly disgusting.

To the healthy-minded wasn't it disgusting, rather than amusing, to hear this old hag say something about dreaming that she was dancing stripped to the waist with Charles Bronson?

Nor did she get anything more than a pained smirk from most viewers in the episode of October 25, 1976. Phyllis's 18-year-old daughter was dating a man twice her age who went around seducing women. When Phyllis expressed concern about her "problem," Mother Dexter's comment was, "What's the problem?"

Then she went on to say that her "first time" was when she was 16, and it was with a man in his sixties.

This is humor?

Equally wearisome is some of the humor in "Hee Haw." Though on the whole it is clean but corny, it incorporates some coarse jokes that are neither very funny nor for that matter very risqué. Mostly they are just vulgar. Example:

QUESTION: "When do we women soldiers get to eat?"
ANSWER: "Oh, you'll probably mess with the officers."
QUESTION: "Yeah, of course, but when do we get to eat?"

Why don't the directors leave that kind of thing on the cutting-room floor?

Probably the answer is that everybody but a few celibates knows about sex and can readily laugh at it even if the joke isn't very funny. It takes more wit and more imagination than the scripters may have to fashion a joke on other subjects that will strike a responsive chord with millions of people.

Even so, the silly, sexy jokes are far better than the serious allusions to irregular sex and sex situations that come up every once in a while in the "good" shows.

"Ivan the Terrible," the series about a Russian family living in Moscow, though not a uniformly good show, was good in the one sense of being about normally sexed people in average situations. Yet it had to include an episode where the anomalous was dragged in. Olga's divorced husband was persuaded to marry a sports champion. Almost immediately after the wedding the bride had to leave her groom for several days to compete in an athletic event. Word came to him that she was disqualified in the event because she failed the chromosome test; that is, she wasn't really a woman, but a transsexual.

Many viewers turned off the set that night with a nasty taste lingering in their mouths.

Keep It Crude

Then there is "Rhoda," still another spinoff from "The Mary Tyler Moore Show." In the beginning it too was clean and decent; it portrayed the antics of Rhoda and her sister, both bachelor gals pushing 30, who were anxious for a good time, for dates, and, above all, for husbands. There was a lighthearted and lightheaded fun and laughter in the show, and nothing suggestive or messy.

Apparently, the viewing public loved it. The scripters married Rhoda to Joe Gerard, and approximately 40 million people watched the wedding episode. Even college-educated viewers wrote in to the network to say, "I cried."

Now that Rhoda and Joe have broken up, the show is still fairly clean and decent, and for the most part is the kind of thing that the detractors of MTM wanted, a show appropriate for everybody from a fifth-grader to a grandmother. However, something new has been added; every once in a while, unexpectedly, a somewhat crude and sexy line seeps in like a minispill to pollute the waters just a wee bit. Then it might be better for the fifth-grader to be in bed.

In one episode after Rhoda and Joe had separated, Rhoda stopped by Joe's apartment. She found him shirtless and said, "So this is separation. If we were divorced you'd have your shirt on. If we were married you'd have your pants off."

The remark wasn't funny. The most adolescent-minded person couldn't get a real chuckle out of it. And it wasn't even titillating. It was just plain crude.

Messing Up Marriage

When this muck finds its way into a show, it often besmirches marriage, makes it seem not much more than a "lost weekend."

After the big Rhoda and Joe wedding episode, viewers probably expected the couple to settle down and live happily, if not ever after (that wouldn't be the TV way), at least long enough to file a joint income tax return. But the show followed the common TV pattern of implying that even the best of marriages can't last long. It separated the couple almost as soon as they had had their first trifling disagreement (just as MTM had separated Lou and his wife a couple of years earlier).

Now Joe and Rhoda's separation provided opportunity to slip into a basically "good" show a few contaminating remarks about marriage.

In one episode (October 25, 1976) Joe and Rhoda consulted a marriage counselor. Joe told the man that although he loved Rhoda, he wasn't sure he wanted to be married. In other words, he would like Rhoda as his mistress, but he didn't want the responsibility of marriage; he didn't want the constraints of monogamy.

"Ivan the Terrible," as we said, wasn't a particularly good show, but it had two partially redeeming features: it pointed out a couple of weeds in the Workers' Garden of Eden and, more important for the discussion at this point, it presented some family harmony. Yet it had to mar the latter on occasion. The housing shortage in Moscow had compelled wife Olga's first husband, of all people, to occupy the family's flat, and this gave the scripters an opportunity to take a few swipes at marriage. In one episode Olga said to Ivan, her present husband, "You like bananas."

He answered, "No, I don't."

"Oh, but you do," the wife insisted. "Remember on our honeymoon, you . . ."

Here the first husband injected himself into the conversation and said, "That was me. You're getting your husbands confused."

This was supposed to be hilarious and no doubt it did get laughs. What harm? Just one little laugh here and there, who would object?

Obviously, few could object and most would applaud, except that TV so often gets its laughs, even in the so-called good shows, at the expense of the institution of marriage, which many Americans hold sacred.

It wasn't really funny, it was sad—and sick—when Phyllis said in one episode, "I haven't had so much fun since my husband's funeral."

The viewer is supposed to laugh and he does—we all do; the canned laughter carries us along. We know that it is not to be taken seriously and yet . . . whatever is downgraded and laughed at, suffers. In the final analysis, there is no more destructive weapon than ridicule.

Remember the old vaudeville mother-in-law jokes? They probably weren't meant to be taken seriously either, but in the long run they gave her a bad name. The word "mother-in-law" is now virtually synonymous with vixen, so when a plant with long sharp leaves like knife blades is called "mother-in-law's tongue" nobody has to ask why.

The blacks, the Jews, and various other ethnic groups have understood the devastating effect of ridicule, and they have complained loudly when jokes were made at their expense. Secretary of Agriculture Earl Butz was forced to resign from the Ford cabinet when he cracked a joke—in private—about the blacks. Why don't those of us who are happily married rear up on our hind legs and yell in protest when marriage and monogamy are made the butt of fun?

Perhaps one reason TV scripters downgrade marriage is that they really don't understand it. To them it has many drawbacks and only two assets, handy sex and for the wife perhaps financial security. In "Hee Haw," that mostly harmless show that leans heavily on slapstick and earthiness, one of the characters declared that there are three secrets to a happy marriage, "Money, money, money."

Stealing Is Fun

Sometimes these same "good" shows go a step further and make a joke of dishonesty.

In "The Harlem Globetrotters" there was a "funny" incident about shoplifting. Then NBC showed a two-hour film, "Fitzwilly," about a larcenous butler who stole to keep his impoverished employer from having to give up the luxurious lifestyle she had always enjoyed. His zany capers climaxed in a big, but unsuccessful attempt to rob a New York department store on Christmas Eve. It had its funny moments, but why must a film give the impression that stealing is a lark and, furthermore, that it might be justified if the motive was "to help somebody else"? Ethics would certainly say that you don't help one person at the expense of another.

In "Laverne and Shirley," Shirley in one episode stole a towel from the hospital where she worked as a volunteer. And she said to Laverne that she would get another one for her when she went back the next time.

Filching a towel or two, that isn't so bad—but it isn't good either. If our children, whom we want to grow up honest, did such a thing, we wouldn't wink at it, yet this "good" show is in effect saying that it is smart and funny.

We are faced with a tough situation when we cannot count on any show, when there is always some strain of pollution creeping through the cracks.

Sweet and Sour

Occasionally a show that we have categorized as good can be good one week and turn sour the next.

"Laverne and Shirley" is just such a Dr. Jekyll and Mr. Hyde. Usually it is decent, though not very intellectually exciting. But now and again it surprises its fans. Take the episode of November 16, 1976, for instance. The two girls went to a party and got so drunk that when they returned home they didn't remember anything that had happened during the course of the evening. As Laverne started to undress, she discovered, to her horror, that she was wearing men's boxer shorts. She jumped to the conclusion that she had had sexual relations with one of the men at the party, and that she might be pregnant. She didn't have the foggiest notion of who the man was. Quickly, she made an appointment to see a doctor for a pregnancy test.

When the test proved negative, she spread the word, and

the episode ended with Laverne, Shirley, and their friends, male and female, in a restaurant celebrating the good news and singing "Alleluia!"

In other words, whether or not Laverne had gotten soused and whether or not she had had sexual relations with an unknown man were completely brushed off; the whole plot hinged on her escape from conception.

Another show in the same category is "Family." It depicts pleasant family life and is, for the most part, the kind of thing that Mom is glad to have the kids look at. It has been called an updated, urbanized "Waltons." The mother and father seem to love one another, and are concerned about decent upbringing for their children. Yet one episode might be high-minded enough for a saint, another questionable. For example, there was an episode where 18-year-old Willie was making home movies. The whole point of the story was the need for family loyalty, and respect for family privacy. Nobody—but nobody—could find fault with it on any score. Yet other episodes not every viewer would cheer. Like the episode where Nancy, the oldest child, who was divorced, slept with two men in the course of three days. And the episode where Willie's divorced girlfriend, who was having a legal battle to retain custody of her baby, was shown in bed with Willie. The sex scene was put there as a stove might be put in the kitchen, because it was standard background. Then there was the episode that pleaded for sympathetic treatment of homosexuals.

Since most TV scripters seem to regard homosexuality as just another lifestyle, it should probably be no surprise to find this perversion featured from time to time on "good" shows. "The Bob Newhart Show" (an MTM production again) was usually pretty wholesome, yet it too had an entire episode built around homosexuality. "Negative attitudes" toward "gays" were called "the kind of Dark Ages thinking that has kept homosexuals in a closet all these years," and the sin that brought down Sodom and Gomorrah was excused with a pathetic cliche: "We're people—different people—and we need each other."

"The Practice," another show designed for a general audience, jumped on the same bandwagon in at least one episode. Yet a few weeks later it ran an episode about a girl with a retarded child, which movingly brought out the generosity and compassion of all who dealt with her, including the crotchety, feisty doctor with the concealed heart of gold. Even the "good" shows are totally unpredictable.

One feels as inadequate as the little Dutch boy with his finger in the dike when it comes to holding back the stream of pollution which touches almost everything. And there is probably more to come, and more "good shows" will be contaminated to some degree.

"Good Times" has not been a consistently "good" show, but at least Florida used to be a conscientious mother. It was rather a surprise, then, to see her in one episode going to a singles' bar and coming home in the wee hours to find her children awake and concerned about where she had been. Could that presage further debasement of a good character and of a comparatively good show?

The pollution current is so strong that it is constantly breaking down old barriers. TV critic Marilyn Beck, writing in the *Philadelphia Bulletin*, said that "Donny and Marie" will no longer be "such Bubblegum Babes." Mrs. Beck quoted their producer, Sid Krofft, as saying, "Though we still are very careful about what we have Donny and Marie say and do, we are making a point of being a little wilder, a little freer with them this year."

Will another "good" show be muddied?

Chapter 6

Liberated Ladies

Producing TV shows isn't quite like cutting out paper dolls of the same shape and size, but as we have said from the beginning, similar thoughts and ideas do seem to be woven into many different shows.

The "liberation" of women is a case in point. If we were to believe what we see on the tube, we would think that any woman who hasn't tasted the dubious delights of abortion and lesbianism must be some kind of dainty maiden from Louisa May Alcott. The liberated ladies we meet on TV know that "personal fulfillment" comes first—before *everything*—and certainly before preserving and nurturing a marriage.

But there is more too. If writers and producers were to draw up guidelines to follow in presenting their entire concept of liberation, the list would run like this:

THE TEN COMMANDMENTS OF WOMEN'S LIB

1. *Don't* ever portray a "mere housewife" unless you caricature her. The "housebound housewife" is a drudge and a dunce.

2. *Don't* ever portray a "stereotype woman." The inhibited, stupid creature went out of style with leg-of-mutton sleeves and wasp waists.
3. *Do* have all women characters engage in as many extramarital affairs as their husbands. This is important to equality.
4. *Do* include some women who skip marriage entirely and indulge in whatever affairs seem convenient and agreeable.
5. *Do* create as many women doctors, lawyers, police, detectives, politicians—and, yes, criminals—as you do men of these professions, not only to show that women are as capable as men, but also to show that there is no such thing as "a man's job."
6. *Do* show that women have the right to lead their own lives and to seek fulfillment (read: sexual satisfaction) regardless of whom their actions may hurt.
7. *Do* allow women to have abortions.
8. *Do* allow women to prefer other women to men as sexual partners.
9. *Do* show that woman is an ersatz man, differing from him in nothing except sexual organs—unless perhaps she is a shade smarter than he is. Unisex is the word.
10. In news programs and interviews, *do* give more time to the proponents of the Equal Rights Amendment (ERA) than to those benighted women who are opposing it.

Prime Time for ERA

Taking the last point first, here's a classic example. It has to do with a program called "Moving Day" (ex–"You Can't Stop Now"), and a local Philadelphia station, WPVI-TV. The station had, as a "public service," been giving a feminist organization, the National Organization of Women (NOW), the prime-time slot 7:30 to 8:00 P.M. of the last Saturday of every month to tout ERA, when the organization Stop ERA asked for time in the same time slot on another Saturday to present its arguments.

After letters back and forth and phone conversations with the station manager that dragged on for eight months, Stop ERA members were finally allowed to appear on TV—twice. Two appearances of Stop ERA members, two years (so far) of ERA backers.

The station manager was within his rights in so apportioning the time; on the other hand, he would also have been within his rights had he given Stop ERA members a great deal more time. His personal bias or station politics could, within the FCC regulations, decide his course.

The Fairness Doctrine simply enjoins a broadcaster to allow a "reasonable time" for "contrasting views on controversial issues of public importance." (This doctrine, incidentally, has nothing to do with the "equal-time" requirement of the Communications Act; that applies only to candidates for public office.) The licensee may decide what constitutes a "controversial issue of public importance" and what is a "reasonable time" for a reply.

Since most TV broadcasters seem to be in favor of the ideas and objectives of the so-called liberation movement, they usually decide, when possible, to give its proponents more time than those who question it.

The Stop ERAers, however, claim to have a case that the majority of women support. They feel that ERA would take more away from women than it would give them. With Reed Irvine of Accuracy in Media they agree that the ERA should be called the TWERP (Terminate Women's Extra Rights and Privileges) Amendment. After all, they argue, nobody has yet found a way for men to bear children; childbirth is exclusively women's responsibility. Therefore, since men don't share childbearing, why should women share (as they would have to under ERA) any financial responsibility for the family?

The Stop ERAers point to states where ERA has already been passed. In Pennsylvania, for instance, under ERA a woman must share the legal obligation to contribute to the support of the family. The old child-support law was invalidated when ERA was enacted.

Shouldn't these facts receive as much emphasis on TV as does the ERA propaganda? A huge number of women think so.

Another example of TV's pro-ERA stand. In April 1977, when the Florida legislature was to vote on ERA, the pros and cons each called for a rally on the capitol steps. Phyllis

Schlafly reported that only 12 pros showed up to 2,500 cons but, she wrote, "TV news gave equal time to both sides" and "showed *no* pictures of our crowd. When the Florida Senate defeated ERA, network TV interviewed the proponents who lost, and did not air a single interview with the opponents who won."

One reason that the television industry favors ERA proponents is that they are frequently more aggressive than their opponents.

Phyllis Schlafly, in her April 1976 *Phyllis Schlafly Report,* spoke of NOW members threatening individual local stations if they refused to sign a contract with NOW. (NOW's official policy, by the way, is to repeal all laws against lesbianism and prostitution.) They said, in effect: "Sign on the dotted line or we will file a petition to deny the station's license renewal." Mrs. Schlafly added, "It would cost at least $50,000 for the station to defend itself. . . . Contracts signed by television and radio stations under such threats have given NOW great influence over broadcast media programming."

The contracts were made quietly. Nobody knew about them until some alert members of Stop ERA and Happiness of Womanhood (HOW) in Detroit uncovered the facts. They found out that WXYZ-TV (an ABC affiliate) in Detroit had signed a contract with NOW, so they asked to see it. The station manager refused, but the women went to the FCC in Washington, which ruled that such an agreement must be open to the public.

On the Same Side of the Fence

But it was not just a matter of being bulldozed by noisy females; the TV moguls themselves, especially in the networks, if not always in affiliate stations, evidently share the same ideas.

A couple of years ago, PBS awarded *Ms.* magazine a $71,000 grant to prepare a one-hour TV program "on subjects of interest to women." Since *Ms.* features articles defending lesbianism, abortion, and the "new morality," PBS must have wanted a program trumpeting such ideas.

At any rate, on October 31, 1976, PBS had a program called "The War Widow," which was rerun on February 10, 1977. It featured a woman whose husband was fighting in France in World War I. During his absence, she and her little girl lived in her mother's home. Lonely, and receiving emotional sustenance only from her husband's letters, she developed a strong attachment to another woman that soon turned into a sexual relationship.

When the Armistice was signed and she realized that her husband would soon be back to claim her as his wife, she walked out of her mother's home and went to live with her woman friend. Saying goodbye to her little daughter, whom she was leaving with the grandmother, she declared, "I love you. I want to take you with me but I can't."

The mother of the "heroine" was shocked at the abandonment of the child, but the lesbian declared that if she stayed, everything that the child would see would be "artificial."

The viewer was supposed to feel sympathy for this love-starved woman who was so honest, as well as independent enough to live *her own life*, regardless of conventional opinion. The other woman and her friends were portrayed as sensitive intellectuals, smart enough to think for themselves. All very admirable!

Twisted thinking was also in evidence a week earlier on October 24, 1976, when ABC ran *The Stepford Wives*. This movie, based on a book by Ira Levin, was a Women's Lib horror tale, about a suburban community where stay-at-home wives turned into complacent blank-eyed automatons. Loud and clear came the message: This is what suburbia does to women if they don't go out and get a job.

The Feminist Philosophy

Most of us remember when NBC in January 1975 put on a special three-hour telecast entitled "Of Women and Men." Barbara Walters and Tom Snyder were co-anchormen.

It showed sex-sans-marriage as SOP, standard operating procedure, whether the couples were teenagers or social-security recipients.

In between these age extremes, the show presented a 25-year-old woman who declared, "I'm into a lot of what's known as casual short-term relationships. And not necessarily with the same guy. . . . Most of the guys I'm sleeping with are single, but not all of them."

She stated too that she had tried and enjoyed group sex. She had not yet tried homosexuality but said, "I'm curious about it like I was curious about group sex a few years ago."

Throughout the three hours there was no mention of holy matrimony, the state where one man and one woman take each other "for better or for worse" and work out over many, many years a precious, soul-satisfying oneness. Nor was there a word about the joys and rewards of parenthood.

Instead, there was talk of "serial" marriage, which Snyder defined as "a series of relationships of a man and a woman," lasting "for a time and then going on to something else." And about children Snyder said, "There aren't going to be as many children born. We've achieved zero population growth in this country," while Walters chimed in that, according to a poll, there was proof that "women don't have to have children to be fulfilled."

These attitudes and ideas are often expressed in soap operas, sitcoms, and teleplays. For example, in "Secrets" (February 20, 1977), the telefilm that producer Jerry Eisenberg said exposed "the bull women have been fed for centuries—the lie that happiness is derived from finding a Prince Charming and spending the rest of their lives acting dumb and sweet and cleaning floors and doing dishes."

To many, if not most TV writers and producers, the "mere housewife" is the lowest form of life on this planet. In a few shows where they do portray her, they make her a cruel caricature, the so-called stereotype woman; in short, she is a pathetically stupid or unstable creature. In "All in the Family" Edith is practically moronic; you wonder sometimes if she can count up to five on the fingers of one hand. Moreover, the poor thing looks like a wilted flower sagging forlornly in a vase.* In MH2, Mary Hartman was both moronic and neurotic. Pigtails,

---

* Jean Stapleton, who plays the part of Edith, crusades in real life for ERA. No wonder she can make the housewife so "mere"—her heart is in it.

gingham dress, and all, she was at one point carted off to spend time in a mental hospital.

In its eagerness to put down the stereotype woman TV seems to sneer at even the skills that traditionally women took pride in. In CBS's "All's Fair" (September 20, 1976) the editor was distressed about ruining the oysters he was cooking, so he turned to the girl photographer and said in effect, "You understand about cooking. You're a woman. Help me with these."

She answered, "I'm a terrible cook. My mother was a terrible cook. How dare you lump all women into one category?"

In "Love of Life" a woman was going to have a baby. Her husband said, "If it's a boy, I'll buy him a train." The mother reminded him, "A girl might like a train too." "Oh!" exclaimed the shamefaced male, "I guess I had a stereotype girl in mind."

In "Chico and the Man" a black feminist declared that God should be depicted not as a man, but as a woman.

Though Maude (of "Maude") isn't *primarily* a feminist (she backs every liberal cause), in one episode she ran for state senator and spouted all the feminist clichés. She made it clear that a husband was a very poor second to a career.

In another "Maude" episode (February 28, 1977) Vivian took up something called "Feminine Fulfillment," which enjoined her to adopt ridiculously frilly clothes, kowtow to her husband, and put on a seduction act every night when he came home.

The theme of the episode was clear: a woman who is not a strident, self-assertive Libber has to be a silly groveling goof. The scripter apparently had never looked around him to see the many reasonably self-confident women who have no neurotic need to be pushy and who, on the other hand, don't grovel. These women would say: In some respects, women are not equal to men, they are superior; just as in some respects men are not equal to women, they are superior. Their roles complement each other—like the needle and the thread, the lock and the key, the right glove and the left—very satisfactorily.

An article in *Ms.* magazine (April 1975) said "Search for Tomorrow" was "the most forthrightly feminist soap on the air." That was before Norman Lear presented "All That Glitters." In this supposed satire (which was mercifully destined for only a short TV life), women were top executives, men either homemakers or typists and file clerks. In one episode the men typists were running around wiggling their fannies, while the women executives came up in back of them and gave them playful pats.

Few TV offerings, especially among the soaps, make women anything but highly successful in business or in the professions. The gals rarely have routine jobs; they have glamorous and glorious careers as foreign correspondents, TV anchorpersons, fashion models, famous psychiatrists, detectives, artists, etc.

It is a neat trick if women can manage it. In real life, eminent careers, whether for men or women, are exceptional. Mr. and Mrs. John Doe hold ordinary salaried positions.

Yet there are still some TV insiders who talk about the medium as though it were a mirror reflecting the world about us. They never ask themselves what happened to all the salespersons, clerks, factory workers, and others? Nor do they ask themselves about the stay-at-home women who make their main concern (even if they do sometimes have a job and hobbies) the care of a sizable family; on TV they are all but an extinct species, first cousin to the dinosaur.

But, amazingly, TV may not be "with it." *Family Circle* (May 1976) ran an article entitled "Back to the Home?" with the subtitle "We Gave Up Jobs to Be Full-Time Mothers."

"Rubbish!" Most TV people would exclaim. Those women don't exist. You find them only in print, and then mostly in Victorian novels.

At the same time, TV often presents "outmoded" men who complain when wives put husband and home in second place. In short, men can be old-fashioned "chauvinistic pigs" but women cannot be old-fashioned enough sincerely to give precedence to the vocation of wife and mother rather than to a salaried occupation.

In fact, TV sometimes makes these men unreasonable to the point of caricature. In "Another World" a husband objected when the wife signed her maiden name to her paintings. This silly "battle of the sexes" (which was seldom waged even before Women's Lib, for most women of the past generation were free in every important sense) goes on in several soaps and sitcoms.

In "Ryan's Hope" Mary, a budding newscaster, was a bride of just weeks when she refused because of her job to go on a short business trip with her husband, Jack. She never considered the possibility of getting a substitute or of making another arrangement. Job first, Jack second, was obviously her credo.

She and Jack quarreled and Jack was made to appear a carbon copy of the Neanderthal man. Of course he went on his trip alone.

Few wives take the non-Lib attitude of Loretta on MH2, who said, "My career comes first, but Charlie comes firster."

Liberation Means License

Another popular TV theme surfaced in "Ryan's Hope." Delia had an affair with Roger, and the implication was not merely that she was no worse than her husband Frank, who had an affair with Jill. It was that she had as much right to carry on an affair as he had.

For those of us who still cling to the Judeo-Christian ethic in this amoral and immoral world, neither Delia nor Frank had the right. It rather offends us that TV implies that everybody has the right to snatch a little pleasure (translate: sex) when he can.

The stability of marriage, or the normalcy of seeking an enduring union, is not often portrayed on television shows. In most of them there is a subtle contrary message. We may not catch it by seeing only one or two episodes of a serial, but after eight or ten it stands out unmistakably. The message is, if you are not finding "fulfillment," that is, "kicks" or continual thrills, something is wrong. You owe it to yourself to look elsewhere.

Shirley MacLaine in her autobiography said her TV show would be significant "if it showed a woman doing more in her life than simply pampering a slow-witted husband, and dealing with a mess of children." She wanted it to center on a professional woman reporter "who wandered the four corners of the world without the protection of men."

On TV sexual license goes with liberation—no doubt about it. And so does female sexual aggressiveness. Phil Donahue (February 7, 1977) interviewed two male prostitutes on his show. One of them explained that it was all part of the women's movement, that more and more women were going out and buying sex.

War on the Unborn

Obviously, abortion is also part of women's liberation. Why let a baby tie you down?

On TV abortions abound. In fact, you would think sometimes that getting an abortion is on a par with having a tooth pulled. In "City of Angels" (now off the air) a telephone-answering service took messages for callgirls. One of the girls mentioned that she had been to a doctor and that "the rabbit died," meaning that the rabbit test proved her pregnant.

The telephone girl answered, "I'll take your name off the list for now" and added, "I know a good doctor who . . ."

She made herself clear; she knew of a good abortionist. It was taken for granted that that was what the pregnant woman wanted.

In "Medical Center" a woman said to her ex-husband's current girlfriend, "If he were ever man enough to get a girl in trouble, he'd give her bus fare and let her go to the abortionist alone."

Again the abortion was taken for granted; the crime was the callous business of letting the girl go off to the abortionist alone.

Maude in "Maude," Phyllis in "Days of Our Lives," Erica in "All My Children," and Summer in "Executive Suite" all had abortions. In "Ryan's Hope" Bobbie advised his sister Delia to have an abortion after she conceived a child by her brother-in-law Pat. In the same show Jill hesitated for a time about whether she should have an abortion; she visited an

70

abortion clinic and discussed abortion at length with several characters on the show.

On TV abortion is often spoken of as "back-up birth control." When Phil Donahue had as guest on his program Louise B. Tyrer, M.D., medical director of Planned Parenthood, she used that phrase several times. "A rose by any other name would smell as sweet"—or a stinkweed as foul.

Now there are many people who are offended by this offhand attitude toward abortion, who don't even like the sound of the word. What about their feelings? TV takes no cognizance of them. But if the Anti-Defamation League can cause the word "nigger" to be banned, and the feminists can rewrite whole scripts to delete so-called sexist words, why shouldn't the pro-life people have their feelings taken into account?

However, in the final analysis, it is the reality, not the word, that matters; and millions regard abortion as a form of murder.

Some people, whether they subscribe to that idea or not, still wish that TV would end its implicit encouragement of abortion. Among these are people who want to adopt a child and are having difficulties finding one available. Some of them will go to almost any lengths to get one. According to a recent UPI report, infants were being sold in Chicago for up to $10,000. The *Chicago Sun Times* carried the sensational story of this traffic in human flesh, the first in this country since the Emancipation Proclamation.

Even television itself has acknowledged that babies are scarce. In MH2, Kathy, an unwed mother, made arrangements to sell her baby. In a special report aired in early November 1976 on NBC's "Eyewitness News," a newscaster declared, "Adopting a baby used to be simple. Sure, you had to wait sometimes, but sooner or later you'd get the child. . . . Today you could wait forever. . . . There just aren't enough babies to go around . . . you sometimes have to look outside the system."

But the people who want babies so desperately and who would plead with unwed mothers to bear the child and put it up for adoption are seldom heard on TV. The "liberation" themes take up too much time to leave more than a pittance for pro-lifers—or for anybody who does not endorse the "new morality."

71

Bending the Facts

Speaking of those pro-lifers recalls a letter to the editor of *TV Time* (February 13, 1977) that discussed the March for Life held in Washington on January 22, 1977.

The letter writer complained that newscaster Terry Ruggels had estimated the number of marchers as 35,000 to 100,000. She commented that he should have been "intelligent enough" to come up with a more accurate estimate. What good is a figure that may have been off by 65,000 people? She concluded that he must have been "reluctant to admit 100,000," which, she said, was the actual number of people who felt so strongly about abortion that they were willing "to suffer the bitter cold and come out and march."

The writer further took Ruggels to task because he had not deigned to mention the fact that President Carter had sent a staff member to the marchers to tell them that he would meet with them at a future date.

This scant coverage the writer contrasted with the extensive coverage of a NOW meeting advocating the repeal of all anti-abortion legislation, and she ended her letter by saying that Ruggels apparently deems "his views on abortion more important than the ethics of unbiased reporting."

Homemakers Get the Brushoff

Not only are the antiabortionists and the non–Women's Libbers given scant coverage, but when they are (as happens on rare occasions) brought before TV cameras for an interview, they are usually handled with anything but kid gloves.

Phil Donahue had a woman named Arlene Rossen Cardozo on his show. She had written a book entitled *Woman at Home*, which argued that women who choose to stay at home and be full-time mothers should not be browbeaten by feminists. They should not be told in subtle ways that in order to do something "meaningful" they must find an outside job; that they are not needed at home.

Admittedly, it was Donahue's duty as interviewer to challenge her thesis so that she could expatiate on her views. This he did with relish.

He also questioned the people in the studio audience who were sympathetic to Mrs. Cardozo's views. To one woman he said incredulously, "You mean to tell me you never have the blahs staying home?"

In reply she mentioned the importance of bringing up children, and spoke of the companionship of a family of kids. Immediately, Donahue voiced the trite complaint of "liberated" women, "But all the people you ever see come up only as far as your knee."

Another woman in the studio audience mentioned that she did a little volunteer work for so many hours a week in a hospital. Instantly Donahue brought up the fact that the doctors in that hospital were making handsome livings, while she, a stay-at-home woman, never saw a paycheck. Then he asked in effect, "Doesn't that irk you?" implying that if it didn't, it should.

Turning to Mrs. Cardozo, he asked, "Don't you think staying at home all the time gives the children too much mother and not enough father?" She silenced him momentarily by answering that if she went out to work, the children wouldn't have any more time with father, only less time with mother.

Donahue talked too about "quality" time as against "quantity" time, using another hackneyed argument: if a woman is at home all the time, she will be with her children more, but only in body; her mind and attention will be on them no longer than if she worked outside the home and then made a special effort to spend time with them while she was at home.

When somebody in the studio brought up the undesirability of children coming home to an empty house after school, Donahue asked in effect, "But should children be so dependent as to mind coming home to an empty house?"

One could go on, but why bother? By this time, we would be glad to hear the last word on the subject. That comes from *Political Affairs*. Writing in that Communist journal, top Communist Party spokesman Henry Winston stated that the Women's Liberation movement is "the most important aspect of the class struggle in the United States today."

If it is important for the Communists' class struggle, it can't be so good for the rest of us, can it?

Chapter 7

The Quiz and Game Shows

On the Hot Seat

When guests come into our home, we expect them to be mannerly, not to insult or offend us.

Elementary, my dear Watson.

But television is one guest that has never bothered with manners and amenities. No category of shows is completely exempt from the boorishness. This includes even quiz shows that at first glance seem innocuous enough.

What could be wrong with them? They are just games. We tune them in to acquire some interesting trivia, or to test our own knowledge, or just to see people win, right?

That may indeed be our motive, but we soon find out that the quiz shows seldom pass along much knowledge; rather they are vehicles to make adolescent-minded adults giggle about silly or suggestive questions.

"Hot Seat" is a good example. Its contestants are couples who work as a team to win money, but during the show they do not stay together. The format is rather clever. The husband (or the wife) steps into a cubicle where his (or her) hand is connected with a polygraph (lie detector).

Let's say the wife remains on stage; the husband goes into the cubicle. In that case the first question goes to the wife, on stage. One question that was asked a wife was, "What would your husband say about swingers? That they are wasting their time? That they have it made? Or that he would like to find out?"

She answers by giving her opinion of how her husband will respond. Then the emcee approaches the man in the cubicle and asks him the questions about swingers, instructing him to answer in all three instances, "No, I wouldn't say that."

Obviously, in one of those instances, he has to be lying, and the lie is quickly spotted. As soon as he speaks, the polygraph registers the stress, and since there is a large black needle mounted on a prominently placed, highly illuminated board, the viewers can see that stress for themselves. So can his wife.

This game or quiz show has tremendous potential as a home wrecker. Suppose the needle indicated that the man really would like to find out about swingers, and that he was lying when he said that swingers were wasting their time. The chances are that another quiz, which might cause considerable hurt and friction, would follow at home between husband and wife.

When the questions aren't that dangerous, they are at least vulgar and suggestive. In another program, where again the husband was on the hot seat while his wife stood outside with the emcee, the emcee posed this question: "When I ask your husband what he thinks about your bosom, what will he say? It's too small? Too big? Or just right?"

To cite one or two questions is not enough to give an idea of what they are like; the cumulative effect is lost. Here is a whole string of them, taken from different installments of "The Hot Seat." Each was presented to the wife:

"The first time your husband told you that you were terrific, would you say he was referring to your personality? Or to your body?"

"After romance, does your husband act as though he were marvelous, or does he act as though you were marvelous?"

"If a sculptor carved a statue of your husband doing what makes you most proud of him, would you want to put it into a closet where only you could see it, or in a park where everybody could see it?"

"What kind of license came to your husband's mind when he first saw you, a hunting license or a wedding license?"

"When you walk into a room, will the part of you that your husband likes best go into the room first, or last?"

"If your husband were a knight going on the Crusades, and he left you at home wearing a chastity belt, would he leave the key in a safe-deposit vault, or leave it with his best friend?"

"What does your husband think about men who tell girls they love them in order to get what they want from them? Would he think they were just using their head? Or would he think they were snakes in the grass?"

"What does your husband do most often: Get angry? Make mistakes? Or make love?"

This list is more than a little bit tiresome. It's worse than a parade of commercials that goes on and on. Time to go out to the kitchen for coffee or a coke?

No, more of it, and worse. The Equal Opportunity Act, or something similar, must apply to males, so here are some of the questions that were thrown at them:

"When your wife is not in the mood for love, does she feel guilty? Or does she feel that a little self-control is good for you?"

"When it comes to the act of love, does she feel that she knows all there is to know, or does she feel she still has a lot to learn?"

"When the TV is on in the bedroom, is most of the sex and violence happening on the set, or in front of it?"

"Since the sexual revolution, whose attitudes have changed more, yours, or your wife's?"

"If your wife, who is a schoolteacher, were marking you on your romantic appetite, would she give you five gold stars on her chart, or would she send you back to kindergarten?"

"What would your wife say when she saw your passion? Would she say that it frightened her, or that it made her smile?"

"As you and your wife went down the road of romantic experience, would she say she was more in need of a road map or that you were?"

Sometimes the contestants on "Hot Seat," catching the spirit of the game, reply with some ribald words of their own.

A wife, asked if her husband would want her bosom smaller, larger, or just as it was, answered, "He has all he can handle now."

In the Same Gutter

In the same gutter with this quiz show is "Celebrity Sweepstakes." Here the contestants are television personalities, and they as well as the host are expected, as a matter of course, to add sexiness to the program by interjecting bawdy one-liners. Recently a male soap-opera star was a contestant. On the soap opera he had the role of a father with a newborn infant. A co-contestant turned to him and asked, "Are you nursing the baby?"

Gales of laughter. Canned or live?

On the same show, the emcee asked, "Fans loved it when Dr. Casey left what unbuttoned?"

A "celebrity" answered, "They had zippers in those days, so it couldn't have been that. I guess it was his doctor's gown."

He could have answered simply, "His doctor's gown," but that would have defeated the object of the show. By answering as he did, he suggested to the audience the picture of a man's pants with the fly open.

Another time the emcee asked the contestants, "What is a more common word for 'conundrum'?"

It sounds like a straight question calling for the straight answer, "Riddle or puzzle."

But who on this show wants things straight? The question evoked snickering and leering and horseplay. Finally the contestants tried to give the audience the impression that they did not know the meaning of "conundrum," but were confusing it with "condom," the word that means a birth-control device. When one of the contestants, a woman, began to answer, another contestant quickly clapped his hand over her mouth, rolled his eyes in mock horror, and exclaimed, "No, no, you can't say it on the air."

A few more questions of this sort, with the accompanying gestures from the contestants, and everybody was conditioned to expect bawdy answers. Hence by the time the emcee asked, "In inclement weather, when most Britishers talk about getting their brolly up, what do they mean?" the viewers, as the producer intended, were thinking about getting up an erection, which has nothing to to do with an umbrella.

Popping Provocative Questions

Similar to these two quiz shows is "Tattletales." The couples, married or "just friends," are separated from one another, and then they are asked, a la "Hot Seat," about the attitudes of their partners.

An ad for the show in *Variety* (February 16, 1977) read in part, "Jerry Stiller and Anne Meara thought they knew all about each other. Until they played "Tattletales"! . . . Host Bert Convy pops provocative questions like these—'Would you pose for a nude centerfold? . . . Could you be in love with two [people] at the same time?' "

And here's a sample of other questions that Convy has asked on the show:

"Would your wife say that she wanted to take an inch off her bust, her waist, or her hips?"

"Would your wife say that you spend more time arguing, or making love?"

"Who would your wife like to see as the centerfold of a magazine?"

Though vulgar, none of these seems quite as irksome as the recent question, "The sexual revolution has changed attitudes toward homosexuality. Would your husband mind it more if he lost you to another man, or to another woman?" Amazingly, two of the men said they would rather lose their wives to another woman.

Cutesy and clever too was the question: "If your husband were going to be stranded on a desert island, would he rather be stranded with a beautiful woman missionary or a beautiful callgirl?"

After the wives gave their answers, the husbands were then asked the same question, "Which would you prefer to be

78

stranded with, a beautiful woman missionary or a beautiful callgirl?"

(Parenthetically, one of the men first parried the question with, "Aren't they both missionaries? They both have a calling.")

This particular question seemed to engender a bit of uneasiness, if not suspicion, in the wives—again, hardly the best thing to bolster a marriage.

Ironically, the aforementioned *Variety* ad spoke of this quiz game as bringing young couples together.

"Match Game" is a cutie too. A sentence with a word, or words, missing is given to contestants and they must fill in the blank. Usually the sentence is such that it can be answered by either a sexy term or some other term. The idea is that the contestant should not say the sexy term aloud, but merely suggest it to the minds of the audience. (Incidentally, this thought-suggestion technique is a practice well known and approved by the Chinese Communists.)

It is quite possible to watch this program once or twice before we realize what is going on. At first we may wonder what all the laughter and leering are about. A novice viewer, for instance, might well supply "kiss" or "spank" when faced with the sentence, "Yesterday was my wife's 30th birthday, so to celebrate I _____ her 30 times."

However, after a viewer has been exposed to the program a couple of times, he will very likely supply, at least in his own mind, another word that the scripters were suggesting all along.

In fact, after listening to that show for a while, viewers become like dumb Dora filling out a job application. When she came to the question "Sex?" instead of writing "Female," she wrote "Yes, often."

So What?

Sometimes the suggestions on "Match Game" are so juvenile that they wouldn't be amusing even to a grade-school kid. Who could get even one genuine chuckle from this question?

"The bartender said, 'There's a new drink made from carrot juice and vodka called Bloody Bunny; one drink and you _____ like a bunny.' "

So somebody says "Hop" and supposedly everybody thinks "Multiply." So what?

Also in the so-what category is this example: "At the department store, one salesperson said to another, 'I don't think that customer has ever worn a bra before; she put it over her _____.' "

Somebody says "Dress," but supposedly everybody is to think "Bottom."

"The Family Circus" had a cartoon showing Dad dozing in his chair before the TV set, while one child says to another, "Daddy watched himself to sleep."

Sominex should sponsor the program.

To make a long story longer, there is "Match Game P.M.," a first cousin of plain "Match Game." It comes on in the evening and surprisingly is a mite cleaner than the afternoon show. But not much. Suffice it to give just one run-of-the-mill example of how contestants are supposed to fill in the blanks: "My wife looks as though she were painted by Picasso; both her _____ were on the same side."

Say "arms" or "eyes"; but think "bosoms" or "breasts."

No wonder Jimmy Carter admitted he lusted after women in his heart. Who wouldn't after watching a few hours of TV quiz shows?

"Match Game P.M." has another quirk. There are six show-biz celebrities present, together with two contestants, and a question is asked of all eight people. The object of the game is for the contestant to match as many of the celebrities' answers as possible. In other words, if one contestant gives an answer which is the same as that given by three celebrities, and the other contestant gives an answer which is the same as that given by two celebrities, the first contestant wins. The game allows for no such thing as an objectively right answer.

For the most part it makes no difference anyhow, because the questions themselves are so silly. A recent question was, "She made her bra out of a piece of string and two _____." Some of the answers were "two buttons," "two coconut shells," and "two egg shells."

The show is similar to ABC's "Family Feud" in one particular. Though "Family Feud" offers much more sensible questions, the winning answer has nothing to do with truth or accuracy. The winning answer on "Family Feud" is the one most popular with the man on the street.

Before the show goes on the air, one hundred people nationwide are asked the same questions, and the "correct" answer is whatever the largest number have given. The technique sounds like that of many demagogic politicians. Truth and principle are irrelevant; all that counts is what the polls say. Everything is relative anyhow. Carried to its logical conclusion, that collectivist philosophy is more destructive than the H-bomb.

One last word about television quiz shows. They are as carefully staged as a Gilbert and Sullivan operetta. On some shows, for example, contestants play games or answer questions to win money, or prizes ranging from major appliances and furniture to motorboats, cars, mink coats, jewelry, and trips to Hawaii or elsewhere. When it is clear who the winner is, he or she must go through an inevitable ritual. First, the winner lets out an ear-piercing yell and begins to jump up and down, screaming and squealing all the while, and generally acting like an escapee from a mental institution.

Then, after a minute or so, the winner rushes to the host, throws his or her arms around him, and goes into paroxysms of joy. If the winner is a woman, the required finale is that she kisses the host.

Are the contestants coached in advance? Well, nobody has ever put on an original act. What would happen if a winning contestant were to say calmly and casually, "Thanks a lot. That's fine"? No doubt the emcee would have a heart attack in full view of millions across the land, or maybe a nervous breakdown a la Mary Hartman.

The time for calmness actually does come afterwards, at an obligatory off-camera meeting in which IRS representatives and production chiefs discuss with the winner his or her tax bracket. The result is usually a cash gift to the winner much smaller than the taxable value of the merchandise seen on screen. Still, the impression that millions of viewers come away with is, "Yes, you can get something for nothing. There *is* such a thing as a free lunch!"

Chapter 8

Commercials: The Crass and the Crude

Deluge of Dollars

"Honesty in TV commercials, is that allowed?"

Nancy Walker asked the question one night on her show.

Honest or not, they are effective. Industry is willing to spend a tidy fortune on them. Here's the figure, $6.6 billion. Yes, that's the sum that industry poured into TV advertising in 1976. And each year the sum escalates.

What kind of advertising does the public see and hear as the result of this deluge of dollars?

The commercials range from Merrill Lynch's thundering herd with its message, "We're bullish on America," to Dr. Pepper's "The most original soft drink in the world"; from the earnest exhortation "Take genuine Bayer aspirin" to singing commercials that urge us to come to McDonald's, where "We do it all for you."

Everything has been tried; the admen are even using the technique of comparing brand-name products. Brand X has gone the way of all flesh. It is no more.

No longer do companies advertise their products as being better, stronger, more economical, or more durable than Brand X. Instead, the advertiser names names, and speaks freely of his competitors. Ultra-Ban Super Dry deodorant comes out flatly and says it "keeps you drier than Right Guard, Arrid Extra Dry, Soft and Dry, or Dial." A woman plugging Dow oven cleaner says, "I tried Arm and Hammer, and Mr. Muscle too. But Dow overnight outcleans them both."

This is the current-style commercial, which pleases some consumers; they say it gives them more information. But who is to know whether some unnamed company hasn't the best product of them all? Naturally, no company is going to come out and say: My product is better than X and Y product, but Z product is better than any of our products. Despite the new seeming openness, there is room for ads to mislead us, and no doubt they sometimes do.

Simple Simon

Not that the Simple Simon ads of yesteryear have disappeared. They are still around and can no more be exorcised than the twin devils of inflation and rising taxes. A word about Simple Simon first.

Visitors step into a kitchen and say to the lady of the house, "Oh, your kitchen smells so fresh!"

Guests would walk into a house and say that? "Not bloody likely," as Liza Doolittle would put it.

And the way the women in the commercials croon over soap powders and detergents—well, it just doesn't happen in real life. If it did, we would leave our TV screens to put in another load of wash; we wouldn't be able to stay away from that ecstatic Dash, Rinse, Fab, or whatever just to see a TV show.

Maybe the ads contain a germ of truth, but they exaggerate to the point of absurdity. If they have their uses, it is mostly because they provide an occasional laugh.

Oddly enough, some of them would elicit groans from the people who appear in them, if the situation were for real. A woman who has paid a fancy price for a professional manicure would surely be annoyed if she were told that her fingers were soaking in Palmolive dishwashing liquid. She could have used that at home for a few cents. Commenting on that particular commercial, *Variety* (November 24, 1976) voices surprise that the woman "doesn't dump the yummy-looking green liquid all over Madge's noodle."

Another commercial that would surely annoy the person in it, if it were for real, is the one where a husband comes home and calls to his wife, "Agnes, I finally got you some help to clean the house."

"A maid?" she asks, but no, he's talking about a can of Klean and Shine.

The laughter, if any, is only from us, the viewers.

We stop laughing when we see the ads that push luxury products as if they were indispensable to the pursuit of happiness. In one commercial, for instance, the woman says that she doesn't mind spending more for L'Oreal's "Preference" (a hair tint) because, she says, "I'm worth it."

Worth it? In one sense, she is worth immeasurably more than any cosmetic ever made. In another sense she may not be anywhere near worth it. Money is relative and how much she spends on a personally gratifying whim should depend on how much money she has after she has taken care of actual needs. It is a matter of "first things first"; obligations before extras.

Along the same lines is the commercial which prates, "Every woman needs a little luxury every day."

Think about that a minute. If something is a luxury, how can it be a need? To say that it is, is a contradiction in terms. Yet we hear that kind of tagline all the time.

Great Expectations

Misleading, if not mendacious, are many other commercials for beauty-care preparations. Naturally, we all want to look as well as we can, and there is no excuse for looking like an unmade bed if a little grooming will spruce us up. On the other hand, some commercials promise no less than bottled beauty, on sale at our friendly corner drugstore.

They show a young boy (or a young girl) talking with a contemporary, who tells him (or her) that the way to get dates, or to attract the attention of a particular person, is to "Put your money where your mouth is, buy Close-Up." In other words, use this brand of toothpaste, and you'll have no trouble getting the dates; Miss America herself (or Mr. America himself) will be knocking on your door. It won't be your kindness or your cordiality, your friendliness or your frankness; it will be toothpaste that wins romance, love, and the happy-ever-after state.

Talk about bargains! It would be cheap at ten times the price. Of course, people rush to buy it. Great expectations as false as the promise that the moon is made of green cheese lure them on.

Are these great expectations one reason that the youth of this country are restless and dissatisfied? Every day, a hundred times a day, they hear promises rarely fulfilled. And do the promises make them cynical as well as restless? Could be. And it could be too that all of us, regardless of age, are affected.

But we can't blame TV alone for this kind of thing. It was going on long before television was even invented, but it is much more beguiling and misleading on TV where we can actually see a living, breathing pretty girl or nice-looking boy.

Small wonder that we buy the aftershave lotion, the bathsalts, or the hairspray; subconsciously we are yearning to be liked, to look like those gorgeous and glamorous personalities and to live similar love-filled lives.

Marvin Kitman, talking about TV commercials in his book *The Marvin Kitman Show*, said, "Boy gets perfume. Boy gets girl. These are the facts that advertising agencies work with in making commercials in the after-shave and cologne genre. It's not much to work with." Much or little, it is used again and again and again.

TV critic Rex Polier described a commercial where Mickey Mantle extolled some male cosmetic and was suddenly "engulfed by mindless groupies who swarm all over him, running their fingers through his hair which looks like seaweed draped over a rock." Polier also cited a beer ad featuring Paul Hornung, in which this football has-been also found himself engulfed by females.

85

Sex for Sale

Whether it's beer or biscuits, perfume or pantyhose, buy it and you're guaranteed romance and sex.

Jovan Musk Oil for men, so the spiel goes, is "unmistakably male." It is "the provocative scent" that "arouses his basic animal desires. It's powerful. Stirring. Unbelievable. And yet legal." Then Jovan has the ad that claims it is "so sensual in its message. It may not put more men into your life, but it will put more life into your men."

The Van Raalte hosiery ad purrs, "Put your legs in our hands." Haines bluntly declares that its hosiery "will make you sexy." A commercial for Black Tie after-shave cologne has a glamorous girl loosen a man's tie and start to unbutton his shirt. It looks just as it is supposed to, like an invitation to go to bed.

Then there's the not-to-be-forgotten Underalls. A girl wearing tight pants walks away from the camera, her rounded little fanny rippling beneath the taut cloth. As she walks she talks, telling how much she likes her Underalls, a form-fitting type of panty hose. She assures viewers that they cling to the skin, creating no bulk at all. Then suddenly she turns around and, as the camera zooms in, stage-whispers with a leering grin, "My Underalls make me look like I'm not wearing *nothin'*."

Don't mind the grammar. All we're supposed to understand is that the naked look is sexy, and we are to run, not walk, to the nearest department store to buy Underalls.

Beautyrest pictures a girl who is actually wearing next to "nothin'." She lies on a mattress, stripped to the waist with her back to the camera, while the narrator tells about the comfort of Beautyrest.

Even products that apparently have no connection with sex are sold with some allusion to it. Worse yet, even products that appeal to children are sold with the same allusion. In one commercial, a boy who looks about 12 years old is shown drinking milk. He remarks, "Milk gives me sex appeal." TV commercials train the kids to be sex-conscious at an early age.

Sometimes the admen have to do a bit of mental acrobatics to work sex into an ad. An ad for Cover Girl makeup by Noxzema declares, "Clean is sexy."

A youngster looking at these commercials would think that

there is absolutely nothing outside the realm of sex. With apologies to Freud, that's not quite true.

And while we are speaking of the Austrian psychiatrist, *Variety* reported that one ad agency told a writer to read Freud's *Analysis of Dreams* in order to find "inspiration for some sort of phallic imagery." He undoubtedly found it.

All the networks run commercials for the TV shows themselves, those come-ons advertising future shows. One mother complained, "I try hard to monitor the viewing of my 10-year-old twin boys. I don't let them look at shows portraying homosexuality or anything like that. Then came this ad for 'Family.' It showed two sisters talking. The older girl, Nancy, asks the 12-year-old Buddy, 'Do you know what a homosexual is?' and Buddy answered, 'Yes, a man who likes another man.' It wasn't a very full answer but it will give the kids some idea, and the next time there is an allusion to homos, they will be all the quicker to catch on."

Some parents would say, so what? The kids have to learn sooner or later. The parent we just quoted, however, said, "Because kids are by nature curious animals, they might go out and seek more information about it. That kind of information is dynamite when kids are too young to know how to handle it. I wouldn't put it past some kids, again because they're normally curious, to experiment."

If she is right, and if only one child in a thousand experimented, and five million children saw the ad (not an unlikely number), that would be plenty—5,000 to be exact.

Bathroom Business

It is said that when a lady told Dr. Johnson, "Sir, you smell," he answered, "No, madam, you smell; I stink." Television commercials would have us believe that everybody stinks.

In one of them a woman is driving a station wagon. All the passengers are sitting in the back; nobody wants to sit beside her. After she uses Shower-to-Shower Deodorant Powder, though, two people crowd onto the front seat. She drives happily off.

A man in a bus is reading an advertisement for a deodorant.

The man beside him remarks, "I don't bother with those things," to which the first man answers, "I know."

The people who talk about "the pasty film" that "covers your mouth" and gives you "the worst breath of the day" wouldn't win any prizes for discretion either.

Then there are those perennial abominations, the ads for laxatives and other patent medicines. It is hard to believe that people anywhere sit around talking about such things. Have you ever heard someone say, with a straight face, "I have a friend who has this irregularity problem"?

The worst in this category is the man who asks earnestly, "Do you mind if I talk to you about diarrhea?" The only answer we can give is to turn off the set. After all, "Yes, I do mind" won't stop him.

We are tempted to turn off the set too when the commercials treat matters of feminine hygiene. This is intimate business, and it could hardly be handled more indelicately. There are commercials for Playtex deodorant tampons, beltless Kotex maxi-pads, Stay-free mini-pads, and Care-free panty shields. And if those aren't enough to make us squirm, there are commercials for "Summer's Eve" and for Massengill disposable douches.

More Than Meets the Eye

It is almost a relief to turn to the commercials that plug away at one of TV's favorite, though by now shopworn, themes, Women's Lib. Of course, there is nothing wrong with a man who polishes up gadgets in the kitchen with Windex or whatever. A cooperative and considerate husband, like a thing of beauty, is a joy forever. And the message of the commercial, "Since my wife works, I had to learn how to make the kitchen shine," is reasonable. Nor is it unreasonable (let's hope) for a man to change the baby's diaper, whether or not he uses Baby Fresh.

However, since TV is always pushing the Lib idea that men and women are like interchangeable parts of a machine, these ads may imply more than they actually say.

Another commercial that carries dubious implications is an ad for Gaines Puppy Choice dog food. It shows a baby and a puppy sitting side by side. The narrator, pointing to each in turn, says, "This is a baby, and this is a baby." The message? Perhaps that the human baby and the dog are both cute little animals that need proper nourishment.

All right, so they are. The statement nonetheless tends to rub the wrong way those of us who believe that man is also something more than an animal because he has an extra spiritual endowment.

Again, there are worse ads. Probably one of the worst to appear on television was not labeled a commercial at all; it appeared on an ABC newscast. It showed a motel in the Pocono Mountains of Pennsylvania where, the narrator said, X-rated movies were shown on closed-circuit televison. These were made available to any room in the motel upon request. The narrator mentioned that rooms were available from $22.00 a day, up.

If that isn't a commercial, what is? Why didn't other motels and hotels in the area protest this "free" advertising? Is there an answer to that?

For the moment, however, let's stick to commercials that are labeled as such. Planned Parenthood had one that boasted, "Planned Parenthood offers *all* the options." Then the narrator went on with the line about every child should be a wanted child.

It was an ad for abortion, no less.

What Next?

Probably it won't be long before there are commercials for abortion clinics. There is already talk of selling contraceptive devices on TV.

In MH2 (fiction to be sure and not a commercial), when Mary Hartman, just before her nervous breakdown, appeared on TV to be interviewed by Susskind as the Typical American Consumer Housewife, she said she wanted to see ads for "more attractive sanitary napkins" and for contraceptives.

So far, contraceptives haven't made it onto the airways, but was this statement in a fictional show a trial balloon?

The Radio Code Board and the Television Code Review Board of the National Association of Broadcasters, which are responsible for recommending changes in Code policies, have begun a review of current policies. These policies today forbid the advertising of contraceptive products on Code-subscribing stations and on the networks. But this may be changed. If there were no thought of change, there would be no review in progress.

The code boards are requesting comments on this subject from interested organizations and individuals. If you are interested, you might write:

Mr. Stockton Helfrich
National Association of Broadcasters
477 Madison Avenue
New York, New York 10022

Chapter 9

Subtle Scoffing

A troupe of men dressed as monks were treading grapes for wine, clowning all the while, sneaking drinks, and making jokes. Later, throwing back their cowls, they donned silly New Year's Eve–type hats. Grabbing noisemakers, they milled about, whooping it up. As accompaniment to their revels, there was background music aping the Gregorian chant that genuine monks use for their daily praying of the Office or the Hours.

Where did all this happen? On "Sonny and Cher," but it could have been a curtain raiser for a number of TV offerings. In fact, similar mocking was in vogue as far back as the early 60s, in "Checkmate" and "The Defenders," among others.

It is not unusual for a television show to feature a skit or to drop a word that makes fun of something or somebody connected with religion.

Despite these monks, Catholics are not particularly singled out. Any Christian person, group, or church is fair game.

By intimation the Baptists were the target when NBC's "Police Story" staged an episode called "Odyssey of Death," Part II, rerun on August 6, 1976. In this show a man and his son-in-law made a practice of robbing and raping young waitresses. While the rapes were in progress, the wives of the two men, mother and daughter, sat in a car, calmly waiting. To pass the time, they prayed and read the Bible. They and their menfolk, these "religious" people, were pictured as ignorant, poor, unscrupulous whites from the "Bible Belt" South. (And this kind of family was depicted before, in 1974, in "Hawaii Five-O.")

The Gospel According to Archie Bunker

It seemed to be the Episcopal church that figured in the baptism incident of CBS's "All in the Family" (August 23, 1976).

Archie wanted to have his infant grandson baptized. The child's parents were not interested, so Archie decided to have the sacrament administered without telling them about it.

He confided his plans to his wife, Edith, who demurred. Archie argued, "You gotta use force, that's the Christian way." In support of this unorthodox statement, he cited the Christian missionaries, as though they made converts at gunpoint.

Naturally, Archie's remarks evoked (canned) laughter. They always do.

When the son-in-law, Mike, entered the room a moment later, he said, "Baptism is just a religious rite," implying that it is mumbo jumbo. Then he asked, "What is the soul?"

Archie, whom the scripters have never yet allowed to give one reasonable or sensible answer, replied with his usual inanities. (More laughter.)

"Meathead," as Archie calls Mike, persisted and next asked, "Where is the soul? And what happens when a person dies?" Archie, as usual, came off looking like a fool—an amusing fool, a butt of fun. The answer he gave was, "The soul jumps out just before the coffin lid slams shut." (Still more laughter.)

There followed a muddled and again an amusing discussion about sin. Mike said something to the effect that the child could not possibly be tainted with sin and thus require baptism. Edith agreed with that view; a dear, innocent baby, who has never done the least wrong, would certainly not stand in need of cleansing sacramental waters.

Archie had no answers. The scripters made sure he had forgotten what original sin was all about.

Finally, when Mike went out with his wife, and only Edith was at home, Archie saw his chance. He sneaked the baby out of the house and took him to the church.

Archie almost changed his mind about the baptism when the minister who greeted him there turned out to be an Oriental. Archie's ever-present racial prejudice came to the fore, and he asked for the "boss preacher." When he found that he could not see the boss, who was not in the rectory, he had to settle for the Oriental, who then proceeded to ask a few questions. Archie had to admit to the man that the baby's parents were inimical to the idea of the christening, whereupon the clergyman refused to administer the sacrament.

The final scene showed Archie in the church by the baptismal font, performing the rite himself. He actually used the very words that are used in the Christian churches, "I baptize thee in the name of the Father, and of the Son, and of the Holy Ghost."

What the audience was supposed to laugh at—and did laugh at—was Archie's naivete, stupidity, and unenlightenment in thinking that these words alone were going to make any difference. Yet perhaps only a comparatively few people stopped to reflect that the whole show was slightly blasphemous, a subtle mockery of *all* Christian rites. Ideas fostered by a show like this seep into the subconscious and weaken belief. Is that the aim of some TV scripters and directors? One cannot help wondering.

God and Man on MH2

Other shows of the same genre abound—and indeed have been worse. In MH2, Loretta was trying to save the soul of a friend, Merle, who had the bad habit, as she said, of "going to houses—sinful houses." When Merle and his son solicited her help, she left home immediately to counsel Merle, although her husband Charlie protested.

"The Reverend Jimmy Joe has called me out to save his daddy's soul," she told Charlie. (Incidentally, "the Reverend Jimmy Joe," Merle's son and a child-prodigy revivalist, was only eight years old.)

Loretta, portrayed as utterly ignorant and stupid, but completely sincere and well intentioned, was chosen by TV scripters to represent the religious person concerned with the salvation of souls.

TV manages to make religion and ignorance seem like two sides of the same coin: Loretta in the soul-saving bit, Archie in the baptism sequence, and "prodigy" Jimmy Joe prove that.

In some cases TV manages to mix religion, ignorance, and sex. Loretta was a "sexpot" if ever there was one, and when Merle urged her to come to him on the double, he wanted her for reasons that had nothing to do with religion. He proved that later; he tried to seduce Loretta, but was interrupted when Charlie burst into the room with a shotgun.

Religion and greed go together too, according to TV. Merle exploited his son's evangelistic work for profit. Moreover, he was involved in some sort of shady housing deal called "Condos for Christ," and after the boy's death, in the interim before he took up politics, Merle planned to devote all his time to this semiswindle while talking about "spreading the message of Christ." He told the ever-gullible Loretta that he had a call from the Lord to promote his condos. He was always able to hoodwink Loretta; at one point she was going to donate to him all the proceeds from the records she cut.

For ridiculing religion, few shows have been worse than MH2. Take Jimmy Joe's death. While the child was in the tub, he was watching a television set rigged up in the bathroom. The evening news was on, showing men perpetrating evil deeds and an airplane crashing into a Presbyterian church, leaving many dead people in its wake.

As Jimmy Joe listened, he sermonized about wickedness and violence, saying it was "like nails driven into our Savior's flesh." But it was not the evildoers or the men of violence who were struck dead. It was the Presbyterian churchgoers, and the innocent eight-year-old when the TV fell into the tub and electrocuted him.

It was the old taunt: So there is a just God? Where is he?

Again, though not more than one person in a thousand is likely to formulate that question in his mind (who would, unless he were compiling a book on TV?), it is suggested to the subconscious.

Loretta's remark at the time seems, upon reflection, to have been tinged with blasphemy. It sounded almost as though Loretta were comparing Jimmy Joe to Christ, who died for human sin, when she said, "He died for the 6:30 news, Lord. For the sins of the 6:30 news."

Twelve Judases

No clergyman on MH2 was ever a decent, conscientious, or intelligent person.

In real life, Christianity has had its rotten apples, beginning with Judas Iscariot. But Judas was only one of the twelve apostles. There were eleven others whom the world has always revered as saints.

MH2 did not even reverse that ratio and create eleven bad to one good; it had none good. The Reverend Mr. Steadfast (*sic*) had an affair with his choirmistress, carried a pint of whiskey in a hollowed-out Bible, and had to be blackmailed before he would help get Mary away from a mass murderer who was holding her hostage.

Frank de Marco, a Roman Catholic priest, told Kathy, "I think about you every day. I love you, Kathy," and the inevitable (for MH2) happened.

A third unsavory clergyman entered the show after Mary had her little sexual fling with Dennis in his hospital bed. When the doctor reprimanded her, saying that romping in bed could have killed Dennis, Mary was disturbed enough to go see a minister. Eagerly—lasciviously, it seemed—he asked to know all the details of the lovemaking.

Potshots at the Bible

The producers of MH2 went to any lengths to make fun of religion. When Loretta was surprised to see so many Bibles around the Hartman house, Mary explained that her sister Kathy had brought them back from her many stays in motels.

Kathy, who met her Toms, Dicks, and Harrys in motels all over the map, took along a Gideon Bible when she checked out of each love nest.

Of course, we were supposed to find funny, funny, funny, the incongruity of promiscuous Kathy snitching a book that admonishes "Thou shalt not commit adultery" and "Thou shalt not steal."

Well, we can laugh at the old joke about the man who didn't know what to do with a Bible so he used it as a doorstop, but MH2's disrespect for sacred things can't be shrugged off as easily, because it did harm. After all, the show reached and affected millions. It was so popular that a book was written about it. Mary Hartman Clubs were formed and "Mary Hartman for President" buttons were sold during the 1976 political campaign. Since many fans were desolate if they had to miss a single episode, it was arranged in some cities for them to phone a certain number to hear a recording giving a one-minute resume of the previous night's happenings.

Nor Are Nuns Neglected

We can hardly leave MH2 without remarking one more slur on religion. While Kathy was engaged to Steve, she discovered him in the act of taking a Hollywood starlet to bed, so she naturally broke off the engagement. Rushing to Mary's house, she tried to calm herself by looking at TV. As luck would have it, the show she tuned in was "The Nun's Story," and forthwith Kathy decided to become a nun.

She abandoned this plan when she met Dennis, but when she broke up with him, it resurfaced. Hoping to take her vows, she went to a priest. He told her that not only were her motives for entering a convent strange, but furthermore she wasn't a Catholic, which made the idea impossible. The priest was Father de Marco, the fellow we spoke of earlier who did not take his own vow of celibacy seriously.

Criminals: Always Catholic?

But enough of MH2. Other shows too have had or have an antireligious bias. Some appear to specialize in anti-Catholic bias. Often crime and detective stories make the underworld characters Catholic.

In ABC's "Baretta" one shady character is portrayed as having a Catholic upbringing and his elderly mother is shown going to Mass.

In an episode of "Serpico" (October 1, 1976) the racketeer whom Serpico was hunting down was a Catholic. Serpico visited a parochial schoolteacher, a Sister, to pump her about the racketeer who had contributed handsomely to the church. Churchgoers are hypocrites—isn't that the intended message here? Whether intended or not, that is what gets through.

Family Portrait

Catholics are put in a bad light too in "Ryan's Hope." This is a well-acted, well-written soap opera about an Irish Catholic family, but the family's religion apparently means little more than keeping rosary beads in the house; it does not affect their morals. Delia, a central character, is completely devoid of conscience. She tops Becky Sharp as a liar, a conniver, a cheat, and an egomaniac. While carrying on an affair with one man, Roger, she inveigles her brother-in-law, Pat, to go to bed with her, and tricks him into marrying her as soon as she gets her divorce.

The other characters are more pleasant, but their sexual

habits are not much better than Delia's. Most of them have frequent, "agonizing" affairs. The agonizing springs from everything but a troubled conscience. When Frank slept with Jill, he was concerned first that the affair might hurt his political career, and then that it might prevent his gaining custody of his child when he divorced Delia. When Jill slept successively with two different men, she was concerned (after she became pregnant) first about which man was the father, and then about whether to have an abortion. When Delia slept with Roger, she was concerned first about losing her husband, Frank, and then about how she could best use Roger to make Pat Ryan jealous and so attract—or entrap—him romantically.

Frank's parents were worried about the whole situation, and when Frank and Delia filed for divorce, one of their concerns was that the Catholic church does not countenance remarriage after divorce, but the script did not call for them to worry about Frank's breaking the commandment regarding adultery.

It is not completely clear whether Jill is a Catholic, or for that matter a member of any church, but she is the only character in the show that ever had a momentary twinge of conscience about adultery. She quickly got over it when Frank argued, speciously, "I can't make peace with God until I make peace with myself." He then demonstrated that making peace with himself meant getting what he wanted, sex with Jill.

Incidentally, Jill, in spite of her short-lived twinge of conscience about sleeping with Frank, previously spent a weekend with the other man, Seneca, which didn't seem to trouble her at the time. It troubled her later only because it resulted in pregnancy. For him to be the father of her child distressed her because it was Frank, not Seneca, whom she loved.*

Distraught, she asked another character in the serial, her sister Faith, who is a doctor, "What'll I do?"

The answer was, "Whatever is right for you," which is like saying, "Abortion, if you can square it with your conscience."

In fact, Faith went further. In a later episode she begged Jill not to rule out abortion and advised, "Don't think about Frank, don't think about Seneca, don't think about the baby, think about Jill Coleridge." In short, think only of yourself.

---

* After the child was born, the story line took a new twist. His blood type matched neither Seneca's nor Jill's, so Seneca concluded the child must be Frank's.

Don't hesitate to snuff out a life if it suits *your* convenience.

Jill did go to an abortion clinic to make inquiries. She returned home more undecided than ever. She had met two women at the clinic, one an unmarried teenager, the other a matron. Both had made a decision. For the teenager it was abortion, for the matron it was no abortion. Both felt happy and relieved, and each believed that she was doing the right thing.

Jill implied that the contrary decisions of these women had left her more at sea than before she visited the clinic, as though she were going to pattern her own behavior on the attitudes and actions of other people.

Whether Jill is supposed to be a Catholic or not doesn't matter here. The idea that in moral matters one simply follows the crowd is both anti-Catholic and anti-Christian.

Religion teaches that objective truth and hence objective commandments exist. It teaches that a person should determine his course of action not by consensus, but by what actually is right. It teaches that doing the right thing many times demands that a person go against, not with, the crowd.

Jill finally did decide against the abortion but, the viewer gathered, it was mainly because Maeve Ryan (Frank's mother) disapproved of abortion.

The relativism and the collectivism running through TV are insidiously undermining all religion, as well as all morality based on objective truth and fixed principles.

Birth Control and Abortion in One Easy Lesson

Another program, quite different in format, offended not only Catholics, but Christians of various denominations. Phil Donahue interviewed on his show Louise B. Tyrer, M.D., medical director of Planned Parenthood, and they discussed vasectomies and tubal ligations as casually as one discusses haircuts. Allegedly, as many women over 25 years old have accepted ligation as have taken the pill. In fact, it was said on

99

the program that three out of 10 couples resort to vasectomy or tubal ligation.

A summary of the other statements that Phil and Dr. Tyrer made might go like this:

Natural forms of birth control, such as the rhythm method, are used negligibly. Only about two percent of Catholics practice them—all older Catholics, relics from pre-Vatican II days.

Some women fear using diaphragms or IUDs, but they shouldn't; the new hormone-releasing IUD is highly satisfactory. Several types of IUDs were actually held up to the camera and shown on the screen. (A few months later, the FDA, citing possible harmful side effects of IUDs, announced a new regulation effective November 7, 1977: women must be told of risks.)

A woman may have a ligation without consulting her husband. (It's part of being liberated!)

If a doctor refuses to sterilize a patient, the patient can always apply to the ACLU for counsel on how to get action.

Abortion is safe. Although Planned Parenthood does not approve abortion as a *primary* form of birth control, it feels that abortion provides a woman with a backup form of birth control. After all, who can tell when other forms of birth control may fail?

Another form of natural birth control, the Billings method, which has been used with great success, was not mentioned. The U. S. National Institute of Child Health and Development sees enough promise in the method to have awarded a $1.4 million grant to the Cedar-Sinai Medical Center in Los Angeles for a three-year comparative study with this thermal-rhythm method.

No doubt Dr. Tyrer knows of the method, but instead of mentioning it, she talked exclusively about artificial methods, which many people do not in conscience feel free to use.

Going to the Devil?

Is television going to the devil? If you watched *Rosemary's Baby*, you might well conclude that it is. This chilling dramatization of Ira Levin's novel was shown over the ABC network on August 29, 1976.

That it was cleverly staged, well written, and expertly acted by a skilled cast including Mia Farrow and Ruth Gordon doesn't make it less pernicious. Worse even than the pop Satanism that we spoke of earlier, it was a parody of religious teaching. The Virgin Mary conceived a Son, the Scriptures teach, not by her husband, a mere man, but by "the power of the Most High" that "overshadowed" her. Rosemary conceived a son, not by her husband, a mere man, but by the power of the evil spirit that overshadowed her.

The names of the two women (does it not seem blasphemous to link them?) were similar, Mary and Rosemary.

Once in the grip of Satan, Rosemary was helpless. Her God could not rescue her. The show definitely was saying that Satan is stronger than God, for Rosemary fought the evil and cried out in desperation and agony, "Oh, God; oh, God," begging His help. She received none. Yes, the message that came through was that God could not help her—cannot help anybody else—and prayer is useless. In the end, evil inevitably triumphs.

Despite all of Rosemary's struggles, she was never released from Satan's grip, and at last she stopped fighting. She looked down at the monster conceived by Satan, lying in the crib; she smiled, content for the time to give in to evil.

The sequel to the film, *What Happened to Rosemary's Baby?*, was equally blasphemous. It opened with the voice of the mother pleading, "Oh, God; oh, God; oh, God."

Again her prayer was unanswered. She wanted to remove her baby, Adrian, from the clutches of the Satanists, but ultimately she failed and died. Adrian was left to be reared by the Satanists.

When he grew up, they prayed to the boy's father, Satan, to help him fulfill his mission. They chanted sometimes in Latin, sometimes in English, using the words, "Hail, Satan! Hail, Adrian!"

Adrian, they said, must bring a new world. After 2,000 years of light must come 2,000 years of darkness. And "there is more joy in hell over the corruption of one innocent than in all the chanting of the ungodly." (Analogous obviously to Luke 15:7: ". . . joy shall be in heaven over one sinner that repenteth, more than over ninety and nine just persons, which need no repentance.")

On Adrian's 21st birthday, the Satanists drugged him and gathered around his stretched-out body. They asked the man who had been husband to Adrian's mother (though not Adrian's father, only his foster father) to kill Adrian. The man raised the knife and was about to plunge it into the youth's body, when somebody stayed his hand, saying that it was only a test. (No doubt this was a perversion of the story of Abraham and Isaac.)

The film ended with another drugging—a partial drugging this time—of Adrian and his seduction by a Satanist so that he might sire a daughter of the same breed. Then Adrian was nearly run down by a speeding car, but by a "miracle" he was not killed. As one character pointed out, it was a "resurrection."

"He's Just a Man"

Speaking of resurrection, NBC ran the movie *Jesus Christ, Superstar*, on October 11, 1976.

In it, Jesus never rose from the dead; the film ended with his crucifixion. The film made him no more than an ordinary human being. Jesus Christ was portrayed as a modern-type revolutionary, a rabblerouser who was uncertain about His mission. Moreover, He was involved romantically with Mary Magdalene, who beguilingly sang over and over, "He's just a man, just a man."

For viewers who accept the divinity of Jesus Christ, the show left a bad taste.

A Dash of Seasoning

All during the 1976–77 TV season, shows that were not necessarily antireligious on the whole were often marked by little slurs against religion.

These slurs were sprinkled here and there for the same reasons that pepper is sprinkled on an egg, to add some zip—or so the scripters and directors thought.

For example, in a "Maude" episode there was a man who invented ridiculous contraptions, sure-fire money losers every one. He even designed self-illuminating bedroom slippers for night wear. Maude quipped, "He's the same guy who invented fluoridated holy water."

Again on "Maude" (October 4, 1976) religion was dragged in unnecessarily and treated flippantly and derisively. Maude had arranged for an elderly and unmarried couple to live in an apartment over her garage, but the man, though he moved in, had qualms about "free love." He said that he was praying to St. Joseph for the manly virtue of self-control. Maude answered that he should be praying to St. Jude, patron of lost causes. To strengthen his chances of self-control, the man hung a blanket up between the twin beds. Maude thought the blanket absurd and wanted to remove it. The man said that if the blanket went, he would have to go to Confession every day. As if Confession were some sort of license to commit sin!

On "The Mike Douglas Show" (February 11, 1977) one of the guests did an impersonation of a priest-pastor who reported to the parishioners that he spent $50,000 for candles, $50,000 for matches, and that Sister Mary Alice had won the mink stole that had been raffled off at the church bazaar.

We have already mentioned that Sisters are frequent targets of antireligious pellets. In "The Tony Randall Show" father and son were discussing their dislike of women and the son said, "We'll have to become nuns."

That the boy did not know that nuns are women, not men, was of trifling concern. But it was not trifling that he thought nuns enter a convent (and he implicitly told viewers this) because they dislike the opposite sex. A nun's consecration of her life to God and to the service of her fellow man was completely ignored.

In "Happy Days" (September 21, 1976) Fonzie's girlfriend with the scanty clothes and the aggressive tactics with boys said that she was reared in a convent after her parents were divorced. This girl seemed a mighty poor specimen of convent upbringing. Whatever the Sisters taught her, it wasn't modesty or meekness.

Still, she was a saint in comparison with Wanda of MH2, whose conversation and behavior were too lewd to recount here. Yet this depraved creature spoke of her nun-teacher in grade school.

After hearing things like that we scarcely notice the milder antireligious tidbits. "One Day at a Time" (January 4, 1977) had an episode where daughter Julie spoke of finding Jesus. Someone said flippantly, "I didn't know he was lost." Another character spoke of "instant faith—add holy water and mix."

"M.A.S.H." has its quota of antireligious wisecracks. An army officer speaking of his wife said, "She's stateside playing bingo with Catholics." A soldier in the same series asked somebody, "Is there a blessing for a new latrine?"

The padre on "M.A.S.H." is portrayed as a blundering, bungling creature who acts as if he could hardly have graduated from "Ding Dong School," much less from any seminary.

Another war show, ABC's "The Rear Guard" (August 10, 1976), was more offensive. In an oblique way it profaned nearly all the Christian churches. Civil Defense men of World War II had captured a group of Germans. One of the captors phoned army headquarters for instructions. They were, "Give the people something to eat."

The caller answered, "Well, we're holding them in a church and there's nothing here but wafers."

Churches figure unnecessarily in other TV shows. In the "Streets of San Francisco" (rerun September 16, 1976) a shoot-out was staged in a Catholic church and money exchanged between criminals who hid in the confessionals.

Like a syncopated beat, the antireligious note repeats itself with irregular regularity throughout television programs.

In an episode of "Welcome Back, Kotter" a teenage girl said that she was pregnant and that one of the "sweathogs" was responsible. All the boys denied having had an intimate relationship with the girl, so somebody said, "We should put a candle in the window because the last time this happened three wise men came from the East."

On "All's Fair," when the then pregnant Charley (she soon had a miscarriage) refused Richard's proposal of marriage, he asked, "Are you telling me this baby is going to be born without a father?" She answered, "No, that happened only once."

In "Block Party," a slapstick comedy show, a stockbroker ended a phone call with, "Give my love to Sister Mary Immaculate." Because it was so incongruous coming in the midst of all the hijinx, everybody laughed.

It was incongruous too when Mary Hartman (MH2, October 15, 1976), while talking to her psychiatrist, referred to the Bible, saying that "The First Corinthians were better sexually adjusted than we are."

TV scripters love to depict a religious hypocrite. In an episode of "All's Fair" (October 18, 1976) a man who hoped to clean up Washington's morals came to see Richard, the editor. Mr. Clean brought with him his homely, frumpy wife and a minister whom Richard had previously met on the golf links. The trio wanted Richard to appear on TV in behalf of their cause.

While they were discussing the idea, in came Charley, the girl photographer. After a few comic lines, Richard bravely or brazenly (you choose the adverb) told all. He was living with Charley.

Shocked, Mrs. Clean jumped up, ready to shake from her feet the dust of this "den of iniquity," but Mr. Clean intervened. He made it clear that he didn't really care whether the men who represented his movement led pure lives; all he wanted was a big name to attract people to the movement and their dollars into his pocket. The "pastor of souls," on leaving, said to Richard that he was not concerned about his morals; that was none of his business.

But for sheer contempt of religion, perhaps nothing tops the first episode of "All's Fair." Charley and Richard were arguing politics and assorted subjects, and Richard made a passing reference to religion. Wide-eyed with surprise and repugnance, Charley exclaimed, "Oh, God, don't tell me you're religious too!"

That is the last straw. For the millions of Americans who are "religious too," it is time to fight back.

Chapter 10

Violent and Vicious

Innocent Action

If you ask the media moguls about violent police or detective, or crime shows, they will look blank, and act as though they did not know what you were talking about. In their lingo, there is no such thing; there are only "action shows," or "action-adventure shows."

Sounds like innocent fun.

·It isn't.

Although nobody wants TV to be all sweetness and light, because life isn't that way, it isn't 99 percent violent and vicious either. Lamentably, as long as man has walked this familiar planet there has been violence. It goes back to Cain and Abel and comes forward to today's newspaper. What is disturbing about TV violence is that it exceeds the demands of reality and the needs of the narrative. It is there just to put more action on the screen. The "action" is like graffiti on a whitewashed wall—useless, ugly, and defacing.

Moreover, producers and directors often depict violence in too explicit a manner. If a man must be killed, we don't have to see a close-up of him spouting blood. But often we do.

Crime shows feature murder and mayhem, torture and spine-tingling horror. Bodies, dead or alive, are thrown from speeding cars, tossed out of windows, toppled down three flights of stairs, or pushed off the roofs of 10-story buildings. Men and women are shot, strangled, stabbed, pistol-whipped, deliberately run down and run over by cars. Too, in crime shows there is usually a race, with cars careening around corners, coming to screeching halts, or hitting other cars, or smashing into walls or tress, or rolling over cliffs and going up in flames as the gasoline ignites and explodes. Sometimes the show ends with a free-for-all shootout of the survivors in which the booming of guns recalls the Normandy beaches on D-day.

In an episode from "Charlie's Angels" there was false arrest, white slavery, seminudity, a lesbian guard at a women's prison, homicide, a flaming car wreck and prisoners pursued by bloodhounds.

Not bad for a single evening! But the feat can be, and often is, duplicated. In fact, there is so much duplication on crime shows that it has become a joke. In the cartoon "The New Neighbors" the man says to his wife, "You know the trouble with the new fall shows? They already seem like reruns."

The reason for the duplication is that the basic ingredients are always the same. The difference between shows comes with the slightly different proportions used in the mix, or with one small distinguishing extra thrown in somewhere. Concocting a crime show is like making a cake. The basics in cake making are flour, eggs, sugar, baking powder, etc., but the proportions of these differ for a pound cake, a sponge cake, a chiffon cake, etc.; and for a devil's food cake a little chocolate is thrown in, for a Lady Baltimore cake some nuts and raisins, and for a banana cake, bananas.

The media men say that people like the basics of blood and gore in any proportion. The extras are comparatively unimportant; they simply keep the shows separate in the viewers' minds.

Pro and Con

Perhaps a few people do like blood and gore, but how many?

It is true, as the networks like to point out, that until modern times there were public hangings in many countries. However, those who attended were at most a few hundred out of the whole populace—nothing when compared with the millions who see violence on TV.

The networks also defend themselves by saying that in action shows, the "good guy" always wins, so the show is teaching a moral lesson.

They do have a point, but as another TV writer comments, this doesn't happen "before the bad guy has been portrayed as a slightly glamorous, high-style, devil-may-care character, who lives a much more exciting life, really, than all us good guys who were watching the good guy catch him."

Occasionally the violence can become sickening, as in "Getaway" (December 15, 1976), when the protagonist beat up his wife.

Knocking the Men in Blue

Distressing too is TV's penchant for portraying crooked cops. After all, the majority of real-life law-enforcement officers are honest. "The Rockford Files," by contrast, has on occasion given the impression that the last person a decent citizen should trust is a policeman. In one episode (October 8, 1976) the law-enforcement man was trying to embezzle no less than $100,000 from government coffers. An episode in "Kojak" (October 3, 1976) portrayed a policeman who was having an affair with a girl described as "a tramp." "The Blue Knight" also has some venal policemen, and it wasn't too edifying to see (September 22, 1976) a violent fight between two officers of the law, one honest, the other a scoundrel. The same show featured police brutality toward citizens—not terribly edifying, and surely exaggerated.

In "Police Woman" (November 9, 1976) there was an episode about a sergeant who had a drinking problem.

In "Serpico" the protagonist had to deal in most episodes with stupid policemen who wrecked his plans. Usually, he was caught between them and the thugs, a situation that was meant to arouse viewer loyalty and sympathy.

In "Delvecchio" the detective, a would-be lawyer, represented a fellow officer suspected of making obscene phone calls.

Sight Effects

Some shows portray among the criminals Vietnam veterans who have become glassy-eyed, lice-infested, unwashed heroin addicts. The parents and wives of men who served honorably over there don't appreciate that—but do any of us? You would never learn from television that the vast majority of Vietnam vets never even tried heroin, much less got hooked on it.

After a while some of this sinks in. We begin to suspect all policemen of venality, stupidity, and brutality, and to wonder if anybody who was in Vietnam might not be a drug taker. As for the constant violence, that must leave a few psychological scars and scratches.

George Gerbner and Larry Gross, writing in *Psychology Today* (April 1976), declared that people who watch a great deal of TV develop fear and timidity, and suspicion of their fellow man: "They think the world is even more dangerous than it really is." And since the dramas are set in urban centers, continued Gerbner and Gross, "The fear they inspire may contribute to the current flight of the middle class from our cities."

These writers believe, as well, that a heavy TV watcher tends to lose perspective. He is unable to see his fellows clearly. "His view of human nature would be shaped by the shallow psychology of TV characters."

In the spring of 1976 psychiatrists Roderic Gorney and Dr. David Loye of the University of California, Los Angeles conducted a study of the effect of violence on adults. They chose at random 260 couples and analyzed the effect of watching so many hours of violence per day. According to the National Association for Better Broadcasting, they found that viewing "antisocial" (violent) television not only increased "unhelpful" behavior, but also "caused a startling difference in values." Dr. Loye reported, according to the NABB, that "change in values was an unexpected and 'almost inconceivable' finding."

Worse yet, the action shows have been accused of fostering an insensitivity in viewers. A person who sees murder after murder is supposedly less likely to be shocked and compassionate when he encounters real-life cruelty. Dr. Victor Cline, professor of psychology at the University of Utah, agreed with this. In an interview published in *People* magazine, Dr. Cline said, "Such constant exposure to violence 'desensitizes' our conscience, blunting our empathy and concern for other human beings."

The doctor gave an example: the famous Kitty Genovese case in New York City. Though 38 people heard her cries or saw her murder, nobody tried to help her. Nobody even bothered to phone the police anonymously.

There are claims that TV does more than simply harden people; that in some cases it makes them relish cruelty as did the ancient Romans who cheered when men and women were thrown to the lions.

Newspapers have reported that crowds standing in the street, gawking upward at a man about to jump off the ledge of a high building, have urged him on by yelling "Jump! Jump!"

Is that the result of TV desensitization?

Maybe. On the other hand, it might have furnished copy for an "All in the Family" (October 14, 1976) episode. Archie climbed out of a window onto the ledge of an office building to try to dissuade a would-be suicide. It was blood-curdling to hear the cries "Jump! Jump!" even on this fictional piece.

Vicious Circle

Which derived from which? The headlines from the TV? Or the TV from the headlines?

On October 13, 1976, the *Philadelphia Bulletin* carried two front-page items that sounded like reenactments of TV shows. One was about a Rolls Royce–driving Miami woman, called "Queen of Shoplifters and Sneakthieves," who operated a nationwide organization of light-fingered gentry. The second item was about a gang that kidnapped a mentally retarded man in San Diego and for two days beat and burned him, etc.

If these news items are not reenactments, then they will very likely be inspiration to some scripters for subsequent shows. This is the vicious circle. TV is both a trend-setter and a trend-follower.

We are concerned here mostly with TV as a trend-setter. Most of us would agree with the words of Paul Simon of the House of Representatives, in the *Congressional Record* of August 3, 1976: "I do not believe it is an infringement of fundamental civil liberties to recognize that excessive violence on our television screens is not healthy for this nation."

Monkey See, Monkey Do

A few psychiatrists would tell Congressman Simon that some TV violence is good because it lets viewers take out these aggressions vicariously. These doctors believe that TV has a cathartic effect, that it gratifies violent impulses without requiring action by the viewers.

The much more widely held opinion, however, is that on-screen violence can turn some viewers into doers who will go out into the real world to enact what they saw on the screen. (More about this when we delve into TV's effect on youth.)

Speaking of this monkey-see-monkey-do effect, Martin A. Russo, representative from Illinois and member of the Communications Subcommittee, said, "Far too often the national press reports serious crimes that have remarkable similarity to fictional crime on television" (*Congressional Record*, September 15, 1976).

TV, it seems, is both an instructor in crime and an abettor of it. During the last ten years, the U.S. felony rate has risen 144 percent. That means crime is increasing six to ten times the rate of population growth. A violent crime is committed every 31 seconds.

Though it would be grossly unfair to blame the entire rise on TV, it is fair to blame some of it on TV.

In a *TV Guide* article (January 29, 1977), Grant H. Hendrick proves that television is at least partially guilty. To gather his data, Hendrick, a prison inmate, interviewed 208 of his peers in the Marquette, Michigan maximum-security prison. The men were probably representative of prisoners in other such institutions, and nine out of ten of them said that TV crime shows taught them new tricks of the trade. The prisoners confided to the writer that television taught them how to steal cars, how to break into a building, how to rob a house, how to roll a drunk, how to fake an ID card, and how to commit murder in a variety of novel ways.

Four hundred fifty-nine prisoners had TV sets in their cells, and, Hendrick said, many sat in front of them taking notes on crime techniques, which they planned to put into practice the minute they were free again.

The shows not only suggested ideas and provided detailed how-to information; they revealed methods policemen used in tracking down criminals.

If the violence and crime on TV do not have this effect on the general population (and admittedly they do not), they are still regrettable. Television treats crime and violence as everyday occurrences and hence almost acceptable.

Nobody can entirely escape seeing TV murder and mayhem. Lee Winfrey, writing in the *Philadelphia Inquirer*, complained that only on Monday night, which the networks consider "women's night," was it possible to dial around and not "get a solid two-hour fix on homicide and gore between 9 and 11 P.M."

The Wild West—At Its Worst

To the crime shows was added for a few months NBC's "Quest," a western that was certainly no less violent than any other show we can mention. The only thing that made it more pleasant than the crime shows was the scenery; that was magnificent. If the people just hadn't been there, it would have been a beautiful travelogue.

Its opening episode (September 22, 1976) included cavalry massacring Indians, Indians massacring cavalry, several brawls and gunfights, and a brutal rape. The second episode (September 29, 1976) was cut from the same cloth. A person watching the show with pad and pencil would have had a hard time tallying the murders, they happened so rapidly. Early on, a horseman rode onto the scene dragging behind him at rope's end an enslaved woman. There followed in quick succession a fight involving several men, a horse theft, and pursuit of the robbers punctuated by a shooting, by the discovery of dead bodies from a previous fight, and by fights with knives, guns, and arrows. Like Hansel and Gretel dropping bread crumbs along the way, the protagonists dropped corpses over hill and dale.

The average lifespan of a man on "Quest" was less than five minutes.

Annie, Get Your Gun

More numerous than in former years are the women criminals on TV. Is this the liberated women's way of saying to men, "Anything you can do, I can do better?" In "Streets of San Francisco" girls often commit murder. In one episode (September 30, 1976) women working with men hijacked a bus carrying the 12 jury members to a court trial.

There are also more policewomen and women detectives than of yore. ABC'S "Charlie's Angels" presents three sexy and glamorous girls who sleuth with the best of men. They see some rough stuff too, like the men, but usually are spared fist-fights and such. *TV Guide* said of the show's debut in the fall of 1976 that the only problems the girls had to contend with during the course of the first episode was "a lecherous tennis pro, an asthmatic thug, a menacing sheriff, a murderous masseuse, one miscellaneous dirty old man, one horse stampede, two screeching car chases, and three violent deaths."

113

"Anything you can do, I can do better!"

The Bad Penny

Violence is not confined to "action shows." Like the bad penny, it turns up almost everywhere.

"Death Wish" was originally a theater movie. With a little laundering of its gruesome beginning, in which the wife was murdered and the daughter raped, CBS put it on the tube. Still there was brutality plus, as the protagonist waged a one-man war on muggers, stalking them in alleys, parks, and subways, and killing them as though they were so many sparrows. Brian Garfield, who wrote the original story, said he was shocked when he heard that it was to be shown on TV.

Nor do the soap operas and sitcoms avoid violence. MH2, which tried not to miss a trick, had a mass murder. A teenager named Davy Jessup wiped out an entire family and then added a little grace note to the affair by slaughtering their livestock.

Violence was rife too on the ABC dramatization of Taylor Caldwell's book *The Captains and the Kings*. A woman was knocked down a long flight of stairs, a man picked up an iron poker and went after another man before they tangled in a vicious fight that scattered and shattered furniture, guns opened up on striking miners . . .

The Gerbner and Gross article in the April 1976 issue of *Psychology Today* stated that more than half of all characters on prime-time TV are involved in some violence and about one tenth in actual killing.

Horrors!

Some programs go beyond the wanton violence of the action shows and try to sate the public's appetite for horror. NABB literature mentions a televised movie shown on KCOP-TV Los Angeles (April 4, 1976) called *The Vampire People*. The film included, NABB said, "ritualistic butcherings and several incidents of drinking blood from the throats of still-living victims."

Indeed, the popular "Starsky and Hutch" had an episode (October 30, 1976) about a vampire. A striptease girl was killed and the police investigation indicated that her jugular vein had been pierced with a sharp instrument after death and less blood was in her body than a normal person would have had. (Incidentally, this was shown on a Friday, 9 P.M. EST, and earlier in the western part of the country—in plenty of time everywhere to catch the kiddies before they went to bed.)

Then there was CBS's "Helter Skelter," shown on the networks on April 1 and 2, 1976 (and rerun January 24, 1977). "Helter Skelter" was too much even for *Newsweek*'s Harry F. Waters, who denounced this grisly production based upon the Manson-clan murders. Waters reminded *Newsweek* readers about the "ritualistic butcherings" of the pregnant actress

115

Sharon Tate and of all the members of her household, which he said the Manson girls spoke of "with orgiastic relish." One of the killers squealed, "We even were going to cut out her baby!" Later, Waters added, the prosecution revealed that one of the girls "drank the dead actress's blood."

Let's hope that TV does not feel that every crime must be reenacted on the screen, and made into a Roman circus. Horrible murders occur, criminals exist, and newscasts have to tell us about them; but they don't have to dramatize them with all the gruesome details.

Variety (December 29, 1976) carried a story about a TV newsman who asked a federal judge to order that a Texas prison allow reporters to attend an execution, the first to take place in many years.

Happily, the petition was denied. We can imagine how mawkishly the networks would have handled the scene. There would have been shots of the chaplain trying to bring spiritual comfort to the condemned man, shots of the prisoner's family, and then a countdown reminiscent of a missile launching—five seconds before the switch is thrown, four seconds . . . three . . . two . . . one.

We can thank the good sense of a few Texans that we were spared—this time. Next time we may not be so lucky.

Chapter 11

Move Over, Mom

Electronic Educator

Napoleon once said, "If France has good mothers, France will have good sons." And Cardinal Mindszenty said, "A mother is the most important person on earth."

Both spoke in pre-TV days.

Mothers now have to move over and make room for TV. No mother can talk to her children as steadily as does the electronic box, nor can she dramatize all her words.

TV, then, is a sort of substitute mother, an electronic educator. Though its methods and its teachings are far different from those of most mothers and those of the traditional pedagogue, it is enormously effective. It draws children to itself more surely than did the Pied Piper.

Normally, childhood is a time of leisure and learning. The whole world is brand new to the youngster, so he is as curious as a kitten in trying to learn pronto. He uses every available moment to sit at the feet of his docent.

A scientific study commissioned by a congressional committee reported that by the time a child is 18 years old, he has
spent 11,000 hours in school and 15,000 hours before a TV
screen, and he has seen approximately 18,000 murders. These
figures have been quoted by many magazines and papers, and
confirmed by the Nielsen Television Index and by the literature put out by Action for Children's Television.

Indeed, other authorities use higher figures. Lloyd Morris-
set, writing the introduction to Gerald S. Lesser's book *Children and Television*, said, "Preschool children up to the age of
six are the single heaviest viewing audience in the United
States. . . . Estimates ranging as high as an average of 50 hours
per week of watching television have been given."

At that rate, 50 (hours) times 52 (weeks) times 6 (years), children by age six will have used up all their 15,000 hours.

Whatever the actual numbers are, we know that children begin watching TV before they are old enough to brush their
teeth or tie their own shoelaces. The 1972 *Report of the Surgeon General* tells us that "by age two or three most American
children have begun to watch and listen to television
regularly."

In his book *Children's TV* William Melody says, "Before 9
A.M. on Saturdays two to five-year-olds control the dial."
(From 9 to 10 A.M., six to 11-year-olds take over.) And he
added that after eight o'clock on a Saturday morning, regardless of the program, there are about 10,000,000 children's eyes
trained on the TV screen.

The *Wall Street Journal* of October 12, 1976 had a front-
page article spotlighting several families' use—or abuse—of
television.

The young son in one family posted himself each day
promptly at 6 A.M. before the TV set. No program as yet was
on the air. He was so mesmerized by the cyclops eye of the
screen that he just sat there staring at the test pattern until the
first cartoon appeared.

The mother of another family said that her five-year-old had
been watching "Sesame Street" "since he was nine months
old and still in his playpen."

The father of the same family gave the daughter her own
color TV set when she graduated from kindergarten.

Granted, it doesn't have to be this way. Parents can limit the

"Thank goodness *my* kids aren't dope addicts!"

child's viewing time. One mother said, "I had an easy time with my oldest child, Johnny. I never turned the set on during the day, and until he was four or five, he didn't think the thing ran until nightfall. It was a different story with my second child. By the time he came along, Johnny had learned TV can run during the day. Then there was no stopping him."

Few mothers try, so it is comforting to recall that not every minute of viewing pours poison into the children's minds. There are great programs like "Wonderful World of Disney," which has collected awards as often and as easily as you and I might collect coat hangers. There is no comment to make about it except Oliver Twist's, "Please, sir, may I have some more."

Deserving honorable mention too are many other programs, among them "Once upon a Classic," "Mister Rogers' Neighborhood," "Captain Noah," and "Captain Kangaroo."

Devil's Advocate

But the object of this book is not to hand out orchids for good shows; it is to play the devil's advocate and point out the bad.

In trying to cultivate the children's imagination and to entertain them, while dispensing crumbs of information along the way, TV for kiddies, with its monsters, puppets, talking-dog McDuff, Pink Panther, Bugs Bunny, Spiderman, Dynamutt, vampires, shark Jabberjaws, computerized wax dummies, fast-moving cartoons, and live-action film, can sometimes overstimulate.

Even the much-praised "Sesame Street" has been criticized for this. Indeed, a Dallas newspaper, the *Morning News*, went so far as to say that the program is breeding "a new generation of drug takers because of the restlessness that it fosters, the lack of discipline, the lack of critical judgment, and what will literally become a fear of a moment's silence."

Few would agree with that sweeping condemnation, but none of us is likely to disagree about the fear of silence part. "Sesame Street" does have a lot of noise—though, come to think of it, "The Electric Company," aimed at the slightly older child, is noisier. The latter, despite its good qualities, does make an awful din; commercials for "The Electric Company" should advise people to wear earplugs.

"The Flintstones," an entirely different type of show (an animated cartoon without any educational pretensions or intentions but still acceptable as entertainment), can also be faulted for noise. Why should our children's musical taste be distorted by rock music at an early age?

"Jabberjaws" too pulsates with raucous rock sound. However, there are definite signs that the popularity of rock music and loud music of all kinds has long since peaked and soon our eardrums will have some rest.

TV critic Lee Winfrey wrote in the *Philadelphia Inquirer* that "Jabberjaws" is "witless and pointless." He called it the kind of children's program that "makes mothers lock themselves in the bedroom" while it is on. Yet this is the TV fare on which we are raising the next generation of Americans.

Frenzied Activity

Frenzied activity often accompanies the noisy programs. Some experts, like psychologist George Gerbner of the University of Pennsylvania, call it violence, but since much of it appears in the cartoons with two-dimensional creatures, it seems that "frenzied activity" would be a better term. Fanciful cats or cows or kangaroos get picked up by the tail or the neck to be swung around in circles or slammed against trees or houses, or flattened to a cardboard-thin slab by falling walls or speeding trains; or a bomb goes off, leaving a bald tiger or a maneless horse; or a piano wired with dynamite blows up in a coyote's face; or a dog is plunged into a vat of molasses or tar; or Bugs Bunny is propelled off a cliff and dashed against rocks hundreds of feet below; or cats endlessly chase mice, dogs endlessly chase cats, or an anteater chases ants.

The Media Action Research Center of Setauket, New York found that during the 1975–76 season an aggressive or frenzied act occurred on the average every two minutes in the Saturday morning "kid-vid ghetto" (as it is called in the industry), and in cartoons the score was even higher—one nearly every minute.

The fevered pitch of activity should make the children dizzy even if the aggressiveness does not dismay them. If mom looked at the stuff for as long as the children do, she would be pleading, "Pass the tranquilizer."

But kids are tougher in some ways than adults; they enjoy the fast action and the slapstick. Still the question is: Is it good for them? Could it really be that we are rearing a generation of drug takers? In the next chapter, we will talk about the effects of TV on children.

For now, however, let's at least note one point: they may sit there benumbed and bemused for hours, and if we say, "Why don't you look at your picture books or go out and play in the sunshine," they don't even hear us; yet the wild activity on the screen makes for later restlessness. Once the TV is off, they don't know what to do with themselves; they suffer from hyperkinesis. They no longer know what it is to sit, lazy and happy, on a grassy knoll and watch the clouds roll by, or to wander in the woods and find with glad surprise the first violets of spring peeping beneath green leaves, or to curl up in a favorite chair and read an adventure story, or just to hop along a sidewalk feeling pleased with themselves for having never once stepped on the cracks.

Some agencies have been working for a long time to tone down children's programs. The government itself has been studying the problem of violence (and frenzied activity) on TV ever since Estes Kefauver's hearings in 1952.

In 1954 a Yale group found that children's programs were the most violent on TV. Fifteen years later the National Commission on the Causes and Prevention of Violence, chaired by Dr. Milton Eisenhower, made another attempt to study the problem.

In 1975 the Rand Corporation compiled a bibliography of the research on television and human behavior and found 2,300 studies or papers on the subject. That number didn't include the papers that grew out of the series of public hearings on violence sponsored by the 6.5-million-member National Parent-Teacher Association in Pittsburgh in the fall of 1976. It did include, however, the major government study, the 1972 *Report of the Surgeon General*, from which we will quote in the next chapter.

Michael B. Rothenberg, M.D., of the University of Washington School of Medicine and the Children's Orthopedic Hospital and Medical Center in Seattle, has described his findings in the *Journal of the American Medical Association*: "One violent act was depicted every minute in television cartoons for children under the age of ten, and there was, on the average, six times more violence during one hour of children's television than there is in one hour of adult programming."

Other Objections

Worse than the violence, perhaps, are the lessons in deceit, vengeance, etc. In a "Bugs Bunny" cartoon, a character talked about getting rid of Bugs and making his death seem like an accident.

Just as adult shows downgrade marriage, so do some kid-vid

shows. "The Jetsons" had an episode about a husband with an eye for the ladies who was conniving to get out of the house and attend a beauty pageant. He succeeded in doing what he wanted, only to find that his wife was a contestant—in fact, the winner.

After seeing that show, the children might wonder if their own daddy is maneuvering to sneak out of the house to see a lot of leggy and bosomy girls—and if mom will outsmart him.

"Porky the Pig" had an episode set in Paris. While Porky and his girlfriend were sitting at a sidewalk cafe, she asked, "Why don't you marry me?"

He answered, "I would, except that I promised the inspector I'd enjoy my vacation."

TV As Moral Mentor

On the other hand, the child does hear something about morals and character development. CBS's "Fat Albert and the Cosby Kids," the creation of Bill Cosby, conveyed such messages as "don't steal" and "don't lie," which is all to the good.

"Captain Noah" advises his little listeners to be good to one another, and he ends his shows with the words, "Don't forget to say your prayers."

ABC's "Afterschool Specials" is, by its very name, not intended for toddlers. However, many of them do look at it with their older sisters and brothers. On the whole, it is a good program but not always appropriate for small children. One episode, for instance, was about two sisters who learned to cope with their mother's alcoholism. That's rather strong stuff for the tricycle crowd.

The same was true of "Muggsby," the show conceived and produced by George Heinemann, NBC vice president of special programming for children. It was about a 13-year-old girl who lived in the ghetto and it attracted some toddlers. It taught social attitudes that occasionally had a moral tie-in; it featured episodes about arson, shoplifting, beatings, vandalism, gang warfare, and guns stolen from a thug. The last-mentioned episode ended with a car chase and a shooting, just like the grown-up crime shows.

123

The National Education Association recommended "Muggsby," and no doubt some parents agree that it is a good idea to make children aware of inner-city problems. Others ask: What's the rush? Why it is necessary to introduce young children to the seamy side of life? These people feel the children will learn that sort of thing soon enough, and they are not anxious to hasten the process. They argue that they are not shielding the children from reality, or failing to prepare them for adulthood; rather, they are starting them off in life on the firm foundation of first seeing and learning good conduct, so that later they can cope, if necessary, with the bad.

Another criticism of "Muggsby": the fact that some acts committed on the program were crimes was not always brought out clearly. That they were (to the God-fearing) sins was not brought out at all.

There were two installments about boys who set fire to their fathers' stores. In one (December 11, 1976) the boy said that he did it to attract his father's attention. Absorbed in his business, the father had not taken time out for his son. The policeman then told the father that he should apologize to his son.

In the other episode, shown a couple of months earlier, the boy at least acknowledged he had done wrong, but his repentance consisted of saying that it was "a mean way" to tell his father that "I hate him."

The hate was passed over—actually defended—with the argument that the boy was trying to send his father "signals," pleas for psychological help and for affection. The scripter made the boy's father an unsympathetic snob who looked down on his son's rowdy pals, whose families were on a financial rung beneath him.

The father was further portrayed as hardhearted and hardheaded. Some neighborhood children saw in his shop a superdeluxe skateboard costing $65.00. They offered to clean the shop for pay, hoping they would earn enough to buy their desideratum. After they had finished, the man told them that they still owed him some cash, and one of the children exclaimed, "That's not fair."

The man replied, "That's business," thereby implying falsely that business is necessarily unfair. He did not explain that one day's work at the minimum wage could not possibly earn them $65.00. He passed up this opportunity to teach the younger generation that one must work for rewards; that effort pays off. Instead, he gave them a false impression of business.

Other shows too give false impressions and false guidance, or no guidance at all. Urie Bronfenbrenner, professor of psychology at Cornell University, complained about the lack of moral training in "Sesame Street." He said its "makers focus on cognitive skills . . . but character development . . . is being taken over by two other institutions as yet unprepared for the task: the children's peer group and the television screen."

By that he seems to mean that "Sesame Street" may teach children their ABCs, but it leaves their character training to their little friends and siblings, and to the other TV shows that they watch.

His criticism is both true and untrue. It is untrue about "Sesame Street," for that program does indeed touch upon social problems that have a moral tie-in. "Sesame Street" constantly shows white and black people together (like "Muggsby" and other children's programs), so it seems to be saying, over and over again, "Don't discriminate for reasons of race." In a general way it also says, "Be nice to everybody, especially other children."

Erosion of Authority

"Sesame Street" promotes its own brand of discrimination: against adults. Quite often it shows adults making mistakes and behaving stupidly (as of course they sometimes do in real life), but it never shows children making mistakes and behaving stupidly (as of course they too sometimes do in real life).

Robert Shayon, professor of communications at the University of Pennsylvania, declared that to show adults blundering on TV saps the child's confidence in the "loving and supportive relationship" with his parents.

It would seem, then, that "Sesame Street" tends to some degree to break down a child's respect for his parents and for any adult authority figure. Do our children need further erosion of legitimate authority?

125

Women's Lib in Nursery School

In some other shows the woman figure is bright and intelligent, while the man figure is a moronic bungler. "The Flintstones," for example, constantly downgrades the husband. If any message at all can break through this very light entertainment, it is: Men are oafs; women (and children?) can for the most part disregard them. Let's hope the children don't pick up this idea. If they fail to respect their fathers as well as their mothers, they are much less likely to develop into well-rounded adults.

In most children's shows the woman is not only smarter than the male; she is the Women's Lib ideal. She doesn't "waste" her talents on rearing children and being a "mere housewife." For example, in early programs of "Sesame Street," which was first aired in March 1968, a character known as Susan was a housewife. Nowadays Susan is a wage earner.

Certainly, a great many mothers do work outside the home; but it doesn't buttress the family to imply that *all* mothers must and do work outside the home. The child who has a stay-at-home mother may then wonder if she is a freak, or lacks enough brains, knowledge, and spunk to cope with the outside world.

Nor does it help the child or society at large implicitly to endorse the widely held falsehood that taking dictation in an office is worthwhile (because you get paid cash for it), whereas helping a child find his bearings in life is a waste of time (because you get paid in intangibles for it).

On the whole, "Sesame Street" deserves praise. Still, like any children's program that hooks the youngsters and implants the television habit at an early age, it does some harm. Though television can be instructive and highly entertaining, it can also, lamentably, be the world's greatest time waster, as well as a debaucher of morals and a fount of false philosophy. The person who does not habitually gravitate toward it, but is selective in his viewing, will have more time to cultivate other interests and in the long run will experience a richer and better life.

Get into the ACT

One more complaint has been leveled at children's programs. The commercials. Few indeed are programs like the excellent "Big Blue Marble" that are put on without any commercials at all.

The vast majority of children's shows are interrupted by candy, cereal, and toy commercials. Action for Children's Television (ACT) particularly has pointed this out. The organization's founder and president, Peggy Charin, argues quite plausibly that children are less able to resist a sales pitch than adults; therefore, commercials on children's programs should be drastically reduced in number, or eliminated entirely. Children want what they see, and any object advertised on the screen, whether it is of good or poor quality, generates the "gimmies."

As some wag put it, adults who live on a budget have learned "to let the world go buy." An excess of commercials

"I'll put it this way, kiddies: Tell your mommy if she doesn't buy
you 'Goodie-Oh Chocolate Yums' you'll have
a traumatic experience."

127

on TV encourages children to think they can have anything they want—right now!

According to literature put out by ACT, the advertising industry spends $400,000,000 a year for messages aimed at children. ACT says it has forced the industry to cut down a staggering 40 percent on the commercials in children's programs. It has also weeded out such advertising ploys as having the hero of a show become the pitchman for a product.

ACT, with others, protested the commercial for Milky Way candy bars. The message ran, "At home, at play, at rest, all day: Milky Way." Timothy Wirth, United States representative from Colorado, remarked that all the sugary stuff advertised on children's shows would give even Spiderman cavities. He also said, "There is, after all, something worse than taking candy from a baby. It's selling candy to a baby."

Along with the American Dental Association, ACT managed the elimination of many ads for sugary foods that speed tooth decay. In 1971, with the American Pharmaceutical Association, it persuaded drug companies to take ads for vitamins and over-the-counter drugs away from children's programs. Hudson Pharmaceutical Corporation stopped pushing "delicious chewable superhero" vitamins, which encouraged kids to find the bottle of pills and down as many as possible, hoping thereby to be strong enough to leap over walls and scale towers a la TV characters.

ACT's pressure on the advertising industry has provided a safeguard to children's health. But ACT has done more. It protested to manufacturers who advertised expensive, guaranteed-to-be-broken-quickly toys on TV.

William Melody, in his book *Children's TV*, warns that such commercials can cause family friction. Let the children see a kite or a doll on the screen a few times and they begin chanting, "Pl-lease, mom, buy me one." The fiftieth time mom hears this, she gets annoyed, to put it mildly.

In deference to ACT, perhaps, Ideal Toy Corporation abandoned kid-vid and put its commercials on family programs where mom and dad could be reached as well as the children. It may have turned out to be a smart move from the company's viewpoint. Ideal is one of the most successful toy manufacturers, and its stock price held up well through the fall 1976 dip in the market.

ACT Could Act Further

It is unlikely that ACT has as yet reviewed the glut of ads. It should, however, keep an eye out for those irritating ads that say this or that toy is "only $7.95," or "only $17.95."

Now money is relative. To one family, $7.95 might be a great deal larger sum than $17.95 to another. All depends upon how much money is available and what are the spending priorities of the family. A family of eight children will not usually have as much money available for toys as a family of one or two children. A family with a crippled child who requires special therapy and medical attention, or for that matter, a family with a very talented child who could profit from special musical training, may not have as much money available as one where all the children are normal and healthy, or one where nobody has extraordinary musical gifts.

Then there are the commercials that tell a child, "Be the first on your block to get XYZ toy," or, "Be the first kid in your school to have an ABC magic-trick set."

The message here is: you'll outshine your friends by having something they don't have. In short, it is not what you *are* that gives you merit, but what you *have*. Logically, youngsters absorbing that philosophy should grow up to be as conniving and acquisitive as the character Joseph Armaugh on "The Captains and the Kings."

The Wealth Within

Fred Rogers of "Mister Rogers' Neighborhood" (a blue-ribbon show for preschoolers) once made essentially the same point.* At an ACT symposium, he said, "Commercialism bombards us all, and all too frequently with messages that say you have to

* As of this writing he is creating a new series called "Old Friends, New Friends."

129

have something besides yourself to get along. . . . Your resources are not enough, so be sure to buy ours."

How right he is! And it is only by developing inner resources, by mining the acres of diamonds within our own minds, that any of us, adults or children, become self-reliant. That means abandoning some of the passive viewing time.

It seems impossible to abandon it all. One mother, however, told this story: "Our set broke down and we deliberately decided not to have it fixed. The first TV-less week was hell. We all suffered withdrawal pains—me too. It wasn't that I was such an addict myself, but at the time my four kids were all little. Getting dinner at night was bedlam without the TV to keep them quiet and out from under my feet. As for the kids themselves—well, they practically went into shock. They didn't know what to do with themselves, and they were a mess. I was about to phone the repairman when, to my surprise, I found the second week was better. The kids got out old toys, forgotten Christmas gifts, and they began to play with them. The third and fourth weeks were still better. The kids devised games of 'Let's pretend,' or they used their coloring books, or they played house—they even told improvised ghost stories."

Did this woman ever go back to TV?

"Yes, I had to," she said. "It's impossible to live in this world without television. It's now an integral part of our modern civilization. But I guess the interval helped a little. The kids learned that TV has its alternatives, and sometimes they turn to them."

Chapter 12

Follow the Leader

Babyhood is over, childhood is here.

We have talked about the viewing habits of the bib and diaper set. Now let's turn to their school-attending sisters and brothers, who look at some very adult programs.

Dr. Robert Liebert, child psychologist at the State University of New York, believes that television "has changed childhood more than any other social innovation in the history of the world."

It succeeds in doing this because the amount of time children devote to it counteracts most other influences in their young lives. Howard Beale, the "mad prophet of the airways," exclaimed in the theater film *Network*, "There is an entire generation right now who never knew anything that didn't come out of this tube! This tube is the gospel! This tube is the ultimate revelation! This tube can make or break presidents, popes, and prime ministers."

Parents, even when they deplore the TV obsession, are often frustrated in attempts to limit their children's viewing time, and to improve selectivity. "I try to monitor Johnny's TV fare when he's here at home," said one mother, "but when he's across the street playing with Jim, or up the street playing with Joe, how do I know what their mothers have tuned in?"

Then many mothers have outside jobs, and they actually encourage the children to look at TV in the interval between school and the time that they themselves get home from work. As one mother said, "That's probably better than letting them play around and get a hand chewed up in the meat grinder—but not much better."

Other parents have long since given up, or else they didn't care in the first place.

Double Whammy

TV is effective, but not just because children see so much of it. There is a second reason: TV uses more graphic methods than any other form of pedagogy.

Harry J. Skornia, Ph.D., author of *Television and Society*, wrote that the army, navy, and air force have done over a hundred carefully documented study projects that "reveal the effectiveness of TV and film" in teaching various skills such as "the assembly and use of guns and other weapons, and in *attitude formation* related to mental, physical, and emotional conditioning" (emphasis added).

He was speaking of the effectiveness of TV for adults, but if his words have any truth at all for adults, the truth is multiplied a hundredfold for children, simply because children's minds are uncluttered with information gathered through many years. Their minds are fresh, as porous as a sponge.

Another authority, Dr. Richard Granger, associate professor of clinical pediatrics at the Yale University Child Center, stated in his book *Who Is Talking to Our Children* that "for a large number of children, television is society at large. Through its powerfully combined audio-visual impact delivered directly into the child's home, it is the face of the adult world, the reflection of society."

Caricature of Life

But what a distorted reflection! It is analogous to what we saw in trick mirrors at the amusement park or at the county fair when we were children ourselves. We stood in front of those mirrors and watched ourselves grow fat or thin, tall or short. We laughed because we knew it was a wild caricature.

Our children who look at television don't realize that its picture of life is an equally wild caricature. They mix up the real and the unreal.

During the first five years of his practice on TV, the fictional Marcus Welby, M.D., played by Robert Young, had 250,000 letters addressed to him. All were from viewers seeking professional advice for their ailments. (When Young, in another capacity, does the spiel for Sanka brand decaffeinated coffee, he starts out by saying, "I can't give you professional advice," then he suggests that people drink Sanka.)

A Japanese TV outfit, convinced that CBS's character Kojak, played by Telly Savalas, was actually a member of the New York police department, asked permission to film him at work in his office.

Now if adults can so easily confuse reality and fantasy, what about children?

One mother told about her son who jumped off the porch railing. "He broke his leg pretending he was the Bionic Man. If that TV creature could jump off cliffs and high buildings with nary a scratch, Danny didn't see why he couldn't jump off our porch rail."

More significant, she added that the nurse in the emergency ward of the hospital where she rushed her son wasn't a bit surprised that the child was imitating a TV character. The nurse said, "We have kids brought in every day because of that kind of program. My first day on the job in emergency we had a kid wearing a Batman cape who jumped off a playground slide."

The horror shows not only give children nightmares, but confuse them. The youngsters cannot always distinguish where fantasy ends and fact begins, or vice versa.

Frank Orme, former editor of *TV News* magazine and now executive vice president of NABB, is concerned about this type of show. Referring to the horror programs, he said, "A

133

child watching television without a guardian is swimming with sharks."

He went on to say that horror shows are more harmful seen in the living room than in a theater; he explained, "In the theater, the child is surrounded by peers and adults. He is consciously aware of their presence, and that he is watching a staged event. . . . At home the child is likely to be alone, or at least without adult accompaniment."

During the first 90 days of 1976, five of the seven VHF stations in Los Angeles broadcast over a hundred "thriller" movies during the day, when small children could see them. The first two things that children usually do upon returning from school are to get something to eat and go sit before the TV set.

Just one station, KCOP-TV, will, according to NABB literature, run about the same number of horror shows in the course of a year. The literature goes on to say, "Assuming the Nielsen stays constant, that means a cumulative child audience of 4,700,000," and it adds up to "9,400,000 hours of child viewing time consumed by KCOP's weekend afternoon horror movies within a single year."

Here are some of the shows' titles—they give a pretty good clue to content—"The Evil Touch," "Scream Theatre," "Carnival of Terror," "Horror Greats," and "Teleworld Chillers." The commercial for "Dark Shadows" boasts, "It starts where your nightmares stop."

It is a relief when the children look at mere detective shows, especially good ones geared to juveniles such as "The Hardy Boys" and "The Nancy Drew Mysteries."

Harmful Hybrids

A certain class of shows is not actually geared to children but has some elements that appeal to children and others that appeal to adults. Among these hybrids are the quiz and game shows. Since we spent a whole chapter talking about them, there is no use going into them at any length here. Suffice it to say that if these shows encourage the "I wanna's" in adults, they encourage them doubly in children. And children love them because they are exciting—or rather the contestants get excited. Moreover, since many of them are purely a matter of luck, children can compete on an equal footing with the adults on the show. Unfortunately, these contests give the children a number of false ideas: you can get something for nothing; sex and material things are the sole components of happiness; and there is no objective truth—rather, truth is what the majority thinks.

Popular too with children are the bionic shows. Kay Mills of Newhouse News Service wrote, "More children under 12 years old watch 'The Six Million Dollar Man' than any other program—including Saturday morning cartoons." Of the six programs that children most frequently watch, she added, " 'The Six Million Dollar Man' draws 9.1 million children viewers. . . . The other five have child audiences of more than seven million."

The bionic spinoffs from "The Six Million Dollar Man" also draw big juvenile audiences.

At first glance all these shows seem merely silly. The characters in them have about as much depth as the comic-strip characters from which they are patterned. "Recycled Superman" is what the NABB calls "The Six Million Dollar Man."

But the NABB has more to say about that show: it portrays "physical superiority as the only way to resolve life's problems." The *Wall Street Journal* (October 19, 1976) pointed out that the show is "replete with karate chops, beatings, brawls, all in studied slow-motion."

Besides the violence, there is the unreality of it all. Is that wholesome?

Well, fairy tales are unreal and they were wholesome enough; they developed imagination and taught children something about perseverance, and tenacity, and facing danger with bravery, because the fairy prince always had to suffer long hardships and slay numerous dragons before he won the golden-haired princess.

But the analogy between the bionic shows and fairy tales is far from perfect. Fairy tales seem to say that man, doing his utmost, can, with the help of some celestial being, triumph over obstacles and at last find happiness. The bionic shows seem to say that man, using science, can achieve power, make himself a sort of god.

135

Ye Gods

The scientific miracles of the bionic shows seem designed as a substitute for divinely wrought miracles that children may hear about in Sunday school or religion class.

Miracles in a religious sense are not a factor on TV; indeed, the name of God is rarely mentioned except in profanity on adult shows. This omission itself brainwashes the children. It gives them the impression that God is not needed—if indeed He exists in the first place.

Ned Scharff, writing in the *Washington Star* (August 8, 1976), said, "Surveys have indicated that the more strongly a person is involved in religious activities, the less television he is likely to watch—a coincidence that has fostered speculation about television having usurped some of the psychological needs for religion."

Sheriff John J. Buckley of Middlesex County, Massachusetts, addressing the National Association of Citizens Crime Commissions, blamed TV for what he called America's "spiritual crisis."

And Larry Gross of the University of Pennsylvania comments, "Television certainly has replaced religion for a lot of people as the thing that tells them how the world works."

The medium is an ersatz god, a stand-in for religion, and a moral mentor.

Social Control?

Dr. Gross elaborated his theory in the April 1976 issue of *Psychology Today.* Writing in collaboration with Dr. George Gerbner, he said, "By mobilizing fear, the medium has replaced the Church as the toughest means of social control."

It is sad indeed if fear engendered by crime shows, horror shows, or action-adventure shows is all that keeps children in line. One would hope that the Ten Commandments and the "good news" of Christianity have some effect too.

Nor does TV always provide the "social control." On the

contrary, it often seems to tempt children to perform all sorts of antisocial—that is to say, wrong—actions.

"All in the Family" had an episode (October 13, 1976) showing Archie and Edith at a supermarket. Archie was complaining about the cost of food, and Edith remarked that if a can was dented, the store allowed two cents off the price. Archie slyly picked up a hammer from a shelf in the store and began denting the cans in his shopping cart.

For some children this might be a great lesson in cheating, because it made getting away with something look like fun. (Admittedly, for other children it might be the opposite, a lesson in honesty. After all, whatever Archie does is supposed to be ridiculed, not copied.)

More certain to have a bad effect was an incident on "Alice" (November 27, 1976). Alice told her 12-year-old son, Tommy, that she loved him, and he answered, "I'm glad, because my teacher caught me cheating on my math test and he wants to see you."

Clever? The boy had his mother cornered.

But since when has genuine maternal love winked at cheating or any other wrongdoing? On the contrary, it would urge corrective measures to keep a child from growing up to be a self-destructive rascal.

TV wants us to laugh at odd things. In an episode of "What's Happening?" a boy planned to go to a party even though his mother had told him to babysit with his little sister. As soon as the mother left the house, the boy started to leave too, but the sister threatened to tell on him.

He asked, "Why would you do that?"

She answered, "Because you haven't paid me a quarter not to." (Bribery is funny?)

Later, his lying about attending the party and his theft (with help from other boys) of a cake were supposed to be funny too.

School for Vandals

TV teaches strange lessons. "Muggsby" had one on vandalism. Though Muggsby herself didn't participate, the episode showed children breaking into a school and systematically wrecking the place. Red paint sprayed on blackboards and furniture, windows broken with baseball bats, papers and records torn up and strewn hither and yon—it was all there on the screen, a complete demonstration.

In fairness, we must add that the show did wag a reproving finger at the hoodlums, but at the same time the episode showed viewers how to do likewise.

Parents, Keep Out!

Other "Muggsby" episodes have irked parents. In its September 11, 1976 segment, a little boy was taken to the hospital with a broken leg. His friends promptly visited him and found his father already there, awaiting word when he might see the boy.

When he came out of the ether after having his leg set, the child asked to see his friends. The father stammered to the nurse something about, "Shouldn't the family go in first?"

The nurse told him that he should love his son enough to let the boy choose his friends and decide whom he wanted to see.

A good way to sap parental influence! The next time mom or dad wants to sound a warning about a companion their children may have chosen, expect the children to argue: "I have a right to choose my own friends. You can't butt in."

Trying to undo this false TV-induced impression is about as difficult as gathering up the scattered beads from a broken pearl necklace.

Here is a second "Muggsby" incident that wouldn't win prizes for discretion or common sense because conceivably it too could have strained the parent-child relationship: Muggsby's much older stepbrother, who was her legal guardian, decided to give her $5 weekly allowance. The two lived in poverty in a trailer behind a garage in the ghetto.

Now, $5 a week in some families is a puny allowance; in other families it might be a near fortune. In the latter sort of family, a child might reason: My parents are mean. Look what they give me! Only $2 a week. And they must have a lot more money than Muggsby's brother. We live in a *real* house.

If the TV scripters had the good of the family in mind, they wouldn't have mentioned the allowance figure at all. Whether they realize it or not, much that they write into teleplays is poison to parents, to the family, to Americanism, to morals. And maybe this poison has a worse effect on children because they do not as often as adults detect the presence of the subtle dose, and so resort less to the antidote of common sense.

A case in point is the way TV treats sex. It not only directs a youngster's mind to sex before he learns to spell that three-letter word; it takes it for granted that all adults exploit sex. In one episode of "Alice," the widowed protagonist was going out for the evening with a man friend, whereupon her 12-year-old son, Tommy, chided her for wearing a modest pantsuit which, he said, hid her figure and cleavage.

In the same serial but in another episode (November 6, 1976), Alice finds the picture of a nude girl in Tommy's wallet. She is a bit disturbed and talks to the teacher who gives sex instruction in Tommy's school. The man tells Alice not to worry. The picture doesn't mean a thing. Tommy carries it only because of peer pressure.

Now children are indeed the world's greatest conformists. That's why it would seem to be the adults' job on television as well as elsewhere to teach the kids that "everybody's doing it" is just about the worst possible criterion for behavior.

In real life one boy may carry such a picture because ten other boys do. Ten million boys may carry such a picture because one boy on television did.

Diet of Violence

By far the most complained about, most discussed, most studied, most criticized, most debated, and most analyzed facet of children's shows is violence. We have talked about violence before and will do so again, because that particular thread keeps reappearing in different contexts. Certainly, no discussion of kid-vid can avoid it.

Hearing the hue and cry, parents ask themselves, "How will the violence affect my kids? Will they really try to imitate some of the stuff they see on the screen?"

139

Well, children do ape their elders in many more ways than just dressing up in mom's long skirts and hobbling around in her high-heeled shoes.

One mother said, "My kids don't watch the regular crime shows or many animated cartoons, but they do go for the slapstick. They see the 'Three Stooges' punch each other, jab each other, whack each other, thump each other over the head, and kick each other in the behind. Sometimes it does make me uneasy. I'm not sure that Johnny might not pick up a hammer and konk his brother with it. Kids don't always have sense enough to realize that the Stooges use a rubber hammer or trick photography."

Another mother complained about this show: "I think it's worse than the animated cartoons because it's real people doing crazy things. When it's a cartoon, the kids have a better chance of recognizing the unreality."

The 1972 *Report of the Surgeon General* warned of children imitating the behavior they saw on the screen. Back in 1969 (when he headed the National Commission on the Causes and Prevention of Violence) Dr. Milton Eisenhower said that "a constant diet of violent behavior on television has an adverse effect on human character."

This "adverse effect" is the same effect that we saw in adults who view violence. It makes the children more likely to be violent themselves, as well as less sympathetic toward victims of violence.

A study at Florida Technological University reported that compared with a control group, fifth-graders who viewed a blood-and-guts show were more more hesitant to call in adult help when younger children got into a scuffle. Ronald S. Drabman, who conducted the study, noted the frightening implications of this decreased sensitivity in children.

Therefore, at least some of the bullying and gang fights that go on in schools may very justly be laid at the door of TV violence. The *New York Times* (March 19, 1976) reported that the federal government was spending "$12.6 million on a program to combat what it described as a virtual reign of schoolhouse terror."

The article said that parents, students, and educators were all concerned about "their schools being trapped in a web of violence and disruption which is destroying their effectiveness as institutions of learning."

But it is not just a matter of some 12-year-old beating up a ten-year-old and so intimidating the younger child that he agrees to pay "protection money." Worse things have happened.

In 1975 NBC ran and in 1977 reran the film "Born Innocent," especially made for TV. It showed a detention home for girls and told the story of how one girl was stripped and raped with a broomhandle.

After it appeared on the screens of America, a San Francisco woman sued NBC and a local station, KRON-TV, for $11,000,000. She said that her little daughter and her daughter's friend, who were eight and nine years old respectively, were assaulted in the same way by children who had seen the program.

Dr. Robert M. Liebert, a psychologist at the State University of New York and one of the investigators who worked on the 1972 *Report of the Surgeon General*, said, "The more violence and aggression a youngster sees on television, regardless of his age, sex, or social background, the more aggressive he is likely to be."

Liebert's conclusion, according to *TV Guide*, stems from analysis of more than 50 studies covering the behavior of 10,000 children between the ages of three and 19.

Throwing Out Emily Post

Enough, and more than enough, about violence! Let's turn to TV's social manners.

We try to train our children to be polite and courteous, and in the average American household it isn't the custom for adult family members to hurl insults at one another.

But more often than the child hears our voice, he hears the voices that come from the tube.

Here are a couple of verbal exchanges from "All in the Family."

MIKE (Archie's son-in-law): Gloria, come on, hurry up! We'll miss the bus.

141

ARCHIE: She missed that the day she said 'I do' to you.

EDITH (Archie's wife): And he's your cousin, Archie. How could I say no?
ARCHIE: This way, Edith, No! But maybe that's too much for you, it's got a whole syllable.

Or we can rerun this bit from "The Practice":

JUDY (to her doctor): Can you recommend a good doctor? Forget it. The last person I asked recommended you.
DR. BEDFORD: Try Sullivan on 54th Street. He'll like you. He's deaf.

Then when Judy's self-assertiveness sounded masculine, Dr. Bedford said sarcastically, "You know something, mister? You're a little effeminate."
JUDY: At your age what difference does it make?

Often the insults are not spoken in a normal tone of voice, but shouted. Producer Norman Lear must believe they are funnier if they are loud, for high-decibel dialogue is a Lear trademark. He hasn't read his Shakespeare: "A low voice is an excellent thing in woman."

The manners of some TV characters are atrocious.

Cookie Monster in "Sesame Street" jams cookies into his mouth in a way that would make us send Junior from the dining-room table if he tried it.

When "The Flintstones" characters say, as they frequently do, "Shut up," we wince, realizing that Junior is learning those two words before he has learned "Thank you" and "You're welcome."

Characters in commercials can be loutish too. In one commercial a mother and her friend sit at a table probing the merits of Spray and Wash. It will take the oily stains from her son's jacket, the mother declares. At this point the boy, without an "Excuse me" or a "May I?" darts between the two women, grabs a cookie from a plate on the table, and darts off again.

Other children looking at the scene probably think this display of bad manners has the seal of adult approval; neither adult at the table objected to it.

Nor did Mr. C of "Happy Days" (rerun December 31, 1976)

object when his teenage daughter called him Buster. Angry at his proposed course of action, she said, "That will leave a scar for the rest of my life. And that's a long time, Buster."

Gruesome Grammar

TV characters are not the people to teach your children good grammar. Some typically sloppy utterances:

"I was doing real good," a girl said about her schoolwork.

"Be sure your child gets their immunization," said a health official.

"That don't happen often," said a sportscaster.

"I don't get no respect," said Jabberjaws.

"Between you and I," said the *schoolteacher* on "Welcome Back, Kotter." When somebody corrected him, he mumbled something about not being an English teacher, as though that were an excuse for his ungrammatical phrase.

"Like I ain't wearin' nothin' " is a tagline from an often-run commercial.

"Doan's Pills work different" blurts another commercial.

"Me and my grandmother can go to Nicaragua," said a character on "Rebop," while another character on the same children's program said, "He watch me real good." In "Rebop" perhaps there was some slight excuse. It might be argued legitimately that bad grammar was more realistic, since the show was depicting children of foreign background who could not be expected to know the English language as well as the rest of us. Still, it is hard on the children viewers who must learn to speak their native language correctly.

The List Lengthens

The list of complaints could stretch to the moon. For well over a decade, scholastic tests have recorded that the performance of American students has deteriorated. TV viewing must bear some share of the blame.

Teachers aver that the attention span of children is shorter than it used to be. Children come to school expecting entertainment—"Sesame Street"–type pedagogy. They have no patience with the necessarily slower, less dramatic type of learning, nor with subjects demanding concentration. Ned Scharff's *Washington Star* article of August 8, 1976 said that despite the fact that programs like "Sesame Street" and "The Electric Company" do introduce a child to his letters, "there is substantial evidence that, after age eight or nine, the more television a child watches, the less well he is likely to do in school."

Not surprising when we stop to realize that many of the shows the child watches are, in the last analysis, intellectually empty. A cartoon in the *Wall Street Journal* showed a boy talking to an adult in a TV production office. The boy said, "I heard that your programs are aimed at a 12-year-old mentality. I'm 12, and I resent that."

We the Parents

We parents might admit we are not entirely blame-free ourselves. If we exerted just a bit more effort we could, by substituting other activity, make a child less dependent on TV.

Other activity! Overworked mothers of America will arise as one to protest that idea. Until another hour is added to present quota of 24, we wouldn't have time for one more thing. We complain now that we're always chauffeuring Junior or Jane to music lessons, to baseball practice, to the dentist, etc.

But we can supply activities that make few demands on mama, quiet ones that the children can pursue at home daytime and evenings. We can even find those that need little or no equipment, and cost little or no money.

Impossible?

No. Listening to music and reading are two that come instantly to mind and both pay fabulous future dividends. Darwin once wrote that if he had his life to relive, he would read more poetry and listen to more music. "The loss of these tastes," he added, "is a loss of happiness, and may possibly be injurious to the intellect."

The mother who plays the piano, or the mother who simply flips on the hi-fi, may awaken in Junior a love of music that becomes a lifelong passion. As for reading, that too a mother can foster—and so can we all, aunts, uncles and grandparents. Before a child learns to read for himself we can hustle him off to the library where shelves stocked with picture books await his eager hands.

After he chooses one or two treasures, we can read aloud to him, and if we do, the chances are that he will sit wide-eyed beside us, hanging on to every word. Soon he will ask when he can read himself and so unlock the precious stories hidden beneath those strange printed symbols on the page.

Once the child learns to read, we can resign. The public library can take over. Children, like us grownups, can have their own cards and take out books charged to their own names. It's a good way to learn responsibility.

Then if we are willing to spend a comparative pittance, there are some good children's magazines. To name a few:

National Geographic School Bulletin
National Geographic Society
17 & M Streets, N.W.
Washington, D.C. 20036

Highlights
2300 W. Fifth Avenue
Columbus, Ohio 43216

Cricket Magazine
LaSalle, Illinois 61301

Three magazines, *Jack and Jill*, *Child Life*, and *Young World*, all put out by the Youth Division of the *Saturday Evening Post*, have the same address:

1110 Waterway Boulevard
Indianapolis, Indiana 46206

A subscription might be cheap at twice the price if it takes our children away from TV at regular intervals.

We might even buy a few books. One bookstore had this sign in its window, "Fight TV; Buy a Book."

But TV will remain with us, and rather than fight it, the better course is to use it, but selectively and sparingly. Actually, there are some good shows, though sometimes we feel that looking for them is hopeless. That's not quite true. If we are persistent, a few will turn up. Carol Rivers pointed out in the *New York Times* (May 16, 1976) that TV can teach "cooperation as well as violence," and she cited an experiment where nursery-school children were observed over a period of nine weeks. One group that watched "Mister Rogers' Neighborhood" were patently more cooperative and less aggressive afterwards than the children who watched the usual potpourri on TV.

Research conducted by Drs. Eli Rubinstein, Robert Liebert, and others backs up that nursery-school study. TV can teach kindness and consideration instead of aggressiveness, *if* the viewing is selective.

"Selective" is the key word. To be selective is to follow the wisdom of the ages. Centuries ago Plato spoke of selectivity when he said in *The Republic*, "Shall we carelessly allow children to hear any casual tale which may be devised by casual persons and to receive into their minds for the most part the very opposite of those ideas that we would wish them to have when they are grown up?"

Chapter 13

TV and the Teen Scene

University in the Home

"The most important educational institution in this country is not Harvard, or Yale, or the University of California, but television."

The man who spoke those words should know. He is Newton N. Minow, former chairman of the FCC.*

Martin A. Russo, then representative from Illinois and a member of the Communications Subcommittee, read into the *Congressional Record* of September 15, 1976 a report from the National Citizens Committee for Broadcasting. It said in part, "Television has become a College of Criminal Instruction. If only college credit were offered, it could become a back-alley 'open university' with its courses in how to commit arson, rape, murder, burglary, and other forms of depravity."

* Quoted in *TV Guide*, October 16, 1976.

Although television is not always that bad, both Russo and Minow were right in saying that it has more power and influence on the junior citizen than does college, or university, or for that matter, high school.

It is easy to see why. After all, once the children enter their teens they are anxious to cut apron strings and find mentors that won't be emotionally involved in their personal lives and that will never take them to task. TV, handy as it has always been, is ready to fill the bill.

Now what kind of shows do teenagers enjoy?

Happily, they watch the boobtube less than either the older or younger people. Still they do watch it more than many parents think is good for them.

Obviously, 12- to 20-year-olds have outgrown kid-vid, so there is nothing left to look at but adult shows, plus a few shows aimed supposedly at adolescents, like "Happy Days," "Welcome Back, Kotter," and "Good Times."

Most parents would give passing grades to all three because as a rule they all end with good triumphing over evil. In a sense, then, it would not be farfetched to say that all three embed a moral of sorts into the story line.

Nielsen's Number One

"Happy Days," a sitcom laid in the 1950s, was by far the most popular of the three during the 1976–77 season. It nearly sent the Nielsen's through the roof, drawing a weekly audience of more than 40,000,000, and on the first run of the Pinky Tuscadero* incidents capturing a whopping 53 percent of the television audience.

It is commanding a fantastic syndication price—about twice what any off-web half-hour has ever received.

It seems almost self-defeating to criticize this sitcom. It is *not* guilty of antifamily, anti-American, or antireligious bias.

* Roz Kelly, who played Pinky, later co-starred with Nancy Walker in "Mrs. Blansky's Beauties."

And it is clean! However, since the object of this chapter is to alert us parents to any hazards, we might as well mention a few not-so-good episodes.

In a rerun, August 30, 1976, the boys, all high school students, made their first foray into a strip joint.

To have high school boys go into such a place isn't the greatest idea of the century, even though the scripter had Richie and his pals find the entertainment dull and disappointing.

There was another objectionable feature. Minors are barred from such places (or certainly were at the time that this sitcom portrays) and the program taught young viewers a way to get around that. The characters on the show borrowed the ID cards of older friends and passed them off as their own. In other words, the episode was a practical demonstration of dishonest maneuvering.

Admittedly, the show had no suggestive seminudity, but it was objectionable on further counts.

Richie was embarrassed to find his own father, Howard Cunningham, in the "joint." Mr. C. explained that Mrs. Cunningham knew he was there; he had gone only because he had to take an out-of-town business associate who wanted that kind of entertainment.

The explanation was supposed to straighten everything out, but it sounded a bit flimsy, if not fishy. In this day of crumbling respect for parents, surely it would be better not to place them in a situation where they have to make excuses for their actions. Parents, on shows aimed primarily at adolescents, should ideally, like Caesar's wife, be above suspicion. For the most part, Howard Cunningham is.

In the episode above, which was a rather old one, the star of the show did not figure prominently. The star, as every TV viewer knows, is The Fonz, or Fonzie. Though he has a tough exterior, and is what the kids call "cool," he is decent and fair, and never bullies those younger or weaker than himself. His father has abandoned him and the Cunninghams have taken him in. Richie Cunningham, the son of the family, is Fonzie's good friend. Fonzie's full name is Arthur Fonzarelli, but nobody dares call him Arthur except Mrs. Cunningham.

For two or three years Fonzie was presented as a high school dropout. This made him less than an ideal hero, despite

149

his good qualities, to hold up to millions of young viewers.

If The Fonz can be such a glittering leader of his contemporaries without a high school diploma, why should anybody plug away at textbooks?

This idea must have eventually dawned on the scripters, for on February 8, 1977 they showed Fonzie graduating. Secretly, so the story ran, he had been boning up at night school in order to accomplish this feat.

In "Happy Days" The Fonz is glib, smart-talking, and slangy. He dresses invariably in a black leather jacket and drives a motorcycle with flair and speed.

In one episode (originally broadcast September 21, 1976, rerun January 25, 1977) he entered a demolition derby. In a demolition derby cars try to cripple each other by repeatedly ramming into one another. The driver of the last car that keeps running, despite crumpled fenders, bashed-in trunk, wobbly wheels, leaking radiator, and the rest, wins.

Now perhaps demolition derbies furnish training in controlled driving or stunt driving, or both, but some parents said of the show that it was just one easy, graphic lesson in driving recklessly. It was also an impressive lesson in wanton waste and destruction.

Fonzie, at the time of this writing, is almost a national hero. Probably more high schoolers and college undergrads know his name than know the name of Thomas Jefferson, Benjamin Franklin, or Robert E. Lee. Because of this, Henry Winkler, who plays Fonzie, is besieged with attention from every quarter. He has been offered six figures to sing on records (though he is not a singer) and to star at nightclubs (though he is not a club entertainer). He has had a movie offer from Universal Pictures.

Newsweek reported that he had been "mobbed on the street" and that girls had written to ask him for "the stubble from his razor."

On sale for both boys and girls are Fonzie T-shirts. Leather jackets are no longer advertised as leather jackets, but as Fonzie jackets.

Whether boys ever carried pink scarves for Pinky Tuscadero is a moot question, but there is no question at all about their having found Pinky attractive. When she appeared on the show, its already ultrahigh rating skyrocketed. The night of the demolition derby, in which she participated, as many people watched the show as vote in some national elections.* The episode and everything: fast action, breathtaking excitement, feminine beauty, and a dramatic ending in which Pinky was struck down mercilessly by the opposing team, the Mallachi brothers, and rushed from the field by an ambulance with screaming sirens. Outnumbered and handicapped, The Fonz went on in vengeful fury to win the derby and vanquish the Mallachis once and for all.

Again, we ask ourselves, Wouldn't we like this "hero" for our offspring revamped a bit? Certainly a few of the plot situations could be rewritten. One of the silliest and also one of the few subtly pernicious episodes (November 30, 1976) was about a stupid sheriff who wanted Fonzie run out of town, mainly, it seemed, because of the boy's haircut and his leather jacket.

To ridicule a law-enforcement officer by making him a petty tyrant was of itself pernicious, but there was more. The sheriff was a rabid anti-Communist who, it was hinted, suspected Fonzie's loyalty to his country. In short, the message of the show seemed to be that anti-Communists are stupid bigots. A few are, but to discredit anti-Communists generally is to jeopardize the security of the land we love.

Black Is Beautiful?

"Good Times," the largely black-cast CBS spinoff from "Maude," is, on the whole, a clean show that plugs family loyalty, decency, and the advantages of getting an education. Moreover, it does not foment racial strife. So far it has portrayed a concerned and conscientious black mother trying to guide her children along the straight-and-narrow. Her problems are as often with members of her own race as with whites. For example, there have been episodes about price gouging in the ghetto involving black against black. It was a black "businessman" who gave J.J., the older son of the family, a job promoting a gambling racket and dope.

* This statement refers to the original run. There was a somewhat less spectacular rerun in January 1977.

But on the critical side, the show often stoops to vulgarities. We quickly get the picture when we see J.J. wearing his T-shirt flaunting the words "Super Lover," and when we hear him addressing his girlfriend as "Hot Mama."

The Contraries of Kotter

Another show that is supposed to have adolescent appeal is "Welcome Back, Kotter." One lad said of its main character, "Kotter is just the kind of teacher I've always longed to have but I've never been that lucky. He's a regular guy."

Kotter, who grew up in the ghetto and was once a "sweathog" like his pupils, somehow managed to get an education and come back to teach the brash, tough, flip young hoodlums of his old neighborhood.

Idealism and humor abound in the show, but unfortunately, so does something else. In one episode, a sweathog defines love as never having to hear from a girl the words "I'm pregnant." In another episode, a student, Hotsy, tells Kotter that she is pregnant. He takes her to his home where he wants his wife to question the girl and find out who the father is. The wife asks her, "How did you get yourself into this? Haven't you ever heard of Family Planning?"

The girl answers, "You can't plan a family very well in the back seat of a 1966 Chevy."

As the show turned out, Hotsy wasn't pregnant at all. But long before she admits that, the teacher questions all the boys. None wants to get into trouble with the teacher, but each on the side boasts to his peers of his sexual exploits, hinting that he has gone all the way with Hotsy.

When the truth comes out that Hotsy is not pregnant, one of the boys turns to his pal and says, "But you bragged that you and Hotsy made an imprint in the sand that the cops are still talking about."

There is a crass sexiness too in the character Vinnie Barbarino (played by John Travolta). Though he is able to project some charm and a touch of tenderness, he is also a master at the vulgar insinuation.

Because of his prominent role in "Welcome Back, Kotter," Travolta is also a hero on high school and college campuses. According to *TV Guide* (January 17, 1977) he receives 7,500 pieces of fan mail a week. His face appears on posters, his voice on records, and his name on T-shirts.

One of his boosters said in *TV Time*, "There is no actor with more animal magnetism than John Travolta." Parents would prefer that TV producers occasionally choose actors who project some intellectual magnetism too.

That Travolta has influence with the younger generation is not to be doubted, but it isn't always the best influence. Once (November 18, 1976) when the sweathogs were looking forward to a big dance, the scripters put these words into his mouth, "If I don't get out Saturday night, think how boring my Confession is going to be. Father O'Malley looks forward all week to hearing me."

Many young viewers immediately envision his sexcapades and may perhaps try to rival them. Then there is the flippant anti-Catholic remark. Tasteless? Not very funny? Of course. But this is the stuff of which televsion "humor" is made.

Travolta, by the way, is the same actor who starred in the United Artists film *Carrie*. TV critic Marilyn Beck, writing of the movie, said that Travolta "admits 'some people get a little upset' when they see 'their lovable Vinnie Barbarino . . . hacking up a pig and slapping around a girl' . . . but he feels the majority . . . 'will get so turned on during his sex scene . . . they won't mind the rest.' "

The Forgotten Age Group

It is sad that there are so few shows geared to young people between 12 and 20. If they watch TV, they are forced to look at strictly adult shows, saturated with sex and crime.

One mother complained, "My 13-year-old babysits for our neighbors a lot, and there is nothing for her to do, once she has put the five-year-old to bed, but look at TV. She sees all the shows she shouldn't see."

Even if teenagers look at so-called family shows, which feature young people in the cast, they see material that not every parent would endorse. An episode of the series called "Family" (November 9, 1976) concerned the oldest child, Nancy, who was divorced and living at home again with her baby. In the course of three days, she slept with two men.

The comments of the mother were questionable as well. She said to Nancy, in effect: You are restless. You were married when you were barely 19, and you didn't do any of the foolish things that most girls do. You didn't have a chance to sort out your ideas and to form a moral code. Now you are trying to find yourself.

Her words might have been interpreted by some young people as a suggestion: Go ahead and sow your wild oats before you marry. It is not only normal, it is necessary procedure if you are to act sensibly later on.

Another installment of "Family" (September 28, 1976), mentioned in Chapter 3, pleaded for tolerance and understanding of homosexuality. Some parents, whether approving or disapproving the tolerance, would not have wanted their children to see the show. They feel that since adolescents are trying to formulate a sexual code for themselves, it would not be wise for them to see homosexuality presented as an alternate lifestyle, that deserves "understanding."

Some parents would also have discouraged the viewing of "Three's Company." Among the characters in this show is Jack, who moves in with some girls because as a homo he is deemed "harmless." The parents of the girls then accept Jack as a proper co-tenant in their daughters' apartment.

Sex at Sixteen

The elastic tolerance and the situation ethics expressed on TV spread confusion (as anybody who has teenage children knows). This moral confusion infects even "straight" sex. Young people are left with a warped sense of right and wrong.

In Neil Simon's *Heartbreak Kid*, shown by ABC on September 7, 1976, the young couple decide to marry. Before the wedding, the boy tries to persuade the girl to go all the way with him and she asks him whether he can wait just two more

"I don't see why we have to get *married*—couldn't we just
live together?"

days, until they are married. He answers, "Nobody waits any
more—nobody does."

When Terry on "The Nancy Walker Show" told Nancy,
"They need someone to play a 17-year-old virgin," Nancy answered, "Must be science fiction."

On "It Happened One Day" the two teenage girls were discussing their divorced mother's upcoming marriage, and one
of them said, "Instead of getting married, she should have
lived together like everybody else."

On "The McLean Stevenson Show" Chris, aged 20, took
girls down to the cellar for lovemaking sessions.

Only about one TV show in a hundred gives the advice that
Florence gave in "The Jeffersons," "Until he says 'I do,' you
don't."

No wonder we have so much premarital sex. Over and over
again TV tells the young people it is the norm. If you remain
chaste, probably you are frigid, or a freak of some kind.

In another show the girl said to the boy she had lured to
bed, "Don't feel bad about losing your virtue. Everybody does
sooner or later."

Again there's the same theme: to wait for marriage is as
absurdly old-fashioned as to wear crinolines on a college
campus.

We find that theme throughout TV. One day on MH2,
Kathy, unwed and pregnant, was talking with Grandpa. Having
slept with numerous men, she admitted somewhat shame-
facedly that she was the "pushover of Fernwood." The old man

155

assured her, "You're sweet, you're kind, and you're fun. These are the things that count, not how many affairs you've had."

Many 16-year-olds believe Grandpa's words and decide that sex is like impulse buying at the supermarket; you pick it up when you see it and like its packaging and price.

And not a few go a step further. Other TV shows have told them, at least implicitly, that free sex is advisable. You should live with a few partners before marriage. You have to find out who is sexually compatible.

The youngsters cannot know that sexual compatibility in marriage depends on many psychological as well as physical factors. A boy and girl who are sexually compatible from the start may in two years or so become bored to death with one another if they are not also compatible in other areas. To begin the relationship without sex and to build a friendship first is the way to build an edifice that has a chance of standing. But does television tell them that?

It doesn't tell them either that some extremely happy marriages have started out with less than perfect sexual compatibility. Newlyweds may need time to mature, to build spiritual, intellectual, and psychological rapport.

That free love isn't a preparation, or a test, or an insurance policy for marriage is not just private opinion. There is scientific evidence to back it. Nancy Moore Clatworthy, an associate professor at Ohio State University, studied 100 young couples. Sixty-five had lived together before marriage; the 35 others had not lived together before marriage. Said Dr. Clatworthy, "The findings do not support the hypothesis that a period of living together before marriage better helps to select a compatible mate or aids in adjustment to marriage." Actually, the study indicated that those who didn't go the cohabitation route were happier than those who did.

But for every young person who hears about that study there are millions who hear TV telling them (as it did through MH2's Grandpa) that sex is just fun, and that a sex relationship is as disposable as a nonreturnable bottle after the soda is gone.

TV assures them that a little sexual fling need not end in pregnancy. They can "protect" themselves. In an episode of "Alice" (November 6, 1976) the mother of a young girl declared, "My daughter has been on the pill since she was 14." The 15-year-old prostitutes in "Little Ladies of the Night"

156

(January 16, 1977) panicked when policewomen confiscated their birth-control pills.

In all this there was naturally no hint of the pill's possible injurious side effects. Nor was there even the gentlest warning that the pill is not foolproof. Twenty out of every 100 babies born to teenagers are illegitimate, according to "The NBC Nightly News" (November 30, 1976). The birth rate among mothers under 17 years of age is climbing at the rate of 10 percent annually. (Incidentally, there are ten times as many cases of child abuse among teenage parents as among older parents.)

With or without pregnancy, promiscuous sex can lead to other complications—venereal disease, for instance. How many 16-year-olds think about that?

The U.S. Public Health Service reports that venereal disease among teenagers has risen 230 percent in the last 15 years. Fr. Dan Lyons predicted that at that rate, "One out of every two high school graduates in Los Angeles County will have venereal disease by 1980."

How can the younger generation hear these warnings when TV drowns them out? Occasionally, we adults may recognize TV drivel for what it is, but our sons and daughters seldom do. They too often prove that Marshall McLuhan of Toronto University was right when he said, "The medium is the message." For lack of experience they believe readily what they hear and see.

In one soap opera, after a couple had intercourse the woman asked the man to drive her home. He answered that he had work to do and couldn't leave. He would call her a cab.

At that, she flared up and said that he surely should give her that much time after what they had just been to one another.

He patted her on the shoulder patronizingly and answered, "You're a beautiful woman and a sensuous woman, but what we did was no big deal."

In other words, grow up and learn to take this kind of thing in stride. No doubt that kind of thinking is largely responsible for the fact that so many young people today feel their lives are meaningless. After all, if the act of love is meaningless, what else is there?

Their parents did not feel that way at their age. Interviewed on "The Today Show" (November 22, 1976), Dr. Pamela Cantor, chairman of the Congress of the American Association of Suicidology and assistant professor of psychology at Boston

157

University, said that suicide rates were up among the young; that in the last ten years for males 20 to 29 years of age they had doubled, and for females they had quadrupled. Another expert on another TV show stated that the leading cause of death between ages 15 and 19 is suicide.

School vs. Screen

As many young people watch the anti-family, anti-marriage programs as adults. *TV Week* (August 22, 1976) published some letters from teenagers talking about soap operas. One letter, signed by four girls, begged ABC to change the time of "Ryan's Hope" to later in the afternoon. They explained, "School will be starting soon and we would like to continue watching this super soap opera." This "super soap opera" certainly has its share and more of extramarital sex.

Another letter complained about the fact that school's opening would mean that she would miss her favorite "One Life to Live." This is a show where Larry walked in one day just as Karen put out a marijuana "joint." When Larry noticed the odor, she blamed it on Lana. It is also the show where Brad sweet-talked Jenny after shacking up with his waitress friend, Lana.

TV-addicted youngsters make the best of the time that is left after school hours. A day or two before Halloween 1976 a 15-year-old girl was having a party for some of her friends. One invitee told her, "Oh, I'd love to come, but that's the night of *What Happened to Rosemary's Baby?* Do you think the party will still be going on after the show is over? I hate to miss *Rosemary*."

God and Mammon

TV dwells on Satanism, but it rarely teaches adolescents to worship God. In fact, most programs teach a philosophy that is frankly anti-God: materialism. Material things and sensual

158

pleasure are all that men should strive for. Well-being, even spiritual well-being, depends on them.

A character in ABC's "All My Children" is a former prostitute. She has had a tragic childhood. Her father beat her repeatedly until she escaped and took up her "profession." In trying to justify her former life, the doctor who has the woman as a patient doesn't mention the beatings. Instead, he explains that she grew up poor in a grubby ghetto, as though that were the important element of the story. Though poverty may make it difficult to lead a good life, poverty alone certainly does not make it impossible. To imply that it does, insults all those who live below the poverty line.

Although TV doesn't advocate stealing, at times it comes close to condoning it. A character in "Police Woman" (rerun August 31, 1976) questioned a man about the legality of his business dealings. He answered, "I don't apologize for my lifestyle to anybody, and it costs money."

In other words, if he had to steal in order to keep up his lifestyle, nobody should blame him.

On "The McLean Stevenson Show" (December 1, 1976) a boy broke into a home and started to ransack it. The incident was handled so lightly that it seemed like fun and games. In the end the *paterfamilias* gave the boy money to travel with his equally young and already pregnant wife to California.

On "Delvecchio" (December 26, 1976) a man stole in order to give Christmas gifts to the "guests" of an old people's home. Because his motive was altruistic, the stealing was made to seem something akin to virtue, and in the end the department store from which he stole donated the ill-gotten merchandise to the home, and everybody, including the thief, supposedly lived happily ever after.

TV certainly makes it easy for the young to rationalize, and thus to end up believing that they have a noble motive for whatever they want to do. Actor Peter Finch (he died in January 1977), who starred in *Network*, a theater movie satirizing TV, spoke of its "power to brainwash." Television "trains us not to think," he continued. "Look what it's done to my 14-year-old son."

159

Tips for Teenage Thugs

Max Rafferty, the distinguished educator, has said: "We are trying to give our children a neon-lit, atomic-powered, air-conditioned nuthouse." TV shows young people how to steal . . . rape . . . murder . . . even how to keep the police at bay in a high-speed auto chase.

A Pennsylvania juvenile-court judge, Patrick Tamilla, recently told a conference of the National Parent-Teacher Association that "seven teenagers were killed here in Allegheny County, Pennsylvania last year trying to outrace the police in auto chases. . . . I believe that the incidence of high-speed automobile chases on TV has convinced many kids to try them too."

Particular heroes with the teen set are the gutsy detectives, like Starsky and Hutch, who drive so madly. *TV Time* printed a letter from a Philadelphia girl that read, "I think Starsky is the most beautiful man in the world. . . . If I had a choice of all the money in the world, or Starsky's telephone number, I would pick the phone number."

Dr. Samuel Silverman, associate professor of psychiatry at Harvard, believes that the war show "Baa Baa Black Sheep" equates antisocial behavior with courage. He said, "This gives the viewer, especially the young and impressionable, the idea that the way to assume leadership is through physical violence and defiance of authority."

Dr. Silverman says too that the police thriller "Delvecchio," by showing how easy it is to commit crime and violence, was "particularly dangerous."

So it would seem that teenagers are encouraged to take up crime and are daily given detailed and graphic lessons on how to commit it.

In February 1976 CBS ran the film *The Taking of Pelham 123*, which showed a gang taking over a New York subway train. The next night five boys between the ages of 16 and 19 put on their own repeat performance. They boarded a subway in Brooklyn and, before transit police could stop them, they terrorized and manhandled the passengers, including a pregnant woman, whom they punched and kicked, and a man trying to defend her, whose teeth they knocked out.

Three years earlier, in 1973, six boys in Boston surrounded a girl and beat her almost to insensibility. They forced her to douse herself with gasoline; then they put a match to her. After four hours of agony she died. The night before ABC had run *Fuzz*, a film that featured boys who poured gasoline over waterfront derelicts and ignited them.

But that was only act one. Act two occurred in Miami three weeks later. Four 12- and 13-year-olds, one of whom had seen *Fuzz*, doused three winos with lighter fluid and set a match to them. The human torches were sober enough to jump up and try to beat out the flames. Even so, one died.

In another chapter we spoke of the rape shown on "Born Innocent," which led to a similar real-life rape.

The Houston horror, which local newspapermen called "The Crime of the Century," had a TV tie-in too. Three youths sexually molested, tortured, and finally murdered, over a period of time, 27 boys between the ages of 13 and 19. One of the three criminals, David Brooks, age 18, admitted that he watched television 14 to 18 hours a day. For him, at least, it was a treasure trove of ideas.

Martin A. Russo former U.S. representative and member of the House Communications Subcommittee, read into the *Congressional Record* examples of crimes first enacted on TV and then in real life. One was committed by a nine-year-old, who dumped ground glass into the family's stew; another was by a 17-year-old, who reenacted a televised rape and murder. The murder was effected by bludgeoning the victim's head and then slashing her throat.

It is possible, of course, for young people to imitate TV without resorting to crime. But they can still hurt themselves for life. Fifteen-year-old Charles Allen saw a fire-breathing act of his favorite rock group, KISS, on TV. Then he tried the fire breathing himself. The result was predictable. He suffered serious burns on his face, chest, and back, and had to undergo extensive plastic surgery. His picture in the *Philadelphia Bulletin* was gruesome.

Producer Marty Pasetta has announced that he signed Evel Knievel to a five-year contract for daredeviling on TV specials. The initial project was the 90-minute "Evel Knievel's Death Defiers," January 31, 1977, in which Knievel jumped his motorcycle over an indoor pool stocked with killer sharks.

Admittedly, most young viewers never get within shouting distance of sharks; many, however, have access to swimming pools and motorcycles. You get the picture.

Max Gunther, writing in *TV Guide* (November 13, 1976), reported that Dr. Stanley Milgram and other social scientists have been unsuccessful in demonstrating the link between antisocial, irrational behavior and TV violence and daredevil stunts. Still, to ordinary people the link seems obvious enough. Dr. Richard Granger, Associate Professor of Clinical Pediatrics at Yale University Children's Center, agrees with parents who would like to see television toned down. He reminds us that "in medicine a basic principle is 'First do no harm,' " and he advises TV producers to adopt this principle as their own.

Upbeat at the End

Can nothing relieve the gloom of this chapter? Is there no good whatever to be said for TV's effect on the adolescent?

Peggy Hudson, in her book *TV 70*, spoke well of a past show, "The Mod Squad." "Some beneficial things," she said, "have come from the series. I saw a letter from a woman who runs a juvenile home. She said the kids had stopped taking drugs because of what they had seen on 'The Mod Squad.' "

Although we suspect that programs like "The Mod Squad" do more harm than good, we are glad to have this one good note to cite, and we had better end this chapter pronto, while we're ahead!

Chapter 14

The News Twisters

Former Mayor LaGuardia of New York used to tell reporters, "Be sure to have your facts straight before you distort them."

Newscasters are not neutral. But how can they be? They have to, or they think they have to, shoot film of only the dramatic and the sensational. That is necessary to produce lively footage. But in so doing, they inevitably must omit shooting the 90 percent which is nondramatic and nonsensational, and with it they often omit the real truth.

Hilaire Belloc wisely wrote, "Truth lies in proportion. You do not tell [the] truth by merely stating a known fact; nor even by stating a number of facts in certain and true order. You can tell it justly only by stating the known things in the order of their values."

Pictures can lie as surely as words. The lying is done whenever certain pictures are shown on the screen and equally important ones are not shown. As Bruce Herschensohn observed in his book *The Gods of Antenna*, the camera is guilty of "educating" the people with half-truths and nontruths. The eve-

163

ning newscasts summarize not the events of the day, but the "filmed record of the day's abnormalities."

This selectivity is peculiarly useful if TV personnel have ulterior motives. A TV cameraman and a film editor can make a person look like a villain without a fleck of decency in his whole makeup. Hitler or Stalin might blush to be seen in the same gutter with such a person after a TV treatment. Or they can make him look like a hero worthy of wild acclaim.

Tricks of the TV Trade

Some people connected with the TV industry admit this readily, and they predict no letup. Marvin Kitman wrote about Roger Ailes, the man who helped sell Richard Nixon via TV to the American people in 1968. Kitman said that Ailes was speculating (facetiously?) that some candidate for office in a future campaign might hire a camera crew to follow his opponent around. The crew could take pictures, Ailes suggested, when the opponent had his "fists in the air, cheering on the home team." Then, said Ailes (according to Kitman), "They cut the film. Take out the fist shot and superimpose it in a crowd of blacks." If racial tension were high, this would be very damaging to the opponent.

There was more of the same: take a shot of the opponent standing in front of a factory smiling as a crowd pressed forward to shake his hand while in the background a smokestack spewed out pollution. With a little editing the camera wielder could "prove" in pictures, and with few, if any, words, that his rival wanted "to destroy our environment."

To cap it all, Ailes explained a potentially devastating technique for embarrassing an opponent. Any photographer who accompanied a man on the banquet circuit night after night would surely be able, at one time or another, to get a shot of him looking awkward with his mouth full, or better still, spilling a glob of gravy or mayonnaise on his tie. The sloven!

Obviously, some sort of picture-prestidigitation has been going on for a long time. For most of us, anything beyond yesterday noon takes effort to recall, because events pile up so quickly that they soon bury the past. But it is worth the effort to prove the point, so let's flash back for an instant to the 1968 Democratic Convention in Chicago. An investigative report of the Committee on Interstate and Foreign Commerce of the House of Representatives said then that "the networks, by manipulating the news coverage, favored the radical mobs. . . . There were incidents shown on videotape and film-out takes, but on the air, which arguably could have presented a different picture of the Convention than the one that was actually conveyed."

Weapons that the *peace*niks used against the police included razor blades affixed to the toe of shoes, spray cans of oven cleaner, and paper bags filled with human waste. TV gave no hint of this.

The committee quoted a Chicago newspaper on how TV gave a distorted picture of what happened. The networks cut away from films of police grappling with disorderly peaceniks in Grant Park, to the Convention Hall where they showed, as though it were of one piece of cloth, "a smiling, obviously pleased Mayor Daley." The newspaper concluded that the "undeniable impression [was] that the mayor was an insensitive sadistic political boss, who had ordered his police to commit acts of brutality."

Another camera trick is sometimes used in photographing crowds. Different lenses give different visual impressions of the size of a crowd. A large crowd can look smaller, a small crowd larger, depending on whether a long or a short lens is used. Bruce Herschensohn noted that CBS's coverage of Nixon's appearance in Jackson, Mississippi on April 25, 1974 made it appear that he had fewer supporters there than he actually did.

When we think of these tricks of the TV trade, it is easy to second what Edith Efron (a contributing editor of *TV Guide*) said in a journalism conference at Pepperdine University: "Broadcast news departments are giving us a shallow, out-of-context, distorted, and often biased view of American political life and of world events—a view that is often nihilistic [and] hostile to this country. . . ."

"Hostile to this country"? We can at least give one example here. During the Vietnam War TV lavished coverage on My Lai while glossing over the Communist bloodbath at Hue. In the 1968 Tet offensive the Communists wantonly murdered thousands of civilians, yet the deed was, as Solzhenitsyn said, "lightly noticed."

165

Camera Power

In his book *News from Nowhere* Edward Jay Epstein speaks of this strange double standard. On one occasion, he recounts, David Brinkley of "The NBC Evening News" said that the song "Ruby, Don't Take Your Love to Town" had been "high on the bestseller list." Brinkley continued that it was "more than a pop song"; rather, it was "a social documentary, a comment on our times and on the war." It was the lament of a man who had returned from Vietnam wounded and who was confined to his bed, lying helpless and anguished as his wife went out at night.

Epstein says that the song that Brinkley called "a comment on our times and on the war" in Vietnam was actually written in 1942. Moreover, the song, at the date of the broadcast, was not a "bestseller." If it became so later, Brinkley's broadcast was responsible.

James Reston wrote of the Vietnam War, "Maybe the historians will agree that the reporters and cameras were decisive in the end. They brought the issue of the war to the people, before Congress and the courts, and forced the withdrawal of American power in Vietnam."

If there are still doubts that camera coverage is powerful, they can be dispelled by reading about plans for the 1980 Olympics in *TV Guide*. One article (September 7, 1976) said that the major networks were bidding for the right to telecast the big events from Moscow, but, it added, "whichever network wins . . . may find itself outslickered by the comrades from the Kremlin, who are interested not only in cash, but in making the 1980 Olympics a propaganda triumph. *This is what they are asking: all coverage would be handled by Soviet cameras*" (emphasis added).

TV Guide (November 6, 1976) asked the networks, "Are you bidding for rights to televise the Moscow Olympic Games, or rights to televise the Soviet version of the Moscow Olympic Games?"

In a later issue, the magazine predicted that the networks would run "Soviet-supervised vignettes of life in the workers' paradise."

The price for this propaganda to be used on us was nearly $100 million. It was the largest sum ever negotiated for a television series, four times what was paid for the Montreal games of 1976.

James Burnham remarked in *National Review* (March 4, 1977) that NBC, the network that signed with the USSR, had "gone way beyond the old selling-them-the-rope-to-hang-us-with routine. NBC is paying them oodles for agreeing to accept the rope."

What is more, NBC is giving them equipment the Soviets do not have. As Burnham says, "The Soviets need both the improved TV system and a non-Soviet cover. NBC is supplying both."

The Soviets may not have the equipment, but they surely have the expertise in handling outsiders. There will be more about this skill in Chapter 17.

Selective Silence

Without being conscious of any Red influence and indeed without any Red pressure, commentators feel it is neither necessary nor desirable to speak of the darker side of Communism. Inadvertently, then, they are helping the Reds, for there is propaganda value in just omitting the unpleasant.

Although CBS, for instance, covered the ending of the Vietnam War reasonably well, the coverage wasn't as full as could be. More about this in another chapter.

Silence greeted Senator John Tower's proposal in 1974 that congressmen submit copies of their federal income tax reports to the Joint Committee on Internal Revenue and Taxation for audit. Bella Abzug, Ted Kennedy, and Tip O'Neill were among those opposing it, but the public, which may have been for it, never knew from TV that it existed.

After the Vietnam War ended, CBS had a special telecast entitled, "Vietnam: A War That Is Finished." It traced American-Vietnamese relations through the administrations of Truman, Eisenhower, Johnson, and Nixon, but strangely omitted mention of Kennedy. Why? It was Kennedy who introduced the Green Berets, and Kennedy who escalated the war by deploying far more American troops in Vietnam than had his predecessor. The only plausible answer seems to be that

Kennedy was a darling of newsmen; the Vietnam War was unpopular, and they didn't want to remind viewers of Kennedy's role in it. They preferred to drop that down an Orwellian "memory hole."

Mum is the word for TV commentators on many other matters. In 1975 the Opinion Research Corporation found that 76 percent of the American people favored our country's maintaining military superiority over the USSR.

Who has heard the views of these people? Or who has heard the views of Dr. Edward Teller, father of the H-bomb? Teller calculates that in an all-out first strike, Moscow could kill 150 million Americans, but he declares, "If we had an ABM defensive missile system, half of those lives could be saved."

In September 1976 the American Security Council Education Foundation was so irked by the silence that it filed a complaint before the Federal Communications Commission, charging CBS-TV News with "massive and continuing violations of the FCC's Fairness Doctrine in reporting national security viewpoints."

The complaint came after 37 months had been spent by the Institute for American Strategy (former name of the present American Security Council Education Foundation) in a study of CBS-TV's news coverage.

John M. Fisher, president of the American Security Council Education Foundation, said, "This pattern of refusal by CBS News to give time to the majority viewpoints, is one of the most serious and effective forms of advocacy journalism practiced by CBS-TV News."

After the ASCEF report was released, Walter Cronkite acknowledged the validity of its findings, but shrugged them off. "There are always groups in Washington expressing views of alarm over the state of our defense," he said. "We don't carry these stories. The story is that there are those who want to cut defense spending."

On January 12, 1977 President Ford gave his last State of the Union address. The most forceful part of it was a plea to keep our defenses strong. NBC commentator John Hart, who immediately followed the speech, supposedly summed it up, but gave not so much as one long word to the subject of defense. A person who didn't hear the whole speech would think from the commentator's remarks that it was mostly a sentimental farewell to Congress.

(Parenthetically, Donald Rumsfeld, then defense secretary,

said in January 1977 that USSR expenditures of the previous year, 1976, were 42 percent above ours.)

The one time (the sole exception that comes to mind) when pro-defense advocates were given a share of the platform was the CBS special "Who's Ahead? The Debate over Defense" (April 20, 1977).

News or Opinion?

But selective silence is not the only complaint; newscasters often give their own opinions as fact. At the Republican Convention in Kansas City in 1976, Senator Jesse Helms of North Carolina expressed a hope that we would restore "nuclear superiority in our defense posture." Bill Moyers branded Helms' idea as "one of the most dangerous concepts around." Solemnly, Eric Sevareid agreed.

As *TV Guide* commented, "We can thank the Lord that Eisenhower, Dulles, and John F. Kennedy disagreed," and according to the polls so do about 76 percent of the American people.

These czars of TV have the final word on what the public shall hear. In her book *The News Twisters* Edith Efron quoted David Brinkley as saying in *TV Guide* (April 11, 1964), "News is what I say it is. It's something worth knowing by my standards."

If the newscasters were truly experts, that statement would be less alarming, but one of their own fraternity, Charles Kuralt, admits that they are not. He was quoted in the October 16, 1976 *TV Guide* as saying, "[America] depends for its life on an informed citizenry . . . most citizens receive most of their information from television. . . . And millions are getting that information from people who just don't know."

What they say over the air is largely a matter of opinion. This is far from the desideratum that Paul White set for newscasting in television's early years. White, World War II head of the CBS news department, said, "Ideally, in the case of controversial issues, the audience should be left with no impression as to what side the analyst himself actually favors."

That notion was jettisoned years ago. Back in December

169

1968 David Brinkley said that to be "objective was to be a vegetable," while Bill Moyers was quoted in *Time* magazine (September 20, 1968) as saying, "Of all the myths of journalism, objectivity is the greatest." More recently Pat Collins of WTOP-TV in Washington, D.C., declared, "I don't think there's such a thing as an objective story. . . . Tell them what *you think* the truth is" (emphasis added).

Admittedly, objectivity is almost impossible to maintain, and admittedly some of us listeners want interpretation. Where TV errs so grievously is in not letting us know when we are getting interpretation and when we are getting straight reporting. A correspondent from Frostburg, Maryland, writing to the editor of *TV Guide* (January 8, 1977), suggested that the commentator's spiel "should be labeled clearly as an editorial." Newspapers differentiate between news and opinion. In fact, they do more. In *The News Twisters* Edith Efron pointed out that "the *Times* and the *New York Post* are liberal and describe themselves as liberal. The *Chicago Tribune* and *Human Events* are conservative and describe themselves as such."

Ninety-nine times out of a hundred, network personnel let us think they are neutral when they are anything but. John Chancellor was the exception when, after Jimmy Carter's first Fireside Chat (February 2, 1977), he used the phrase, "In the opinion of this observer."

Fred Friendly, author of the book *Circumstances beyond Our Control. . .* , said, "The guidelines on news analysis that I laid down for editors in the newsroom was that a full understanding of certain stories required interpretation."

Since Friendly, then head of the CBS news department and later president of CBS, was surely known to his employees as the confirmed and ardent liberal that he is, they were not likely to have jeopardized their jobs by giving a conservative interpretation of anything.

In fairness to Friendly, he does say in his book that the newscaster should stop short of "making up the viewers' mind on a recommended course of action."

But newscasters pontificate with such solemn assurance that they impress, and perhaps intimidate, viewers. Eric Sevareid usually sounds more certain than the Pope speaking *ex cathedra*. In just a sentence or a phrase he and other newscasters can put over their ideas. On Labor Day 1976 NBC's "Today Show" mentioned the kickoff of the presidential campaign and Jimmy Carter's opening speech in Warm Springs, Georgia. The newscaster added, "But President Ford will stay in the White House at the moment, *in the pose of* a president hard at work." A few weeks later another NBC commentator spoke of Ford "waiting *safely* in the White House." (Emphasis added in both cases.)

Wizards of Words

Commentators can also add weight to their pronouncements with introductory phrases like "It is widely thought" or "Critics feel" or "Observers point out." There is no way to check these phrases, so we viewers tend to take them on faith.

Or a phrase can harbor a concealed slur. Herschensohn, in *The Gods of Antenna*, said that NBC and CBS both referred to the *"group that calls itself"* the National Citizens Committee for Fairness to the Presidency. That sounds as though the group were not really national, or not actually composed of citizens, or not truly interested in fairness. Herschensohn pointed out that the networks never apply this prefatory phrase to the ADA, the ACLU, or the SLA.

The newscasters are using their wizardry with words to maneuver us. Before the 1976 presidential campaign began, a number of men were vying for the Democratic nomination, and at first it seemed quite unlikely that Jimmy Carter would get it. After he did *U.S. News and World Report* (August 2, 1976) commented, "The campaign manager of one of the Democratic presidential dropouts argued that Jimmy Carter 'was a creation of the press.'. . . Television has given news a cutting and immediate impact that it seldom attained when journalism relied exclusively on print."

The Kingmakers

Though the networks were not markedly pro-Carter, they leaned his way and helped get him elected. On October 24, 1976, for instance, CBS's "60 Minutes" devoted a large segment of the program to Carter's son, who spoke in behalf of his father. Not a minute was given to a Ford spokesman.

Kevin Phillips, in his *TV Guide* column (November 27, 1976), said people decided how to vote not by what they saw or heard on the debates and in the candidates' speeches, but by what "newscasters chose to single out, ignore, emphasize, or criticize."

In proof of this statement Phillips cited Carter's *Playboy* interview, saying that "the people were reacting less to what Carter said than to what the networks . . . *said* he said."

The *Playboy* flap hurt Carter a bit, but in the end, Phillips believes, the TV commentators handed Carter the victory. Phillips supported his opinion with the following facts: in the second debate, he said, the networks gave a pro-Carter verdict, even though some immediate postdebate sampling gave Ford an 11 percent margin of victory. More important, the networks not only repeated and repeated Ford's remark about Eastern Europe, but also repeated and repeated their disapproval of it. With the repetition Ford's stock went down and Carter's stock began to climb, going up, said Phillips, "first by 12 points, then by 27, and finally by 45."

Phillips' estimate of TV's power in the campaign was corroborated by a test that psychologist Lloyd Sloan conducted at Notre Dame University. Before the second debate he recorded the voting preferences of 254 people, then divided them into three separate groups. The first group heard the debate, but did not hear any commentators. Dr. Sloan recorded "an overall shift of 20 percent to Ford. The other two groups listened to commentators of ABC and CBS, and they changed 22 percent and 27 percent respectively in favor of Carter."

Another bit of TV news coverage during the campaign concerned the long-delayed report about the courageous freeing of the ship *Mayaguez*.

When the coup occurred in May 1975 it made most Americans lift their heads with pride. But when the report appeared in 1976, the newsmen who did not ignore it tried to imply that most Americans thought the raid reckless and foolhardy, too costly to have been of worth. Since many people didn't remember what had happened (memories are extraordinarily short), they believed what they were told.

But now a word about the long Watergate imbroglio, which most of us do remember. The self-righteousness of the commentators, as they passed judgment, was nauseating. So was the hypocrisy. Long before the matter was resolved, Daniel Schorr and Dan Rather went about the country lecturing and collecting fat fees for attacking Nixon, while at the same time they were appearing on television and reporting the news in a supposedly objective way.

Perhaps there was additional hypocrisy. Quadrangle Books, a division of the New York Times Company, published *At That Point in Time* by Fred D. Thompson, chief minority counsel of the Ervin Committee. The book stated that the Democratic National Committee and columnist Jack Anderson knew about plans for the Watergate break-in before it happened. Why didn't some TV newscaster ask about this? Where were the usually ubiquitous TV sleuths to sniff out the story?

Possibly Thompson's statement was incorrect, but if it was correct, TV's failure to investigate it leaves the American people with the impression that the Democrats were taken unawares and that "dirty tricks" were mainly a Nixon phenomenon.

Despite all the efforts of the press and TV, a number of citizens vaguely sense the bias, and have for a long time. That is why they shake their heads in doubt when Walter Cronkite ends a broadcast saying, "And that's the way it is."

Agnew, while wrong about many things, wasn't wrong when he criticized the media. He particularly attacked the "instant analysis and querulous criticism" of TV commentators, and said that a tiny group of men, perhaps "not more than a dozen anchormen, commentators and executive producers . . . represent a concentration of power over American opinion unknown in history."

The *Christian Science Monitor* in the fall of 1976 commented, "Though Mr. Agnew's attack was partisan and although he has since met his downfall, he raised issues that still trouble many . . . the concentration of electronic power."

More up to date is a criticism of the media by Sam Ervin of North Carolina. Although the ex-senator is known as a friend of civil liberties (and most TV people have a perennial love affair going with all civil libertarians), his words were not heeded.

When taken to task for bias or inaccuracy, the TV industry, instead of answering the charge, reflexively appeals to the First Amendment, which certainly was never intended to serve as a shield for distortion.

An item in *Variety* (November 24, 1976) noted that a proposal had been made in the state legislature of North Carolina for punishing newsmen who publish "grossly inaccurate" accounts of court proceedings. *Variety* went on to say that counsel for the North Carolina Broadcast Association said, "It certainly appears to be an unlawful restriction on the First Amendment."

News vs. Entertainment

Accurate or inaccurate, TV news is attractively presented. Whenever possible it is made to resemble a show-biz offering.

Sometimes there is no harm in that, and maybe some good. It adds to viewer interest. Since much of the content of news programs is filmed in advance, there is plenty of time for the film to go to the cutting room, where it is edited and its dramatic qualities are accented.

Human-interest tidbits are also played up, so that we may get more of Billy Carter's hijinx than we do of a dry statistical report on economics that influences our lives. There may be harm in that. It is what Ron Nessen, press secretary during the Ford administration, called "junk news." He expressed fear that it often may drive out "the substantive news."

Some TV newsmen admit this and even deplore it. *Variety* (February 16, 1977) quoted a newsman who said, "The trend of the last decade has been to emphasize the frivolous, to denigrate the intelligence of the audience, to discourage the development of a tough, aggressive news tradition."

A *Wall Street Journal* article (October 15, 1976) also spoke of the news, especially local TV news, as being "pure entertainment," and it complained that the "less visual daily doings of politicians, bureaucrats, and jurists which can powerfully affect people's lives, often are crowded out."

Personality Cult

What is said and how it is said are sometimes less important than who says it. That's evident from the fact that ABC was willing to pay Barbara Walters a million dollars yearly for five years.

TV Guide (October 19, 1976) took dead aim on the networks' personality cult: "If you want a performer, buy him. . . . The losers may be the viewers who could end up with less substance and more personality in their news."

The emphasis on personality affects not only the networks but the local stations as well. Veteran New York TV newsman Gabe Pressman charged that newscasting's top management men "fuss and fret about coiffures and telephone popularity surveys of their newscasters."

A familiar name is also important. According to a UPI report, Henry Kissinger, former secretary of state, has signed a five-year contract with NBC to appear on documentaries and interview shows and to act as the network's special consultant on foreign affairs. The contract also gives the network exclusive rights to special programs based on Kissinger's memoirs after their publication, probably in 1979.

No doubt about it, Kissinger is knowledgeable, but while in office he was a controversial figure, distrusted by some, admired by others. In retirement, however, his word on TV will probably be taken as gospel truth.

Documentaries: Fact or Fancy?

Not only do TV newscasts and specials flaunt tinsel trimmings and glamorous anchorpersons, so do documentaries.

A *Wall Street Journal* article (August 5, 1976) quoted John O'Connor of the *New York Times*, who said, "A seeming anxiety to construct production values for a 'hot story' . . . [may] raise unfortunate but legitimate questions about the journalism of '60 Minutes.'"

One of the most trumped-up "documentaries" shown on "60 Minutes" was "The Guns of Autumn." Even the liberal *Washington Post*, which owns CBS's affiliate station WTOP, criticized it, saying it "should receive an award for the most biased TV reporting of the year, possibly of the decade."

It showed supposedly typical hunters going to a garbage dump to shoot down tame bears. Actually, the dump was in a town that had asked that the bears be shot because people who had brought uneatable trash to the dump had been mauled by the animals.

However, when a senior vice president of CBS announced the show, he said, as though he did not know the facts, "This is purely and simply a broadcast about hunting. It is about how deeply the urge to hunt reaches into the American psyche —about the incredible efforts men and women make to fulfill that urge to chase, hunt, and to kill."

Staged TV scenes, passed off as the real thing, are not rare. Epstein, in his book *News from Nowhere*, tells about "one of the most impressive CBS News efforts," called "Hunger in America." It began with the picture of an emaciated, malformed, dying baby. Charles Kuralt said on the air, "Hunger is easy to recognize when it looks like this. The baby is dying of starvation. He was an American. Now he is dead."

Epstein went on to say that a government investigation later uncovered the fact that the dying baby "actually was a three months premature baby, weighing less than three pounds . . . those parents were neither poor nor starving. The mother . . . had the premature birth after an automobile accident."

Both liberals and conservatives complained about the show. Representative Henry B. Gonzales (Dem., Texas), a liberal, denounced the documentary as "inaccurate and misleading."

The show asserted that the majority of the Mexican-Americans in the city of San Antonio were hungry all the time, and that they accounted for 50 percent of the population.

Marilyn Beck of the *Philadelphia Bulletin* wrote an excellent article (April 1, 1977) entitled "Beware 'Objective' TV Documentaries." She quoted William Kromick, a producer-writer-director, as saying, "The word 'documentary' . . . leads people to believe reality is represented. But that's seldom true."

Rewriting History

Besides the documentaries, there are TV docu-dramas, which claim to dramatize historical truth. Often they not only dramatize it they fictionalize it. Richard Reeves, a liberal maverick, wrote a piece entitled "Kennedy Drama Turned History into a Fairy Tale" for the February 12, 1977 *TV Guide*. In it he complained about the "pseudohistory" that is replacing documentaries on TV, and commented glumly, "I doubt that there is much I can do but grumble about being fed fiction-as-facts on John Kennedy, Harry S. Truman, Joseph McCarthy, Charles Manson, Babe Didrikson Zaharias, Entebbe—and Kunta Kinte."

In an article appropriately captioned "Gunning for Joe," the *Philadelphia Bulletin* of February 8, 1977 rapped NBC's "Tail Gunner Joe," the docu-drama about Senator McCarthy.

The article quoted Roy Cohn, counsel to the Senate Government Operations Committee under McCarthy, who called the show a "smear job." Cohn continued, "If McCarthyism is the dirty word they say it is, this was McCarthyism at its worst." Cohn said he believed it was "part of a concentrated effort of Hollywood and the television industry to rewrite history of the 50s, to make out there was no Communist menace."

Even Arthur Unger of the *Christian Science Monitor* called this docu-drama "a simplistic production," which was "no more likely to bring about an understanding of the McCarthy phenomenon than a reading of Westbrook Pegler columns of the Roosevelt period would aid in an understanding of Eleanor Roosevelt."

Whatever faults McCarthy had, this "historical" show blew them up to fantastic and utterly ridiculous proportions. The show also took an unfair dig at Nixon's role in the Alger Hiss trial. Watergate does not alter the fact that Nixon helped rid our country of a traitor; yet this show seemed to imply that Nixon had wronged an innocent man for the sake of boosting his own career.

Then there was "Roots." Professor John Bracey, head of the Afro-American Studies Department at the University of Massachusetts, said, "It was a fantasy, a Garden of Eden-like program that was no better than Tarzan in its depiction of Africa." Professor Philip Curtin of Johns Hopkins University disliked the film's "fairy tale" approach to African society, where warriors were often slaves, not free men. British journalist Mark Ottaway (who according to the *New York Times* has "a reputation for integrity") questioned the authenticity of Alex Haley's research in an article for the Sunday *Times* of London. Ottaway's findings, as reported in *TV Guide* (May 28, 1977), were that " 'the oral historian' in Kunta Kinte's home village

177

had hoodwinked Haley" and that if inhabitants of Haley's supposed African ancestral home were involved in slave trading, "It was not as victims but as collaborators."

Professor Wolf Schmokel of the University of Vermont criticized the film for failing to mention that only about 20 percent of southern whites owned slaves.

Yet people usually believe their TV instructor. One particularly glaring example of semifiction masquerading as fact was a CBS program aired the evening of September 9, 1976, following Mao Tse-tung's death. One would expect *some* recognition of the fact that he was a bloody dictator who for 27 years kept a fourth of mankind in thrall. One was not prepared for an eulogy. But CBS viewers heard Mao compared to the world's great heroes. The narrator actually made him sound like a combination of Washington, Jefferson, and Lincoln, with a soupçon of Joan of Arc, St. George, and Prince Charming thrown in for good measure. In another chapter we will examine that strange TV adulation of this bloody-handed Red leader.

Privilege and Power

Apparently, TV personnel can get away with almost anything.

Small wonder that FBI Director Clarence Kelley said, "If there is an institution in our society with power that approaches unlimited power, that institution is the news media."

Theodore White, author of *The Making of the President* books, put it more dramatically: "You can take a compass with a one-mile radius and put it down at the corner of Fifth Avenue and Fifty-second Street, and you can control 95 percent of the entire opinion and influence making in the USA."

It conjures up Edmund Burke's words as he stood in the House of Commons in London. He said, "There are the three estates in Parliament, but in the reporters' gallery yonder [in the anchorman's booth] there sit the Fourth Estate, more important than they all."

Chapter 15

America? Ugh!

"George Washington crossed the Delaware. I think he was looking for broads." So spoke one TV character.

Another TV character, a prostitute, joking that she had been doing the same sort of work for 500 years, said, "I made out with George Washington."

Ruth Gordon, who played the part of a 105-year-old congressional secretary in NBC's "That Was the Year That Was— 1976" (December 26, 1976), claimed to have had an affair with every American president since Abraham Lincoln.

Moscow housewife Mama Olga, in "Ivan the Terrible," told her little son that "the father of his country," Lenin, when he was a boy, cut down his father's cherry tree, using a hammer and sickle. Afterwards he admitted his misdeed, saying, "I cannot tell a lie."

The boys in "Welcome Back, Kotter" (March 3, 1977) were asked to draw a picture. Kotter, the teacher, said they were at liberty to draw whatever they wanted "as long as it isn't a naked picture of George Washington."

"Who wants a naked picture of George Washington?" a sweathog demanded.

"Maybe Martha," answered another.

Many of us wrinkle our noses when we hear these sallies. Like Queen Victoria, "We are not amused." They are flip but are not really funny.

It seems the networks want to prove that they are much too sophisticated to express love and loyalty to our country and to our country's heroes. They are like college freshmen who want to show how blasé and brash they are, or like little boys on a bicycle who want to prove their nonchalance and daring: "Look, mom, no hands!"

'Too Sentimental'

Early in 1976 Tony Orlando was interviewed at Las Vegas. He had recently played there to an audience that broke attendance records. Although on December 28, 1976 his television show, "Tony Orlando and Dawn," was cancelled, the previous year he was a top TV personality. In 1975 he won the People's Choice Award for the best male entertainer, beating out such TV bigs as Bob Hope and Johnny Carson.

In the interview Orlando expressed pique. He felt that he didn't receive the publicity of many lesser TV stars. Whether his anger was justified, or whether it was only his show-biz ego squawking, there's no knowing. But he does occasionally express pro-American sentiments and it is certainly conceivable that this penchant does not ingratiate him with some TV moguls who are scared of that sort of thing.

When he taped a show at Camp Pendleton, the U.S. Marine base, he asked a group of marines about their New Year's resolutions. Three men, one right after another, said, "To be a perfect marine, sir." The fourth, a black man, answered, "To be a perfect American, sir."

Orlando then handed the man the mike. He sang "Happy Days are Here Again" and broke down in tears. Orlando said, "It was one of the most touching and humane things I've ever seen. And the networks cut it out of the show. 'Too sentimental,' they said."

On television, mom, country, and apple pie are out. Patriotism is passé.

180

Bicentennial Blues

Kevin Phillips charged in *TV Guide* (August 28, 1976) that, aside from the great day of July 4, 1976, the networks largely ignored the Bicentennial. He wrote, "Historical pageants? No coverage. Battle reenactments and ethnic festivals? Nothing . . . evening newsclips of Americana have been few enough to count on your fingers."

Among newsmen Charles Kuralt was the "exception that proves the rule." "Otherwise," said Phillips, "lack of interest in America's geography, countryside, and folklore is pervasive."

Maybe he forgot the "Adams Chronicles." But aside from that series, plus the "Bicentennial Minutes," which were too short to tell a dramatic story, and the visits to the various states on "The Today Show," there was indeed pitifully little from January to July, and once the Fourth of July passed, even that little (with the exception of "Bicentennial Minutes") disappeared.

What a waste of material! So many dramatic but comparatively little-known stories would have made exciting TV sequences: the story of Francis Marion, the "Swamp Fox," onetime Indian fighter and later the American general who raised several all-volunteer companies among the country lads of South Carolina and marched to the relief of General Horatio Gates; the story of George Rogers Clark, who secured for the colonists what is now the state of Kentucky and who went northeast to capture Detroit; the story of the battle of Charleston (a British defeat) and of Sergeant Jasper, who rescued the colors of Fort Moultrie and began there his brave and romantic career; the story of Colonel Isaac Shelby and Colonel John Sevier who, after General Clinton defeated the revolutionary army in North Carolina, defeated the British veterans on Kings Mountain.

When the War of Independence was mentioned at all, only its familiar events were brought up. Or if anything less familiar was mentioned, Phillips said, it was designed to make viewers believe, if they didn't know better, that the Revolution "was sparked by women, minorities, and young activists."

When the country celebrates its next centennial, all of us will be dead. Meantime, why doesn't TV give us some patriotic programs?

Every single one of the fifty states has a history that could be written up into a fascinating TV series. How many people know that Tennessee was once a free and independent nation? In 1772 the English established the Watauga settlement there, and for its government, the first written constitution in America. The government preserved its independence of all other governments, including that of North Carolina, its mother colony, until 1775.

How many know of the painful divisions and heartaches that beset the families of Maryland during the War between the States, as one brother fought for the North, another for the South? A Margaret Mitchell–type genius could make a superb "Gone with the Wind" out of the idea.

How many know about the Russian settlement in California?

And we might give the networks another idea, *gratis*. Why not a children's program on the landmarks of the USA? There is no dearth of material. How many children have visited Fort McHenry in Baltimore where Francis Scott Key wrote the "Star-Spangled Banner" by the light of "the rockets' red glare" over the harbor? It is a dramatic story. Key was held on a British ship, that is, an enemy ship, while the battle raged, and in great suspense about its outcome he wrote our national anthem.

How many children have visited our Space Center at Cape Kennedy? Science fiction cannot top it for interest. How many children have visited South Dakota's Mount Rushmore, emblazoned with the colossal sculpture of Washington, Jefferson, Lincoln, and Theodore Roosevelt?

It took the British to give us a look into our colonial past; it was they who brought up James Fenimore Cooper's *The Last of the Mohicans*, and they brought to WTOP-TV in Washington a top-notch series on the ethnic diversity of the United States.

On the Road

Perhaps Charles Kuralt can again be mentioned as an exception. His program "On the Road," which focuses on people throughout the land, has at least shown our ethnic diversity—

and shown too that we are not a nation of sex maniacs, neu-
rotics, and killers as some other programs imply.

Kuralt was written up in *TV Guide* (November 20, 1976)
when he filmed a family in New England. In the article he
was quoted as saying about the USA, "Where else in the world
could you find yourself eating in a Japanese restaurant with
a fundamentalist minister and his wife from Hartford with
their Muslim daughter-in-law from Phoenix who's an airline
stewardess studying to be a veterinarian?"

There is much that is interesting and inspiring about our
country, but the TV cameramen seldom catch it. When they
do find something that verges on the inspiring they are likely
to distort it or ignore it. If they had existed in the 18th century,
they probably would not have focused on Patrick Henry when
he said, "Give me liberty or give me death," or on Nathan
Hale when he said, "I regret that I have but one life to give
for my country."

Soldiers, Sailers, Marines

On TV a man who gives his life for his country is a dupe of
the government and the establishment. In another chapter we
will discuss TV's handling of the Vietnam debacle, but here
let's just point out that TV repeatedly slurs the armed forces.

Variety (November 17, 1976) ran a story about a retired
army colonel who had filed suit against NBC because he objected to the way he was portrayed in the web TV feature
"Judge Horton and the Scottsboro Boys." He said that Joe
Burleson was shown as a cowardly and prejudiced National
Guard commander who shirked his duty of defending the
black defendants in the celebrated rape case.

NBC asked a circuit court in Alabama to dismiss the suit because of a technicality; the network claimed the suit was filed
in the wrong county.

TV also has a way of choosing comic, stupid, or slightly
disreputable characters for servicemen.

In MH2, Grandpa Larkin, the Fernwood Flasher, is a navy
veteran. In "M.A.S.H." one of the men said of a relative back
home, "He can name 24 of the 48 states; he has an appoint-

ment to West Point." In the "Nancy Walker Show" Terry had for his homosexual partner a much-decorated naval officer, who appeared in full uniform on the show.

"M.A.S.H." hardly inspires much respect for the army. We all know that there are cases where men shoot themselves in nonvital spots to avoid military duty, but "M.A.S.H." included one such shooting in the episode of November 11, 1976, the very day we dedicate to remembrance of veterans.

And "Baa Baa Black Sheep" did not exactly serve as a recruiting vehicle for the military. It provided no models of military courtesy or discipline.

Police Too

TV seems to be anti any public servant, including even the police. Chapter 10 on violence mentioned that many crime shows portray corrupt policemen. In "Joe Forrester" Captain Tragar was corrupt. In "Law and Order" (May 6, 1976) deputy chief of public affairs first tried to downplay charges of corruption that beset the police force, but his son convinced him to denounce the corruption. Policemen in "City of Angels" appeared as sadists who routinely slugged and beat people with rubber truncheons. In the episode entitled "A Lonely Way to Die" (March 2, 1976) they beat a man so badly that he could hardly walk.

But worse than this kind of thing, TV has on occasion made real-life policemen look more like rabid dogs than decent men. In his book *The Marvin Kitman Show*, Kitman revealed how TV covered the hippie rioters who infested Chicago at the time of the 1968 Democratic Convention. He said that cameras and sound trucks were on the scene and originally recorded one two-minute sequence showing the rowdy young people using the expression "mother f——" no fewer than 18 times. They also threatened in that short time "to kill a cop." When the film was shown, the offensive word was bleeped out, as well as the threat to kill, so the police, said Kitman, looked as though they were roughhousing kids for no reason.

Odd that the TV people should be so careful to delete an

obscene word in this case when it alone would explain the action of the police. Though quite properly the word is *rarely* used on TV, it has been used. But this time, the one time when it might have been justified, it was bleeped out.

Sticking Close to Schorr

The networks have revealed their double standard on other occasions too. Because so many TV hirelings seem to have a shallow love for this country, they are willing to let their own men get away with actions that not too many years ago might have precipitated a storm of criticism.

A former employee of CBS was the ultraliberal Daniel Schorr. Most of us remember his story. He somehow obtained a copy of a classified congressional document, used the material in a broadcast, then passed it on to the antiestablishment New York weekly, the *Village Voice*. At first he lied about all this and hinted that his colleague Lesley Stahl had been the guilty one.

Now if a Republican campaign operative got hold of a secret document belonging to the Democratic National Committee by some unknown and presumably underhand method, and then publicized it, the TV networks would (as we know) scream about it over the air, public opinion would be aroused, and the man would land in jail. Against Schorr (and Ellsberg before him) not a squeak was heard.

For a while Schorr did not even lose his salary, and when Dick Salant, CBS News president, did accept Schorr's resignation, he publicly thanked him for a "superb job and eloquent service to all of us in journalism."

Why did Schorr do what he did?

Merrill Panitt, writing in *TV Guide* (October 16, 1976), answered, "Possibly because Schorr never was an objective reporter. He is a man with a mission, [it] usually being, by his own admission, aggrandizement of Schorr." The same writer went on to say that this far-from-objective TV reporter once suggested that Barry Goldwater go to Germany to "join up" with right-wing elements there.

185

When Schorr was called up before the House committee investigating his action, he spoke grandiosely of the First Amendment, though the First Amendment was never meant to apply to information that might help the enemies of this country.

Too bad there aren't more honest liberals like John P. Roche who don't mind crying out against this kind of thing. Roche wrote in *TV Guide* (December 25, 1976), "What really burns me up is a persistent addiction to a phony adversary culture, to unjustified anti-Americanism."

Miasma over the Medium

But aside from these individual cases where TV seems anti-American, there is a general anti-American miasma that hangs over much of the medium.

The serial that purportedly satirizes TV soap operas and sitcoms uses a character like Mary Hartman as the prototype of the American TV housewife. Is this not an insult to American women, and indeed to all Americans? The episode in which the publicity men came to tell Mary that she had been chosen to go to New York to represent the Typical Consumer Housewife was the episode in which, screaming hysterically, she threw the inebriated Tom out of the house.

In a later episode Gore Vidal interviewed Mary and said that the book he would write about her would also be about the emptiness of America, about the promises not kept. It would be a book about survival, despite the world we live in. And Gore Vidal in real life said, according to *Time* magazine, "To understand Mary Hartman is to understand America."

Stephanie Harrington, writing in *Ms.* magazine, called MH2 "the unedited all-American unconscious." John Leonard, cultural affairs reporter for the *New York Times*, called MH2 "the American interior monologue." Gerald Nachman of the New York News Service wrote that it "perfectly captures the neuroses, insecurities and frustrations of modern life. . . . Mary represents today's woman caught in a consumer-oriented society while searching for a meaningful life." A

186

critic writing in the *Nation* said the show "chronicles the decline of our capitalistic society." And Daniel Lockwood, who wrote *The Mary Hartman Story*, pontificated, "In the year of our bicentennial, with all the stirring speeches about . . . the American way of life, we still recognize the truth of our lives is something less grand; it is a husband without a rising sign, a closet queen, a corrupt D.A." He added that the tremendous success of the show proves that most Americans believe in their own helplessness.

God preserve us if we form our ideas about America from TV!

Chapter 16

Blitzing the Conservatives

To cite the sins of TV at such length is to feel like Jonah preaching against wicked Nineveh.

Often the medium is not only anti-America, but also antiestablishment, antibusiness, and anti anything that is conservative with either a small "c" or a capital "C."

True, in "All's Fair" TV balanced the conservative Richard with the far-out Charley, but it was Charley's remarks that were the more outrageous and the more attention-grabbing. The first line of this book was one of them.

Since the chapters on sex shenanigans have already proved that TV is ultraliberal when it comes to sexual morals, there is no need to say more on the subject. Let us turn then to the ultraliberal political attitudes we see on TV.

We can begin with Richard and Charley. Liberals of Charley's stripe (and these are the types generally portrayed on TV) use extravagant epithets in speaking to and about more conservative people. When Charley first walked into Richard's comfortable, well-furnished home, she said, "What a cute little pad. You'd never know a fascist lived here."

True, Richard hurled an epithet of his own when he answered, "Would you stop talking like a sorority-house socialist?"

Of course, we were not supposed to take Richard and Charley's dialogue seriously. It is only a parlor game. At the same time, it is worth noting that "fascist" is considered a more pejorative term than "socialist." (Mussolini was a fascist. Kindly old Sir Harold Wilson, with his pipe and Oxford accent, is a socialist.) If "fascist" through this kind of use becomes associated in our minds with "conservative," it will obviously make conservatism disreputable.

As a rule, though, "All's Fair" was not strongly biased. Few other shows on TV have even made an attempt to balance the so-called liberal and the so-called conservative.

"All in the Family" does have both Mike and Archie, but there is no attempt at balance. Archie Bunker, the caricatured archconservative, is portrayed as stupid, bigoted, and unreasonable. He is the object of special ridicule. Mike, the son-in-law who is liberal beyond the norm, indeed to the point of being Left-leaning, is portrayed as far better educated and more sympathetic, logical, and understanding than Archie.

Archie is suspicious of Puerto Ricans, all of whom he fears carry knives; he looks down on blacks, all of whom he is sure are shiftless; and he dislikes Jews, all of whom he thinks are Shylocks. In short, Archie is a brother to the Ku Klux Klansman, and by TV implication, so are all conservatives.

No wonder Lee Winfrey, writing in the *Philadelphia Inquirer* (November 19, 1976), said some programs display "no more honesty than a poker dealer in a bust-out gambling joint."

The Hot War

However, "All in the Family" (or for that matter "All's Fair") is not representative of TV's usual treatment of conservatives. One fairly common treatment is to make conservatives nonpersons. Whatever their beliefs regarding morals or politics or anything else, conservatives are deemed irrelevant, reactionary, and nonsensical, not worthy of a hearing in this enlightened age.

When TV can neither ridicule conservatives nor ignore them, it uses a third technique: the openly hostile attack or hot war, especially in news-related programs.

The hot war goes back even to a time before the current television era began. It raged during the Goldwater campaign of 1964. Barry Goldwater was a conservative and therefore sported horns and a tail. It was amazing how slyly and how well newscasters managed to paint this picture of him.

Granted, we cannot blame TV alone for the famous commercial about the little girl with a daisy who was blown up by a nuclear bomb. The advertising firm of Tony Schwartz (incidentally, the same firm that handled Jimmy Carter's publicity for the last three weeks of his campaign) created it, and the Johnson forces accepted it.

Apparently, though, the TV moguls had no qualms about running the commercial. And it was TV's attitude (and that of the press), as much as anything else, that was responsible for surrounding Goldwater with an aura of madness; he was the unstable creature who lusted to start an atomic war and, on the side, to snatch social security from the needy.

Many people thought the whole performance as disgraceful, in its way, as the Watergate antics years later.

Speaking of Watergate, we must wonder why the TV newscasters who were calling so loudly for an investigation of Nixon and "the president's men" didn't call for an investigation of the original reason for the bugging of Watergate. Government agencies had heard rumors that McGovern was accepting money from North Vietnam and from Fidel Castro. The Cubans, who actually did the bugging job, were themselves concerned about the rumors. Were they true? The TV people did not ask.

Newscasters scarcely mentioned the fact that bugging is standard procedure in government, with or without the provocation of a possible security risk. Kennedy was the first president to bug the White House, and the record of his conversations with everybody who entered the Oval Office is on tapes now in the private possession of the Kennedy family. No doubt the tapes would reveal interesting details about the lifestyle of the man whom syndicated columnist Earl Wilson called "the swingingest president of the century."

Now nobody is suggesting, or should suggest, digging up sex scandals for no good purpose. The point is that if TV had regarded Kennedy as a conservative, it probably would have called for an exposé of the scandals. But for a certain liberalism that TV moguls saw in Truman and LBJ, they might have asked for an investigation of them, the first man being a product of the unsavory Kansas City political machine, the other a buddy of notorious Bobby Baker. In short, anybody who pleases the liberal TV people can usually count on comparatively gentle treatment; anybody who displeases them by evincing a tinge of conservatism can count on comparatively rough treatment.

The Bible Belt

Because, on the whole, religious bodies have a conservative influence, they too, as we said in an earlier chapter, come in for some TV digs. And perhaps because the southern part of the country, the Bible Belt, has in the past been a conservative stronghold, both religiously and politically, TV programs have often had an anti-South bias.

Since Carter's election, things are changing a bit. Whether this is just a temporary letup or a permanent change is at this writing too early to say.

A few years back, a TV fan who had never lived in the South would get the impression from looking at the boobtube that the South was mainly populated by two groups of people, the vicious and the ignorant.

Often in crime shows if there was one person who had a southern accent, while all the other characters had northern, eastern, or western accents, the southern accent was the clue to who-dun-it. For example, in a "Police Woman" episode the southern accent was the distinguishing mark of a man just released from prison and reunited with his wife, who also had a southern accent and who had just kidnapped a baby, killed her landlady, etc.

An installment of "Charlie's Angels" that dealt with white slavery was laid in the South. There was a prison farm with

191

a lesbian matron, and threats of rape, enforced prostitution, and all the rest. Still, on several counts it was not as objectionable as *Nightmare in Badham County*, also set in the South. It was a wonder that the film didn't start a second Civil War—except that the southern people could not blame the thing on the North, but on TV.

At that, it was supposedly somewhat cleaned up for TV! The censors did anything but a complete scouring job, and a number of ABC affiliates refused to carry the film because of its depravity and violence. Notwithstanding, about 180 affiliates throughout the country did carry it.

If the conditions depicted in that film exist in any American prison, we should think twice before we point a finger at the Nazi or the Soviet concentration camps.

And if the hatred between the whites and the blacks of the South, or of any place, was ever as bad as "Roots" depicted it, then we all would have to give up on the entire human race. The telefilm was based on Alex Haley's book. Haley is a former writer for *Playboy* and the author of an admiring biography of radical Black Muslim leader Malcolm X.

Happily, other people besides Haley have roots and can remember hearing about love and loyalty going both ways between whites and blacks. Mammies were often treated as second mothers by white men and women who had been fortunate enough to be under their care as children. The descendants of these men and women are still retelling tales of fond and affectionate relationships between blacks and whites.

Then TV's idea that the typical southerner is an ignoramus turns up time after time. For example, there was Loretta of MH2. Though Loretta was not a villain, but instead one of the few sympathetic characters in the serial, she was completely untouched by book learning. Her language would have driven an English teacher to drink—except that it was often amusing, and definitely *ad rem*.

Every region has its ignorant and evil citizens, as well as its cultured citizens; but if manners are a gauge of civilization (some sages say they are), then the South is by far the most civilized part of the country. One has to conclude that it is the South's conservatism which makes it a TV whipping boy.

It is or has been a whipping boy in newscasts too. According to Paul Good (*TV Guide*, March 5, 1977), TV covered the black push for racial equality in the South during the 60s, but coverage virtually ceased "when blacks started raising issues that threatened non-Southern whites."

Small Towns: A Bad Place to Be

Small towns, wherever they may be, North, East, South, or West, are also TV whipping boys. Benjamin Stein noted in the *Public Interest* that TV portrays small towns as "evil . . . the innocent wayfarer [or] naive families have a tire blowout outside a small town and completely disappear into the maw of a townwide criminal conspiracy." Stein thinks this hostility exists because small-town citizens are "resistant to the political currents which move [TV] writers." In short, they are too conservative for the scripters.

Big, Bad Business

Business too is conservative—for the most part. Predictably, TV tends to be antibusiness.

In 1976 Kevin Phillips studied two months of network coverage of business on the evening news and was surprised at the unrelieved black picture that emerged.

Since 1968 Vanderbilt University Television News Service has been videotaping the network news and accumulating a tape library. Phillips drew on abstracts in the Vanderbilt collection for evidence of how the networks portray business. Patrick Buchanan (*TV Guide*, November 13, 1976) wrote that "for years CBS's lawyers have been waging war in the courts to get control of the Vanderbilt tapes." (Recently, however, CBS, dropped its lawsuit.)

The antibusiness bias reared its head when Bill Buckley hosted long-time TV big wheel Fred Friendly on "Firing

Line" (August 7, 1976). Friendly said, "The argument from Mobil is that socialists like Barry Commoner, as they call him, get . . . on television, and they, Mobil, and they, Exxon, can't buy time or space to argue back."

When one of the studio guests asked him, "Would you favor their buying time?" Friendly answered, "Well, I'm nervous about big companies buying time to do propaganda."

But he didn't believe it was "propaganda" for antibusiness people to talk?

Now nobody would assert that business is as pure as new-fallen snow. Business has its share of scoundrels, and, granted too, big business can be as ruthless as big government. In fact, it can, and sometimes does, work hand in glove with government on an international scale. It then manipulates all of us and helps our enemies by meeting their trade requests for sophisticated machinery and technological secrets.

Nonetheless, the ordinary businessman—even the smashingly successful businessman—is not necessarily crooked, ruthless, or decadent, and he tries to give the public a fair shake, if for no other reason than that "honesty is the best policy" for him personally. Thomas A. Murphy wrote in the *New York Times* that businessmen "who offer substandard quality, inadequate service and poor response to customers will be steadily and inexorably moved off the board by those who offer better quality, better service, and more complete customer satisfaction." He regretted that some forces both within and without the business community, seek to "replace the corrective forces of competition with the discipline of government."

Moreover, there are forces (and some of them are TV personnel) that would do away with the possibility of an ordinary person making a normal profit, investing his savings, collecting dividends, or clipping coupons.

On "The Moneychangers" (Ross Hunter's adaptation of Arthur Hailey's book), which premiered on NBC on December 1, 1976, the mistress of one of the principal male characters spoke disdainfully of what was "good for coupon clippers."

Do we envision a bloated capitalist? Well, elderly widows who do not want to take the risk of buying stocks are a large proportion of the people who buy bonds and hence are "coupon clippers." Institutions like orphanages and hospitals also buy bonds. They are coupon clippers too.

194

The Filthy Rich

Residents of the ghetto and the "filthy rich" receive dispro-portionately more time on TV than the vast majority of middle-income people, and the businessman, when portrayed at all, is often a character like Joseph Armaugh in "The Captains and the Kings," out to scalp the workingman.

A possible exception to that statement was ABC's adaptation of Irwin Shaw's *Rich Man, Poor Man* (RMPM). This saga of a self-made millionaire had its faults, but its main character was portrayed (particularly in Book I) as a decent fellow who cared not only for profits, but for his employees as well.

At times it seems as if the TV scripters are trying to foment class warfare, the way they depict corporation executives and bankers. In "The Moneychangers" the wife of banking ty-coon Roscoe Heyward said to him, "My father was something no businessman can hope to understand: he was a man of style and breeding."

The same derogatory tone prevailed throughout the series. These were unsavory people with the possible exception of one man. That one man, Alex Vandervoort, was of course a far-out liberal who, greatly influenced by his activist mistress, wanted to commit millions of bank funds (not a cent of his own) to a civic project, the rebuilding of the city's principal slum.

His opposite number and rival in a power struggle, Roscoe Heyward, was a conservative and a humorless stuffed shirt. Real-life conservative Bill Buckley wouldn't want to be caught dead (and certainly not alive) in his boring presence.

The banking-business crowd, in this series, was a dissolute bunch. When super-tycoon George Quartermain wanted to establish a $50 million line of credit at the bank, he arranged, as a little persuader for the bankers, a trip to an exotic Carib-bean retreat. The group traveled to the island paradise aboard Quartermain's private jetliner, which was equipped with a sauna bath and boasted three sexy stewardesses. Once they had arrived, Heyward was told that there was a button above his bed that he might press if he got lonely at night. He did, and as quickly as a genie pops from a bottle, one of the beauti-ful girls appeared with an at-your-service-sir smile. Quartermain had instructed this sultry siren to soften up the banker so that the $50 million would be forthcoming.

Quartermain proved himself an accomplished con artist in other ways too. He rigged figures to make his business interests appear financially sound, while his vast empire was about to collapse and he was preparing to skip the country.

Rex Polier described the series in the *Philadelphia Bulletin* (December 9, 1976) as "a merry and unprincipled romp for profits in a whoopeedo atmosphere of broads and booze." He added, "The story is simply preposterous."

Not much more realistic or more favorable to business was the series "Executive Suite." It too was loosely based on a novel.

Its main characters were executives of a multinational conglomerate. Almost without exception they were rascals of one kind or another, definitely "enemies of the people." TV writers allowed them to have no sense of civic responsibility. One of the insecticides they manufactured was suspected of inducing cancer. Only under pressure did the firm suspend production of the item, and the senior vice president, a callous curmudgeon, opposed the move, saying, "Mice get cancer when you look at them cross-eyed."

When 95 employees were laid off, it was without unemployment compensation—hardly plausible in today's world. The shop steward told the president that he should hire those 95 men back as safety inspectors, because working conditions were unsafe. Today it is a rare plant that does not take every safety precaution possible, and our record on that score in America is the best in the world.

Then the board turned down a union proposal for a new health plan, so the workers staged a slowdown.

Topping all this, the president's daughter (patterned after Patty Hearst?) had joined a group of radicals and had bombed her father's factory. While the show did tap her on the wrist for this, her action was made to seem understandable, maybe even justified.

It is hard to believe that any successful company ever had such a board of directors. The bright-eyed boy-genius who was the youngest member of the board was pretending, for the sake of respectability, to be married, but in fact was merely living with a woman—a former porn-film queen at that; the senior vice president was as tight as Scrooge and twice as mean;

196

another vice president had made his secretary his mistress; another was a secret drinker whose wife had a close friendship with a lesbian; a woman board member had an affair with an industrial spy who, unbeknown to her, was stealing the company's formulas and blueprints; and the consumer-affairs director had found another employee for his cute little sex partner. Wags nicknamed the show "Executive Sweeties," and *Newsweek* spoke of it as "a boardroom to bedroom melodrama."

Dick Griffin of the *Chicago Daily News* interviewed some businessmen who had seen the series; he quoted Leo H. Schoenhofen, chairman of Marcor (owner of Montgomery Ward and Container Corporation), as saying that he thought the show was so ridiculous, so flagrantly inaccurate that he didn't believe anybody would pay any attention to it.

John S. Reed, chairman and president of Santa Fe Industries (parent of the Santa Fe Railroad), disagreed with Schoenhofen. He thought people would pay attention and said that his 13-year-old son would "sort out . . . the good and the bad guys. And I'm a bad guy."

Samuel B. Casey, Jr., president of Pullman, went right to the point: "It galls me to see a TV program that doesn't say a single good thing about America. . . . Profits aren't bad. Let them visit Sweden or Russia and see how those societies work and they'll find we have a great thing going here for the people."

The Profit Picture

Television itself is far from being a nonprofit industry. The teleplay scripts may decry profits, but the people responsible for putting on the teleplays are as profit-happy as any in the country.

In 1976 the networks raked in nearly three billion dollars in advertising revenue ($2,991,280,700). NBC collected $235,000 for a single one-minute commercial on *Gone with the Wind*. According to *Variety* (April 13, 1977), profits were up a whopping 25.8 percent from 1975, and pretax profits were up 44.5 percent.

Variety further remarked that TV's "economic health . . . is the envy of practically every industry in the country." TV tycoons get stratospheric salaries, and even the "performers" like Barbara Walters don't do badly. She makes exactly five times as much as the president of the United States.

Comedian Donald Harron of "Hee Haw" is quite pleased with television's monetary rewards. Said he, "This is an age when a 'fool' is better paid than a king." *Time* (January 10, 1977) quoted NBC's vice president Joseph Taritero as saying, "There is just no limit to what a network will pay if they want someone."

Before Senator Henry Jackson decried profits in the oil industry, he should have taken a look at the profits in the television industry. Syndicated columnist Patrick J. Buchanan wrote in the *New York Times* that "the wealth and salaries of Big Bill Paley [former chairman of the board of CBS] and Uncle Walter Cronkite compare favorably with the men who run the oil industry. Toss in ABC's Million-Dollar-Baby and some of the fellows at the Petroleum Club look positively middle class."

Many people realized at the time that Jackson's diatribes were pure political hokum. When TV teleplays impugn profits, however, we are more likely to take the message seriously.

Would it not be refreshing if some TV show acknowledged a few facts that even a kid-vid addict knows? Profits are what enables companies to expand and to provide jobs as well as meet the payroll on existing jobs. Corporate profits pay taxes, and these taxes in turn fund government programs and services. The same TV commentators who seem to decry profits the loudest are often the ones who champion federal health and welfare programs. Government cannot spend any money until it first collects from citizens—unless it prints more paper dollars and further inflates the currency.

The few TV people who do acknowledge the need for profits seem to be saying in effect: Yes, we realize the need for some profits, but profits are too high. That message came through on "Executive Suite" and on "The Moneychangers," both of which portrayed tycoons living in unbelievable opulence and voluptuousness.

Well, maybe profits are too high for those mythical people and maybe they are too high in some super-businesses that have international tentacles, but in many average businesses, they are too *small*. Warren Brookes of the *Boston Herald-American* did a study of comparative profits and came up with these results: pretax profits between 1973 and 1975 for food retailers were a pitiful 1.3 percent, for the oil industry 8.2 percent—and for the TV industry an elephantine 19.1 percent.

And Louis Rukeyser, syndicated columnist, financier, and TV personality, reported in the fall of 1976 that "the average profit on each dollar of sales last year was less than a nickel." Speaking of food profits, he said that they had risen to 1.7 percent. On each dollar of sales the supermarket earns a profit of two cents. State sales taxes often top that amount. In Pennsylvania, for instance, a customer pays six cents in taxes on every dollar purchase, and Governor Shapp wants to raise that to seven cents.

"Executive Suite" could have brought out that point, and it could have mentioned another truth: when profits dip so low that entrepreneurs lose their incentive to expand—or to engage in business in the first place—the whole economy stagnates, jobs become scarce, and lower-income people suffer more than anybody else.

Exceptions That Prove the Rule

Maybe TV is beginning to see the light. Amazingly, NBC-owned stations in Los Angeles, Cleveland, Chicago, Washington, and New York are running (as of this writing) a series of 20 half-hour shows that laud the free economy, profits and all. The series, called "America: The Super Market," was produced by KNBC, Los Angeles, in collaboration with the Law and Economics Center of the University of Miami. *TV Guide* (December 18, 1976) called it "an extraordinary series" and added, "It is even more extraordinary to see it on NBC."

Early in 1977 PBS introduced a series titled "In Search of the Real America." Political writer and demographer Ben J. Wattenberg, its scripter, actually argued that American corporations aren't necessarily sinister, that the U.S. doesn't exploit the third world, and that our way of life isn't meaningless. In short, Wattenberg lent support to the conservative view. He said of the program, "This is the only advocacy television that calls itself advocacy television. There's a lot of advocacy television that calls itself reportage. We are saying this is one man's opinion."

Wattenberg did not confine himself to defending free enterprise. He treated foreign and defense policies and said unabashedly that the U.S. is a bastion of freedom.

Down on the Farm

Since attacks on business far outnumber defense of it, however, we had better return to them and note that TV's dislike of business and profits includes "agribusiness," as PBS called farming in its January 1976 documentary, "A Day Without Sunshine." The message of this show on migrant farm workers in Florida was that farmers and food processors exploit the workers.

Since the message was not supported by fact, the program had to spring full blown from the antibusiness bias of the TV people—that, coupled with a blind pro-labor orientation that made them accept without investigation what certain labor bosses told them.

The American Farm Bureau Federation, representing the producers of about 80 percent of the country's commercial crops, asked for time to tell its side of the story on TV. Request denied.

The Farm Bureau then put out a printed rebuttal (which few people read), asserting that the program was "not authentic journalism but a propaganda instrument for Cesar Chavez' United Farm Workers." The same men who had put out a pro-Chavez booklet months before had served as producer and associate producer of the documentary. Moreover, the key men interviewed on the program were Chavez supporters and allies, although no emcee identified them as such.

Edith Efron called the documentary "an unreliable piece of political advocacy" and, in *TV Guide* (September 11, 1976), said that one of the three men, Dr. Marshall Barry, former assistant professor of economics at New College, Sarasota, Florida, "posted an appeal to students to get jobs cutting cane in Florida for 'a couple of days' in order to walk out on strike in support of Chavez and the UFW."

She noted further that the narrator on the show quoted the chief of the Child Labor section of Florida's Department of Commerce as saying that forty to fifty thousand children work in the citrus fields. Farm Bureau people retorted that this man had told them that he had said no such thing. He averred he could not have said it, because that would mean there were twice as many youngsters working in the groves as there were in the total citrus work force.

The executive producer finally acknowledged in a postprogram meeting that Miss Efron attended that "Chavez supporters had indeed directed and produced 'Sunshine' and provided its dominant interpretations and solutions."

Chavez seems to be a pet of the TV networks. When they aren't hitting the orange growers of Florida, they are extolling Chavez and his California grape boycott. Even sitcoms have referred to the boycott favorably, among them "All's Fair" and "McLean Stevenson."

Like a Dry Martini

Why don't more businessmen and farmers demand time to present their side of the story? Many of them feel that anything they say the glib TV commentators will twist, so that they will still come off looking like the enemies of workingmen. Edith Efron, who understands the businessman's plight, said of the American free-enterprise system, "Throughout the whole history of the human race, no other system has fed, clothed, and housed the common man so well as the individualistic, private-property, competitive free-enterprise or capitalistic system. And anybody who claims . . . to be concerned with the material wellbeing of the common man, and who is not an advocate of capitalism, is one of two things: he is ignorant or he is a fraud."

That is a rather strong statement, but the facts bear it out. We label as "poverty" an income that is higher than the average family income of the world's second most powerful nation. Moreover, that "poverty" income is 800 percent above the world average. With but six percent of the world's population, the U.S. produces one third of the goods and services of the whole world.

Moreover, our system is more efficient. Anybody who has tried to make a telephone call in Europe knows that good old privately run AT&T is better than state-run phone companies elsewhere. It is not unusual for a hotel guest in Europe to be told by the operator that there will be a half-hour or so wait on his call. New home telephone service in our country costs between $10 and $35; in France it can cost up to $1,720.

Plumbing in the USA is . . . but why labor the point?

The *Wall Street Journal* published a speech by a Major Steve Richie (ret.) in which he said, "Despite the unprecedented achievements of our free market system, it is under attack from all quarters, and it is being defended with an ineptness which is unparalleled."

Certainly, TV rarely defends it; on the contrary, it often attacks it.

The words of Dr. Nicholas Nyardi, former finance minister of Hungary, fittingly close this chapter. Comparing America's economic system with those of other countries, he said, "American business is like a dry martini cocktail. When it is good, it is very good, and when it is bad, it is still good."

Chapter 17

Sounding Board
for Socialism

An Ancient Ideology

"I don't believe in God because I don't believe in Mother Goose."

Clarence Darrow said it, but many TV shows say essentially the same thing every day—see Chapter 9, "Subtle Scoffing."

Substituting for the religion that is scoffed at or ignored is a brand of materialism. Although materialism too has already been covered in these pages, one popular brand, socialism, has not as yet come in for a word. TV fosters that ism indirectly, by creating a climate favorable to socialistic aims.

These aims haven't changed over the centuries. Plato wrote about socialism in *The Republic*. His system called for abolition of the family, state care of children, and the sharing of mates among the "guardian" or warrior class. Once the responsible family unit disappeared, there would be no pressing need for private property, or private initiative in trade or public affairs.

Now television takes an antifamily stance. It has been known to showcase wifeswapping. And it doesn't bolster private property either.

Socialism generally, whether ancient or modern, calls for an oppressive kind of equality, which levels individual people into compact, faceless masses. Nobody is outstanding for any quality. Since TV tends to downgrade historical heroes, as well as current authority figures from prelates to policemen, it helps further this key socialistic goal. We are all common men with earthy passions and appetites over which we have little control. That is the TV message.

Dostoyevsky explained in *The Possessed* how the socialists hope to achieve their "paradise": "We shall unleash drunkenness, scandal, denunciations; we shall unleash unprecedented debauchery; we shall extinguish every genius in his infancy. Everything must be reduced to the common denominator, total equality."

Many TV shows seem bent on debauching America and leveling us all to Dostoyevsky's "common denominator." In fact, Shirley MacLaine used that very term. In her autobiography she said that she and other performers were "expected to appeal to the largest number of people, which meant figuring out the lowest common denominator."

Time (November 22, 1976) used the term too in writing about "Charlie's Angels." It said, "The ABC gang has finally found television's Holy Grail—the one true least common denominator."

Share and Share Alike

TV's anti-free-enterprise bias gives a false luster to socialist economics. If free enterprise is to be curbed or destroyed, we have to find an alternative. Socialism is standing in the wings, ready to move stage-center-front when free enterprise exits.

In economic terms socialism means the state controls business, power is concentrated in government, and businessmen become puppets, following endless regulations and making out forms in triplicate to register their every move.

We already have a mixed economy, part capitalist and part socialist, for more than a dash of socialism has been stirred into our free-enterprise system. Slowly we are moving toward pure socialism, which is more devastating than most of us realize. Let's review a little American history.

Two groups of early colonists, the Pilgrims in New England and the Cavaliers in Virginia, tried socialism. Land in each colony was held in common, and farm produce was community property from which everybody drew according to his needs—in theory.

The system failed in both cases. Surely these sincerely God-fearing folk meant to shoulder their share of responsibility, but when they saw that they could fare just as well by slacking off a bit (without perhaps conscious thought or intent), a few of them did slack off.

Their harder-working friends noticed this and (again, perhaps only half-consciously) told themselves: If so-and-so is idling, I will too. Why should I work this hard so that other people, who are as capable of work as I, can take it easy?

In Jamestown the stores ran so low that Captain Smith called a town meeting to discuss the threat of starvation. It didn't take the colonists long to decide what to do; they changed the system.

Captain Smith wrote in his records that after ridding themselves of socialism, the families produced as much in one day as they had in a full week under the old regimen.

Plymouth Plantation in New England had a similar experience, and private ownership of land and produce had to be established to ward off disaster.

Watch Your Step, America

When Sweden in the fall of 1976 repudiated its unworkable socialism and ended 44 years of rule by the Social Democratic Party, TV newscasters announced the fact but gave it little notice. True, the Swedes have not yet dismantled their welfare state; but if the newscasters had not been pro-socialism and anti–free enterprise, they would have commented at greater length on this qualified setback for socialism.

If they continue to create a climate favorable to socialism, where will America end up?

Let us hope that we will have as much sense as the Swedes and put the brakes on socialism. We could, instead, accelerate it and tomorrow find ourselves, like Britain, on the brink of bankruptcy. Within a year after the British people chose the socialistic policy of nationalizing the coal mines after World War II, England had its first coal famine, which brought the wheels of industry almost to a dead stop. It would seem that from that point on, *Great* Britain ceased to be so great. In the lifetime of a large segment of our population, it has sunk from a first-rate to a third-rate nation.

If America does not follow the same path, we will hardly have TV to thank. James Keogh, former executive editor of *Time*, conceded in his book *President Nixon and the Press* that TV reporting "too often showed an obsession with the negative [and] a left-of-center ideological conformity . . ."

The Leftward Slide

It isn't the "right-wing lunatic fringe" alone that declares that leftish ideas and socialism can, and sometimes do, lead to Communism. In 1920 Lenin boasted that in Russia the Communists were "taking the first steps in the transition from capitalism to socialism, or the lowest form of Communism."

The late Earl Browder in his book *What Is Communism?* called socialism "the next stage in the historical march of humanity toward the classless Communist society."

TV is doing nothing to halt that possibility. In fact, a series like "Ivan the Terrible" (1976 summer replacement) seemed inadvertently to encourage it.

Now hastily let me say that "Ivan the Terrible" did *not* laud Communism. In fact, it sharply gibed bureaucracy and housing in the USSR. Still, its picture of life under Communism was almost indistinguishable from life in the USA (though possibly in a leaner era, like that of the Great Depression).

Joe Adcock, *TV Time* editor, wrote that although we thought of Moscow as a miserable place, "beset with secret police," the producers of the show, Rupert Hitzig and Alan

King, "didn't see it that way." Adcock quoted Hitzig as saying, "People are alike everywhere."

Maybe people are alike, but the systems under which they live are not alike, and the Red system does cramp the lifestyle more than "Ivan" implied.

For this reason the September 1976 *Mindszenty Report* (of the Cardinal Mindszenty Foundation) was quite critical of the show. It said, "Brave men like Solzhenitsyn and Cardinal Mindszenty spent their lives trying to warn the free world about the evils of the Communist system. Producers like Alan King ridicule their sacrifices by turning Communism into idiotic situation comedy."

This show was vehemently anti-Communist, however, in comparison with other TV offerings. Ralph de Toledano, writing for Copley News Service, commented on the current spate of teleplays about the Hollywood Ten, whom the House Committee on Un-American Activities in November 1947 cited for contempt of Congress. These TV films seem to be telling us that HUAC was trying, back in the Dark Ages, to suppress legitimate political dissent. De Toledano particularly cited *The Way We Were*, starring Barbra Streisand, which portrayed the Hollywood Marxists as heroes, "defending the philosophy of Thomas Jefferson and Tom Paine." What actually prompted HUAC action, de Toledano explained, "was the fact, well-documented, that Communists were using Hollywood and the tremendous salaries it paid as a great employment agency for brothers-in-arms—and doing their utmost to exclude anti-Communists from the movie colony's plush acres." The earnings of these men, not Moscow's gold, were largely funding the Communist Party, USA and its espionage.

Though the Hollywood Ten spent a short time in prison, de Toledano noted that most of them returned to their old jobs. Apparently, many movie moguls do not believe in the evils of Communism. Nor do many TV bigshots today, including newscasters.

Seeing Is Believing

Those who live under Communism have no difficulty believing. In September 1976 four men and one woman from

Croatia, Yugoslavia, commandeered a TWA jet in New York and forced the pilot to fly to Montreal and Paris where the French gave them a choice: Go to the United States and stand trial for your crime, or we will hand you over to the Yugoslavian Communists.

They chose to go to the United States.

TV reported the hijacking of the plane, the arrival of the plane in the United States, and the fact that a bomb left in a locker had killed a policeman; but that the Croatians chose the United States over their native land was all but ignored. Certainly, that fact speaks ill of Communism, and well of our system.

Why did TV give it so little attention? Many commentators lean so far over backwards in trying to be fair to the Communists that at times they are in danger of falling for the Red line.

Some mighty baron of broadcast fell for the Red line when PBS put on a special about I. F. Stone. John P. Roche, noted in *TV Guide* (December 25, 1976) that the program called Stone " 'the conscience of the Washington press corps,' without mentioning Stone's conscience was elastic enough to justify Stalin's butchery of the 1930s."

Roche spoke too of the TV drama "The Great Cherub Knitwear Strike," which told the story of a Stalinist labor organizer in the Depression years. The moral of the story was, said Roche, that in those days "only a Stalinist had the guts to take on the slave-driving management."

Perhaps too somebody is falling for the Red line when commentators consistently brand countries like South Africa and Rhodesia as racist, while other countries where Red influence is strong, like Kenya or Uganda, which are at least equally racist, receive only a tap on the wrist.

With regard to South Africa, newscasters shed copious tears over the 300 or so people killed during the rioting in June 1976 but had few tears for the butchery of thousands of Africans by other African governments, Uganda, Nigeria, Zaire, Angola, to name some. They didn't mention the fact that the Soviet Union has been heavily supporting the Rhodesian guerrilla groups fighting out of Mozambique. Nor did they add that the Reds, after their successful Cuban blitzkrieg in the Angolan civil war, have expanded their influence in Africa.

The *Philadelphia Bulletin* (November 9, 1976) quoted black Rhodesian leader Joshua Nkome as saying, "We get our assistance, especially military assistance, from the Soviet Union. . . . We are working with them."

Did any of the networks air that fact? If they did, they certainly did not play it up.

Commentators have referred to non-Communist South Korea as a "repressive dictatorship," but when do they use such harsh language about Communist North Korea?

Nor are the commentators alone the culprits. Some of the people who are responsible for sitcoms are equally biased. In "All's Fair" the girl photographer, Charley (in the episode of February 28, 1977), went through a marriage ceremony with a South Korean to save him from being deported. Afterwards there were swipes at the government of South Korea (its book burners were said to have burned, among other things, a volume that "conservative" Richard had written). What about North Korea? It was mentioned in the episode, but there was nary a barb thrown at this Workers' Paradise.

Wrote Kevin Phillips, in *TV Guide* (January 8, 1977), "It's OK to slash at bribery of U.S. Congressmen by the [right-wing] Korean regime, but the . . . networks have shown no interest in pursuing FBI Director Clarence Kelley's blunt indication of 'extensive activity' by the Soviet KGB trying to penetrate Capitol Hill offices."

Rightist dictatorships, like the Spanish regime under Franco, are bluntly called dictatorships, while leftist dictatorships usually rate milder terminology.

Even after Franco's death, Spain has remained on the newscasters' Hate List. In comparison with other countries it fares rather badly. When Uganda's madman, Idi Amin, murdered thousands, the criticism meted out to him was gentle compared with the firestorm that descended on the Spanish government some time before when it executed five convicted political killers.

No Comparison

If TV presented the full facts, we would see that there is no comparison between Communist dictatorships and other dictatorships. Solzhenitsyn has presented what he calls the "calculations of specialists": "During the 80 years before the Revolution [in Russia] . . . about 17 persons a year were executed. The famous Spanish Inquisition at the height destroyed perhaps 10 persons a month." Solzhenitsyn then quoted figures taken from a book published in 1920 by Chekhov. That author said that in the years just preceding, 1918–19, "more than 1,000 persons a month" were executed without a trial. In addition, at the height of Stalin's terror, "in '37 and '38, more than 40,000 a month." (Some experts say these figures are low.)

And we all know what happened in Cambodia. Or do we? Although CBS did give the affair reasonably good coverage, we couldn't have learned all the facts from TV.

The Maoist Khmer Rouge ordered the mass evacuation of Phnom Penh, and the forced march from the city resulted in the death of thousands upon thousands. Even nonambulatory hospital patients had to go, and reports told that relatives pushed the wheeled hospital beds of their loved ones while they tried to hold up infusion bottles. There were also reports of massacres, purges of whole villages, and accounts of people being buried alive to save ammunition. Others who fell by the way were not always buried and the countryside became a corpse-strewn charnel house.

Time estimated that upwards of 600,000 Cambodians died; the French newspaper *Le Monde* set the figure at 800,000; and a Cambodian chief of state, Khieu, interviewed by an Italian newspaper, spoke glibly of a million or more, commenting, "It's incredible how concerned you Westerns are about war criminals."

The Khmer Rouge, like other Rouges or Reds, must believe in Stalin's dictum, "One death is a tragedy; a million deaths are a statistic."

TV cameras caught comparatively little of the misery and death. In all fairness, much of it they could not have caught; they would have been debarred. But cameras alone were not the culprits. Commentators had a part in playing down this particular news item. The people who often bandy about the word "compassion," and who claim to champion "the poor," hardly said a word about the Cambodians.

If as many dumb animals—cats, dogs, flamingos, or whatever—had been rounded up and killed, nearly every commentator on TV would still be talking about it.

Kowtowing to Mao

Even worse than inadequate coverage is distorted coverage. We had a dose of that on newscasts immediately following Mao Tse-tung's death on September 9, 1976. In an hour-long CBS broadcast not one full minute was devoted to the man's crimes, or to his belligerent aphorisms like "Political power grows out of the barrel of a gun." It took only about 20 seconds for the ambassador of Taiwan to say, "Mao was the worst despot of all history." He was given no chance to say more; the cameras moved on to somebody or something else.

The gist of the narrator's remarks was this. Perennial poverty existed in China under the feudal lords. In modern times Western nations came to exploit China. America, he said, had a "noble name" for its policy, "The Open Door," which meant, said the narrator, that "no one country could rule China—not even the Chinese."

China was humiliated and revolution was its only recourse. Chiang Kai-shek attacked the revolutionists in '27, killing untold thousands. (No mention of the fact that Chiang was trying to prevent the Communists, whom he recognized as traitors and oppressors of the people, from taking over.) Mao performed the fantastic feat of marching about 100,000 people across the vast country.

Believing that Communism would help China, Mao formed the Chinese Communist Party and developed social and economic programs aimed at ending the misery of the past. His schedule was disrupted by World War II. After the war, civil conflict broke out in China and Chiang Kai-shek tried unsuccessfully to stop Mao's Communists. The Nationalists under Chiang lost popular support and were defeated.

Here the narrator injected this gem: "Bewildered voices spoke of the loss of China, but China was never ours to lose." (Certainly, by going Communist, China was lost to the whole Western world.)

So the People's Republic of China arose.

Here came a second derogatory word about Mao, which perhaps took another 20 seconds: "Inevitably there were victims —about 2,000,000 people were killed." One sentence for the pitiful hordes who were enslaved, terrorized, imprisoned, beaten, tortured, starved, and finally done to death.

211

Nobody knows for sure how many were killed. If it were 2,000,000 it would be awful enough, but that figure is ridiculously low. All estimates, *including those of the Chinese themselves*, are enormously higher. The United States Senate Committee on the Judiciary put the total Chinese death roll in all the purges since 1949, the year Mao became chairman, at somewhere between 32,000,000 and 61,000,000.

The *Guinness Book of World Records* lists Mao as the greatest murderer of all time, and sets the figure at 26,300,000.

As the film rolled on, showing people working in droves (slave laborers every last one of them), the narrator's remark was, "The use of men instead of machinery was not a Communist idea. It was age old." (True enough, but it certainly doesn't show that Mao improved the situation.)

The narrator's conclusion? If in the Cultural Revolution there were inevitably some excesses, the educational progress and the study of Marxist philosophy that it provoked were beneficial. (Here the camera planed in on a group sitting around tables reading Mao's little red book.) Mao changed a weak country dominated by foreigners into an independent country. Remarkably, in a land where people were hungry, people are now being fed.

If we didn't know that Mao outdid Hitler and Mussolini in cruelty and despotism, if we didn't know about the rotting corpses he piled sky-high, if we didn't know about the people who have braved shark-infested waters to try to swim away from the "paradise" he created, we might, after listening to that CBS documentary, feel like petitioning our congressmen to erect a monument to Mao in our own capital, perhaps on the White House lawn.

It is interesting to note, by the way, that the CBS narrator's spiel may have been put together in advance of Mao's death. Edward Epstein, in his book *News from Nowhere*, said of news programs in general that in most cases "immediacy is illusory. A four-month analysis of the logs of the NBC "Evening News" showed that 47 percent of the news film depicted events of the day they occurred, while 36 percent of the news film was more than two days old, and 12 percent was more than a week old."

Morbid Fascination

Why did CBS put on such a program?

It seems that some TV people are fascinated by Communists and find them more absorbing than mere non-Communists. They cannot bring themselves to think of Communists as anything but glamorous guys, maybe even good guys. Alan Alda, writer and director of "M.A.S.H.," as well as actor in this series about the Korean "conflict," must have some such idea. In five seasons of running "M.A.S.H." has never once identified the North Koreans or the Red Chinese as "enemies." By contrast, the scripters of "Hogan's Heroes" leave no doubt that the Nazis are the enemy.

This same strange dichotomy shows up elsewhere. On August 22, 1976, the *Seattle Post Intelligencer* carried a story about an anti-Communist, Oskar Bruesewitz, who set himself on fire and burned to death in East Berlin. His action was a protest against religious persecution in East Germany. He carried a poster reading, "The Churches Accuse the Communists of Oppressing Young Christians."

Where was TV's usual prompt and copious coverage of a dramatic incident? Where were the powerful pictures? When the pro-Marxist Buddhist monks some years ago set themselves on fire in Vietnam, the newsmen and cameramen were Johnny-on-the-spot.

Vietnam Revisited

Speaking of Vietnam, some may recall that on November 14, 1976 ABC put on a program about that country on "Visions." From start to finish it not only was antidefense spending, anti-USA, but also seemed pro–North Vietnamese. It showed action pictures from war-ravaged Vietnam. There were men dying, or men with arms and legs shot off; there were Vietnamese children confused and crying because they were separated from parents.

While the pitiful pictures flashed on the screen, a voice kept saying, "The question is why." Then came the plaintive song: "Children lost lives in war . . . They don't know why . . . They don't know what we're fighting for . . . Shouting freedom every day, while trying to save your life you lost your sanity . . . Stop the killing."

A message followed about cutting defense spending.

Some people would say it was a fraudulent message, arguing that a strong defense would save lives, not take them. Among such people might be Dr. Edward Teller, father of the H-bomb. In Chapter 14 he is quoted as saying that an ABM defensive missile would help protect us and save lives in the event of a first strike from an enemy. Surely too, some people would argue, a strong defense might deter our enemies from making even the first strike.

To "balance" the program, one army officer was allowed a word in favor of defense spending. He was not a forceful speaker, nor a scintillating personality to begin with, but even if he had been, there were on the program approximately ten other people who offset his remarks and the gruesome pictures that spoke more loudly than everybody put together.

The pictures too spoke a fraudulent message. Oh, they were genuine enough in the sense that they were taken in Vietnam of real people who really suffered. The fraud was the implication that the United States caused all this suffering. The war was going on before we got there, and the North Vietnamese were killing the South Vietnamese and vice versa. We entered the war with the idealistic hope of saving the country from a Red takeover; we made a horrendous mistake and caused the useless death of thousands of Americans when we adopted what Senator Strom Thurmond called a "no-win" war policy.

If we had had the will to win, we would have saved the lives of many Americans and many Vietnamese, and we would have saved the South Vietnamese from Communist slavery—and if the domino theory is correct, we would have saved others yet to be enslaved.

Yes, the death toll and the tremendous suffering that the Vietnamese people endured can be laid principally and primarily at the doors of North Vietnam, the instigator of the fight, and the USSR, which aided North Vietnam even as far back as when Ho Chi Minh was fighting the French.

Now that we have withdrawn from the country, "peace" supposedly reigns, but a CIA document reveals that the Reds have killed over 250,000 people.

There have been similar TV programs. The August 2, 1976 issue of *U.S. News and World Report* said, "Military leaders maintain that cameramen played a large role in undermining home-front support for Vietnam by close-ups of isolated but bloody episodes seen—often in living color—by home viewers. . . . Broadcasts that seemed to portray Americans as mindless killers."

Patrick Buchanan, writing in *TV Guide* (November 13, 1976), said that CBS "portrayed the U.S. military and fighting forces in Vietnam in a negative light two thirds of the time."

Of all the commentators, Howard K. Smith was about the only one who supported U.S. policy in Vietnam. Indeed, some TV newsmen went so far as to try to sap the morale of our fighting men. Bruce Herschensohn, in his book *The Gods of Antenna*, said that in May 1970 a CBS correspondent interviewing troops asked them four questions:

"What are you going to do?"

"Do you realize what can happen to you?"

"Are you scared?"

"Do you say the morale is pretty low in Alpha Company?"

Herschensohn said that Senator Robert Dole of Kansas, hearing about these questions, asked, "Does freedom of the press include the right to incite mutiny?"

Of course, if America was not going to try for victory, everybody no doubt agrees that we should have gotten out—and the sooner the better. But why didn't TV in the beginning boost our will to fight a winning war? Surely, that would have made all the difference.

Even the Ads

TV can be blamed only partially for the no-win industry-sponsored commercials that it ran. However, one can imagine the anti-TV furor that would have erupted if that type of ad had been run during World War II.

Take the Bacchus commercial. Marvin Kitman speaks of it in his book. A bottle identical in shape with, but much larger than, the one that holds the Bacchus after-shave lotion was constructed and placed on a flatbed wagon, outside a walled city, supposedly (but not actually) the city of Troy. Townspeople dragged the giant flagon through the gates. Entranced with its fragrance, men and women alike fell into one another's arms. Then a Greek soldier who had been hiding in the bottle climbed out, his sword between his teeth. Through the power of Bacchus he was the victor.

A narrator explained, "The after-shave lotion that conquered the world. Created by the Greeks to make their enemies irresistible to women. Because when a man is irresistible, he has better things to do with his time than fight."

Kitman said of this ad, which appeared while our forces were in Vietnam, "It was perhaps the most powerful antiwar statement to come out of Madison Avenue."

TV had no qualms about running it.

If we had won in Vietnam, we might be able to sleep more soundly in our beds. Ernest Schier of the *Philadelphia Bulletin* wrote on October 31, 1976 about an incident that had occurred the week before. Between the late-late show and the signoff of the "Star-Spangled Banner" came a paid commercial. Though the presidential campaign was in full swing, the commercial had nothing to do with either Gerald Ford or Jimmy Carter. It was a commercial in behalf of the Communist Party, USA.

Chapter 18

Interviews and Guest Appearances

Pecking Order

An antiestablishment activist is better than a square, a liberal better than a conservative, a striking labor boss better than a businessman, a sensationalist better than a plain, sensible everyday guy, a Gloria Steinem feminist better than a Phyllis Schlafly traditionalist.

Better for what?

For interviews and guest appearances.

After all, TV people would naturally want the guests on their shows to reflect the ideas that they themselves believe in. We have discussed these ideas in previous chapters. TV people wouldn't want to champion one point of view themselves, only to have a guest come on the show and challenge their punditry.

Bestselling author Allen Drury said in *Book Digest* (June 1976) that liberals have "been in the 'in' position in the media for about 10 years. This group goes around telling each other

217

how good they are, and how they have the answer to everything. They feed on each other, promote each other, and help each other."

We could hardly expect anything then, but the lionizing of liberals. Sometimes, though, TV emcees, either to prove their broadmindedness or to give the show a derring-do appeal, go further and feature leftists and Marxists.

Left of Liberal

A decade ago the networks refused to provide a soapbox for such people. Then came the Smothers Brothers, who invited to their comedy hour longtime Communist fronter Pete Seeger.

Not to be outdone, other TV entertainers also requested a guest appearance from the redoubtable Mr. Seeger.

Later he appeared on an ABC program in cooperation with the National Council of Churches and was introduced as a "folksinger and conservationist." Certainly, he is a folksinger. Maybe he is a conservationist too, who knows? Anyway, Marxists are trained to champion legitimate causes in order to curry public favor. But the night he appeared, he talked, not about conservation, but about the then popular subject of Vietnam from a radical point of view.

A parallel case is that of Malvina Reynolds. Former undercover agent Karl Prussion said of Ms. Reynolds, "She has been part of the Communist conspiracy all her life . . . and attended the National Training School of the Communist Party."

When CBS's Roger Mudd had her on his program, he identified her simply as another "conservationist," a DDT fighter.

Convicted atom-bomb spy Morton Sobell was invited to tell "his side" of the Rosenberg spy case on the "Mike Douglas Show." Although Sobell admitted that he had belonged to the Young Communist League, and other leftist groups, he spoke mainly about being a victim of rabid and unreasonable anti-Communist feeling.

Other Odd Balls

Communists and out-and-out Communist sympathizers are of course comparatively rare on TV. Commonplace, however, are the weirdoes who challenge traditional values, manners, or morals.

Phil Donahue (January 4, 1977) interviewed antiestablishment radical feminist Florynce Kennedy, who had bitter words for the church, which doesn't allow women positions of power; for business, which "rips off" the people; for government, etc. At one point, Donahue referred to a song she had sung on a former appearance.

Although she didn't sing it again, she repeated the words that she sang before:

> My country 'tis of thee,
> Sour land of bigotry

When Donahue mentioned the book that she had written, *The Case against Marriage,* Ms. Kennedy cracked: "Marriage is like locking yourself in the bathroom because you have to go three times a day."

Her shallow hedonistic philosophy was further revealed when she talked of ending her life in two years. She said, "I ain't goin' to stay till I ain't having fun."

Donahue has had many other far-outs on his show—too many to list here. One obnoxious guest was feminist Jessie Harline, who discussed: Should wives be paid for working in the home? (Obviously, Dr. Harline meant paid in cash, for most wives would say they are already pain in intangibles.)

"The Today Show" (September 1, 1976) hosted a Jesuit who questioned the Pope's pronouncement that "homosexual acts are intrinsically disordered and can in no case be approved." (Ironically, Jesuits take a special vow to serve and uphold the Papacy.)

David Susskind has also showcased countless far-outs. Among them have been ex-cons and prostitutes, drug addicts discussing fellow addicts in the medical profession, and a former pro football player, a homo, discussing homosexuality among players.

"Some Are More Equal Than Others"

Most talk-show hosts do not even invite "squares" for balance. In her April 1976 *Report* Phyllis Schlafly wrote of the strange balance of TV interviews. Apparently it isn't one for one, but one for ten. She said that after it has given time to ten Women's Libbers, a station will invite her to appear and discuss why she thinks ERA will deprive women of rights and privileges rather than give them additional rights.

It seems to viewers that when people like Mrs. Schlafly do get on TV, they are not always accorded fair treatment. On August 9, 1976, when Joel Spivak interviewed Mrs. Schlafly, he said before she had a chance to say more than a word or two that he was pro-ERA and that he completely disagreed with her.

However, Mrs. Schlafly probably thought herself lucky to be interviewed. As she said in the *Phyllis Schlafly Report,* she is usually expected to debate with others on a program; seldom is she given "the soft-and-easy interviewing given to the libs."

About the only time that the welcome mat is put out for her is on debate-type or panel-discussion-type shows. A few squares are then needed to have an argument and to add liveliness to the program.

In a debate there are ways of stacking the deck. Patrick Buchanan, writing in *TV Guide* (February 26, 1977) about the program "ERA: The War between the Women," commented on "the disproportionate time [within the show] allotted the contending sides." The organization Accuracy in Media clocked the first half-hour that it ran and found that ERA spokespersons had almost 17 minutes to hold forth, Stop ERAers 3.5 minutes. Buchanan said that if that count is correct, "ABC has a moral, if not a legal, obligation to provide the Stop ERA movement with 15 minutes of prime time." The day that happens salt will be sugar and sugar will be pepper.

Following a pro-con debate over ERA, TV people, it seems, have invited a string of pro-ERAers as solo guests to counteract any possible favorable impression the cons may have made in debate.

If anybody then objects and asks where the latter have gone, the answer is, according to Mrs. Schlafly, "We had Phyllis Schlafly on last year—what do you people want?"

What about the Fairness Doctrine?

Chapter 6, on Women's Lib, explained that the station manager may decide what is "reasonable time" for rebuttal. It doesn't have to be equal time, and if it had to be the TV people would, no doubt, agree with the statement in George Orwell's famed book *Animal Farm*, "Some are more equal than others."

A Full and Fair Hearing

If a program is really balanced, and three of one persuasion and three of the other participate in a discussion, some emcees tend to be about as hospitable to the conservatives as they would be to Typhoid Mary.

On one occasion David Susskind hosted Jews who had left the Soviet Union. When one of the men said that America should not kowtow to Russia and should be leery of detente, Susskind changed the subject. When the man persisted and said, "Let them [the Reds] be afraid of you [the USA]," Susskind looked down at the man from the lofty heights of self-righteousness and tried to shame him by saying, "You're saying we should rattle our sword!"

Unabashed the man answered, "Yes, why not? I don't want a hot war, but you need not be afraid of the USSR."

Somehow, Susskind shifted the conversation to another track and the pros and cons of detente, or the possibility of an alternative policy, was never again mentioned.

Even if Susskind were right about detente, the fact remains that since most TV people are liberal in their views, only the liberal views of others are likely to get a full and fair hearing. If there is a non-war-provoking alternative to submission or detente, or both, such an alternative is rarely, if ever, explored on TV debates or talk shows.

Intimidating Interviews

People who try to discuss this or any other subject from a conservative standpoint are often not only silenced, but ridiculed, browbeaten, or upbraided.

Ridiculed? Tom Pettit covered the floor of the 1976 Republican National Convention for NBC. At the time Ronald Reagan was within an eyelash of getting his party's nomination and almost up to the last moment there was suspense. Certainly, nobody was a stubborn idiot for believing that Reagan had a chance.

Yet *Newsweek* (August 30, 1976) reported that Pettit "seemed to be upbraiding Mississippi delegate Gail Healy as he interviewed her about her vote for Reagan. 'I felt it was my best choice,' she explained. 'Your best choice for what, I wonder?' Pettit pressed. 'Do you still harbor some conviction that Reagan could win?' "

Who's Crazy?

Even when a conservative states a long-proven universal truth that one would think is noncontroversial, TV people hesitate to accept it. If the statement is made on a talk show, the TV people are likely to call in, the next week, some radical professor or far-out "expert" to dispute the truth and to dredge up "arguments" against it.

Indeed, Marvin Kitman quipped, "If Jesus Christ came back to life on public television, they would put Pontius Pilate and an MIT professor on to give the show balance."

The trouble is that all of this has an effect. We are human and the repetition of such tactics gets to us. It often dulls our common sense and after a while we begin to question our own convictions and the age-old convictions of society. As one viewer put it, "If the supposed experts think so differently from me, are they crazy or am I?"

And often the viewer subconsciously continues that reasoning: Their prestige and their salaries top mine, so *I* must be the crazy one.

These "experts," chosen by TV men, often preach that all truth is relative; that yesterday's morals are as outmoded as yesterday's potbellied stoves and gas-burning lampposts; that collectivism is unselfish and progressive; that to be liberal is to be enlightened and loving; and that prosperity has nothing to do with industry and self-reliance but depends on the bounty of Big Brother, who mysteriously doles out dollars that he didn't first get from our pockets.

In short, the experts chosen to appear on TV mirror the message that the TV people themselves believe in, and want to propagandize.

If by some miracle a viewer should remain uninfluenced, and should disagree with what he sees and hears on TV, he often ends up being called, by his brainwashed fellow viewers, bigoted, reactionary, illiberal, and insensitive. He lacks "compassion."

Body Language

The TV people themselves, however, rarely use such words. Their approach is usually more subtle. They convey their feelings with no more than a quizzical smile, the faintest suggestion of a sneer, the raising of an eyebrow, or at most a word or two.

To be fair, we should concede the possibility that some of this message-conveying is unintentional. TV is an intimate medium; a close-up camera catches the slightest change of expression and automatically a person's facial muscles register his inner feelings.

A tone of voice too is sometimes unconsciously revealing, so it is difficult to say when a television personality actually intended beforehand to put down a conservative. But whether deliberate or reflexive, expressions of face or voice show where most TV people stand.

Once Joel Spivak was interviewing a Philadelphian about the campaign to recall Mayor Rizzo. The interviewee made a pro-Rizzo remark and Spivak said, "Is that so?" The tone conveyed that Spivak was sure it was not so.

Oases in the Desert

On the whole, though, Spivak seems to be fair, and, it must be said at least in passing, there are indeed a few other TV interviewers who have been fair to conservatives. Fair treatment was given Milton Friedman, Nobel Prize winner and author of *Capitalism and Freedom,* when he appeared on "60 Minutes." He spoke freely, saying in effect that the welfare state in England had brought that once-proud country to the brink of economic ruin. He declared that New York City is America's Britain, but fortunately New York, unlike a sovereign state, cannot print money and so add to its woes with runaway inflation.

Bill Buckley usually has liberals and leftists on his show, "Firing Line," but he doesn't really conduct an interview. His ploy is a two-way conversation, which gives him the opportunity to present conservative alternatives to the ideas of his guests.

Unfortunately, that kind of oasis in the desert of talk shows doesn't come as often as we would like.

Impertinent and Insensitive

Gail Magruder (Mrs. Jeb Stuart Magruder), when interviewed by Spivak, spoke about the indelicacy, the impertinence, and the insensitivity of TV reporters. She was referring not to Spivak, but to those who interviewed her and her family after Watergate. She said that they even tried to waylay her 12-year-old child and pump her for information.

A TV reporter interviewed Senator and Mrs. Howard Baker just before the Republican National Convention of 1976, Tennesseeans commented later that the interview lost Gerald Ford the presidency. One explained, "At that time Ford was considering Baker as his running mate. Now Baker is mighty popular around here and I'd bet plenty he would have carried this, his home state, for Ford. That would have put Ford over the top. But Ford couldn't choose Baker after that TV reporter got through with Mrs. Baker. She admitted a drinking problem in her comparatively distant past, and said that she had told Mr. Ford about it. The reporter kept probing for details about her drinking until I and, I guess, lots of other people too were embarrassed for her."

A few years ago when Barbara Walters interviewed Mamie Eisenhower on "The Today Show," some of us cringed at Walters' impertinence. She asked Mrs. Eisenhower about her "drinking problem."

Walters' treatment of the Carters was hardly less snoopy. Interviewing the president-elect and his wife in their Plains, Georgia home on December 21, 1976, Ms. Walters asked Mrs. Carter if Jimmy was "romantic." Did they plan to sleep in the same room in the White House? In a double bed?

False Impressions

Bad as this is, there is worse.

Interviewers and moderators of debates have been known to maneuver so that the viewer is deliberately left with a false impression. This is a grave charge, but there is evidence to support it.

In her *Report* of November 1973 Phyllis Schlafly wrote that on October 18, 1973 she had appeared on "The Today Show" to debate ERA with Mrs. Lucy Wilson Benson.

Mrs. Schlafly presented the stronger arguments and the more convincing evidence, and so apparently won the debate. Barbara Walters must have been piqued at this, so about two weeks later (October 30, 1973) she read on the show a letter that she said was from the attorney general of Pennsylvania, purportedly negating Mrs. Schlafly's arguments.

According to Mrs. Schlafly's *Report,* the letter (which was written not by the attorney general but by a young woman who worked in his office) was a tissue of half-truths. In the *Report* Mrs. Schlafly went into great detail refuting them.

Moreover, Mrs. Schlafly accused Barbara Walters of deleting one crucial line from the letter in order to give the impression that the letter refuted what she had said about the Weigand case, when in fact it did not.

Phyllis is not the only person who has dared to accuse TV programs of deception.

Maybe television personnel are self-deceived to such a degree that they compulsively bend facts to make them square with what they perceive as truth.

Certainly, most TV people do not see Communism as an evil, and if an interviewee mentions it, that irks them. Indeed some of the TV crowd think the evil is a kind of virtue and believe that some Communist leaders are heroes of a sort.

In October 1974 CBS put on an hour-long documentary called "Castro, Cuba, and the USA." It included an interview with Castro by Dan Rather. In his commentary Rather implied that Cuba no longer supported revolutionary action in other Latin American countries, and said that today Castro talks "more of conciliation and trade."

Accuracy in Media (AIM) challenged the program. Rather excerpted trivial bits from a taped interview with Castro and two other Americans. He neglected to excerpt a vital portion in which the Americans had asked Castro about his support of revolution elsewhere and the latter had replied, "Do we sympathize with revolutionaries? Yes, we do. Have we aided revolutionaries as much as we have been able to? Yes, we have . . . when they fight, we back them." Instead, Rather opined that Castro was more interested in "conciliation and trade."

Human Events quoted AIM's conclusion: "That comes close to being deliberate falsification with intent to mislead."

Chapter 19

Behind the Screen

"Considering the number of hours that television has to fill, I'm surprised there is enough mediocrity to go around."

Eric Sevareid may not have been entirely accurate when he said that. After all, there cannot be enough mediocrity to go around; otherwise, we would not have, as indeed we do have, some excellent shows, and some that are atrocious. The atrocious get the spotlight here.

When TV is atrocious, the problem is not slim budgets or unskilled performers; rather, it is a dearth of behind-screen people with reasonably high standards of morals and taste.

In the hidden hierarchy the top man is the packager or the entrepreneur of complete shows for sale to the networks or the affiliates. Under him come the executive producer and the producer or producers who hire the next-level people, the scripters and the director. (The director hires the cast.)

Many of this group are brilliant men and women, but alas, their brilliance has nothing to do with their ethics, nor does it prevent their concentrating on just one aim: attaining high ratings by any available means.

Doctoring the Drama

Let's discuss writers first. Don Segall, producer of CBS's (now axed) baseball comedy "Ball Four," declared that a TV series "thrives or falters on the quality of writing."

These writers, or scripters, as they are usually called, are a breed apart. Other writers resemble the cat who walked by himself; generally they themselves dream up what they want to write about and then spin their yarns in quiet with nobody looking over their shoulders. Not so the TV scripter. Often the producer brings the scripter the idea and says, "Get busy on it. See what you can come up with."

Then the scripter writes his piece, which may be pulled to bits when the producer and, later, the director get to it. These kibitzers make changes freely, or ask the writer to make changes under their guidance, so that the finished product is likely to be a potpourri of the ideas of producer, scripter, and director.

Commercials too are a horrible handicap for the scripter. Before each advertisement the scripter must build enough suspense to hold the viewer in his seat until the story resumes. As producer-writer Richard Alan Simmons put it, the action has to "peak every 15 minutes."

Moreover, the non-TV writer has better control of his characters; they do what he wants them to. The characters of a scripter may not be so obliging. Norman Alden, who played the part of Leroy Fedder in MH2's early episodes, decided to leave the show to accept a movie role so the MH2 scripters had to find a way to write him out of the serial. Their device was unique: Fedder drowned in chicken soup. Suffering from flu, he used the whiskey cure and imbibed so heavily that he passed out and his head fell forward into a bowl of soup.

Non-TV writers go to their typewriters in the first place with a different motivation. Aside from seeking (sometimes even *instead* of seeking) monetary rewards, they may be filled with a wonder and a joy that they want to share, or they may have a compulsion to express their vision of truth, or they may just enjoy fashioning readable sentences as a florist enjoys arranging a bouquet. Again, not so scripters. If they contract to write for TV at all, the Nielsen ratings and the attitudes of their producer and director are the only considerations they can afford to think about.

228

If their inner convictions differ from those of the producer, they usually put them aside and write what he wants; if they don't do that, he will probably change their script anyhow.

To make it big in the Nielsen's means they must write whatever will catch at least the fleeting attention of people as widely divergent as the erudite Ph.D. and the illiterate grade-school dropout. As CBS president Frank Stanton put it, they must "appeal to most of the people most of the time." The story, then, must be overt, it must be melodramatic, it must have conflict.

Script-Ease

Admittedly, even the simplest boy-meets-girl magazine story has to have conflict or obstacles to overcome before the couple end in each other's arms. But the best stories depend on character; or on the kind of person who is in the story, what code he adheres to, what he wants from life, and what he believes in his soul of souls.

For scripters to develop character in the disjointed 26-minute segments allotted (four minutes of the 30 go to commercials) would indeed be a feat worthy of Shakespeare. For script-ease they resort to violence, lust, perverted sex, crime, and cruelty. Making the final result attention-catching is paramount.

Obviously, the thing must escalate. To catch attention today, the episode has to be more shocking, more sexy, more gory, or more something-or-other than it was yesterday. The scripters fear a smooth period in the lives of any of their *dramatis personae*. For instance, if they find that they have inadvertently created a smooth marriage, they have to doctor it with discord. Rarely, even in a serial that goes on from year to year, do the scripters show a basically happy marriage where the couple struggle with problems and somehow manage in the process to make their love grow to new heights.

In an earlier chapter the point was made that even "good" shows sometimes toss in an atrocious bit to roil the waters, and "Rhoda," with its separation of Joe and Rhoda, was mentioned. It is also a case in point here.

Reference Library

Though there is an unwritten law in TV that scripters and producers do not tinker with any story line as long as a show is popular, while "Rhoda" was sitting triumphantly among the first 20 of the Nielsen's, the scripters twisted the story line around to arrange the breakup of Rhoda's basically happy marriage.

TV Guide (December 11, 1976) quoted producer Charlotte Brown, who explained, "We all suddenly realized we were getting bored with our show. Everything was so *nice* for our Rhoda in her happily married life."

And producer Dave Davis talked about inventing "something to spice up Rhoda's placid existence."

Executive producer Jim Brooks added, "I guess we had the conceit that we could do a show about marriage that was different. We couldn't."

Where was their imagination? Scripters of the 1950s and 60s managed to write some popular shows with happily married people.

Silent Editorial

But scripters and producers do worse things than break up marriages. Kay Gardella of the New York News Service wrote that young students in ABC's film "Boy in the Plastic Bubble" smoked pot freely and "not once did the script make a moral issue of it. It was like a silent editorial condoning such practice. How easy . . . it is for a writer to subliminally impose his views on an unsuspecting public."

As a matter of policy, some scripters make violence graphic. The policeman-novelist Joseph Wambaugh, who has written some original treatments and has acted as script supervisor for series like "Police Story" and "Charlie's Angels," said, "If you show violence, you must show it as it really is. People must feel it, be in awe of it, frightened by it. It is not a throwaway joke."

Wambaugh, who appeared on the NBC special "Violence in America" (January 5, 1977), complained about the unreality of some cop shows.

Everybody agrees that violence is not a throwaway joke, but why show so much of it unnecessarily?

Who's in Charge Here?

Some scripters (and producers and directors too) say, "Don't blame me. I'm just a hireling. The higher-ups crack the whip."

Under a pen name a successful TV scripter wrote a spoof for *TV Guide* (January 15, 1977), not necessarily about Joseph Wambaugh, but about any man who might write for "Charlie's Angels." A mythical producer, "Harry," tells the writer to jeopardize the life of each of the three Angels four times in each episode, "a total of 12 jeopardies per show." Then Harry instructs the writer not to let the girls ride in cars where the camera can catch only heads and shoulders. "Show them off as girls," he suggests. Make them scantily clad "go-go girls, callgirls, swimsuit models, ballerinas."

When at last the writer got his "jeopardy" count right, his

shapely girls sufficiently displayed, and his producer satisfied, word came "from the top" that "the concept had been altered."

Exaggerated?

Of course, but there is probably some truth in it: word from network chiefs can upset the best-laid plans of scripters and directors.

Probably exaggerated too is the testimony that Larry Gelbart (former producer of "M.A.S.H.") and David W. Rintels (TV writer and president of the Writers Guild of America West) gave before a congressional committee.

Gelbart said (*Congressional Record,* October 1, 1976) that the problem of inferior-quality television "lies principally with the networks who control every aspect of programming. . . ."

He added that no writer, producer, director, or story editor is hired without the approbation of the network executives, nor do any of them keep their jobs without that approbation. He put it succinctly, "Only the pencil is in our hands. The networks tell us rigidly and explicitly what we can and cannot write, what they will buy and schedule and show, and what they will not."

Rintels testified that most writers "despise gratuitous violence." He added, "Violence and cop shows work as a Gresham's law, driving out quieter and more human drama. . . . Given free choice, we would . . . rather write about the human and intellectual concerns."

And *TV Guide* (June 4, 1977) quoted Stan Kallis and Bill O'Brien (former producers of "Hawaii Five-O") as saying, "We were told to juice it up," so they complied. On the next round of the show, said O'Brien, "You never saw more blood."

Another Point of View

Despite what these gentlemen say, scripters, producers, directors, and other behind-screen persons often have a rather free rein, and they do usually make the detailed and specific choices. For the most part, the executives dictate only broad policy.

Jason Bonderoff, in his book *Daytime TV, 1977*, said that Irna Phillips, head scripter for the soap opera "As the World Turns," was "indomitable," and that "she ruled the roost . . . with an iron telephone, cracking out orders and directives over her long-distance hotline. . . . This frail old lady . . . could make sponsors wince, networks cringe, and actors cry (for real)."

Producer Freddie Bartholomew told one actress, Judith Mc-Gilligan, not to "get too comfortable here" because "Irna is losing interest in your character." In other words, a particular scripter might decide on his own to put a character on the chopping block.

The public too makes its voice heard. When Liz, the character that Ms. McGilligan played, became ill as a prelude to Irna's plan to kill her off, the switchboard lit up like a Christmas tree with calls from viewers. They didn't want Liz to die.

Though she wouldn't bow to TV people, Irna bowed to public opinion. Instead of having Liz die immediately, she had her undergo emergency surgery. At the time she was uncertain whether to make the surgery successful or not.

Actually, she let Liz recover, and it was some time later when Irna decided again to have Liz die—this time as the result of a fire. But still it was not to be.

Irna found out that "Search for Tomorrow" was having a similar fire episode, so once more she changed the script. Even rival shows can sometimes dictate story lines. A cat has nine lives and Irna had to give Liz almost that many before she finally managed her death.

As long as Irna Phillips wrote "As the World Turns," there was measureless melodrama, but there was also a grim morality. In her scripts the sluts and the sinners (whom she "reckoned up by dozens") proved that "the wages of sin is death."

Another writer who seems to run her own show is Agnes Nixon. This soap-queen scripter for such shows as "All My Children" and "One Life to Live" said recently, "I've had a show on every day for 52 weeks a year for 20 years." Though she follows the usual soap-opera formula, mixing, in generous proportions, divorce, infidelity, abortion, miscarriage, sudden death, illegitimate children, amnesia, and "social questions" that make the newspaper headlines, Ms. Nixon has averred that she always tries to combine timely problems with traditional values. Of late she has added teenage prostitution, male infertility, and child abuse. (Incidentally, she is one of those scripters who are afraid to let a happy marriage last. Ruth in "All My Children" was the happy wife of Dr. Joe Martin until Nixon involved her in a sizzling romance with a younger man.)

Producer Power

But if some writers seem to have a free rein, certainly so do some producers, packagers, and directors.

In *News from Nowhere* author Edward Jay Epstein relates this tale. During a strike of New York City teachers an NBC correspondent covered the story for a newscast, saying that the issue was the rejection of integration by black educators, because they wanted to control their own neighborhood schools.

The producer declared that this was "not the way to play the story." He insisted the strike be defined as a move to get "more responsive schools."

Epstein comments, "Although it is a moot point whose interpretation of the strike was correct, the correspondent . . . had to yield to the producer."

In February 1977 a producer threatened that Anita Bryant would lose her job because of her fight against a pro-homosexual ordinance in Florida. Shortly afterward Bryant lost a $250,000 contract with Singer Sewing Machine Co. to host a nationwide television show. If the producer was the main cause of the cancellation, he has power plus.

Potentate of Prime Time

But it is impossible to talk about powerful producers without mentioning the biggest name of all. Norman Lear—"King Lear," as he is known in the industry—is one producer and packager who does not knuckle under to network bigwigs.

Admittedly, this may not always have been the case. Back in 1969 he was less potent. That was when ABC advanced him money to develop two shows, "All in the Family" and MH2, but later turned thumbs down on both. He soon found a home for "All in the Family," but it took him seven years to do the same for MH2. He brought in new writers, Ann Marcus and Gail Parent, to rework MH2.

As an aside, Gail Parent (who wrote for the "Carol Burnett Show" during its first five years on the air), when interviewed by Phil Donahue (January 19, 1977), said that she worked on the concept of MH2 rather than writing the script. Hearing her talk on the Donahue show, however, convinced viewers that her personality strongly marked the show. She even looks and talks a little like Louise Lasser, who played the Mary Hartman role.

When Ann and Gail had done their job, Lear presented the result to Lin Bolen, chief of NBC's daytime programming. Lin didn't like what she saw. She thought it insulted women who watch soaps and said, "I couldn't commit to a show that depicted my women as fools."

Eventually, all three networks turned down the show, and Lear had to peddle it to affiliates.

The rest of the Lear story is well known, but no chapter about TV personnel can omit it. Lear has had more shows on prime-time television than any other independent producer. Besides MH2 they include, or have included, "All in the Family," "The Jeffersons," "Sanford and Son," "The Dumplings," "Good Times," "Maude," "All's Fair," "The Nancy Walker Show," "Hot L Baltimore," "All That Glitters," and "Soap."

In a routine week about 150 million man-hours are spent watching Lear shows, which is more time per week than it takes for all government employees throughout our land to deliver mail, negotiate with foreign countries, run our federal reserve system, or send out welfare checks. An NABB brochure (summer 1976) stated flatly that Lear "talks" by television "to more people each week than any other person in history."

What kinds of shows does the Baron of Broadcast produce?

Many kinds. "Hot L Baltimore" was probably one of the most lewd and vulgar ever on television. It was about prostitutes and sexual weirdoes living in a fleabag hotel.

The first episode envisioned marriage for one of the girls to a man who she thought was a Hollywood producer. Actually, he was a cigarette-lighter salesman who had, in the past, promised girls phony movie contracts.

An older and more experienced prostitute filled in the bottom line with, "All any girl ever got from him was two Zippos —and a very bad rash."

In case the viewer didn't understand, it was made clear that "rash" was a venereal disease.

Another installment showed the death of a "customer" of one of the girls. The girl sighed and said, "I guess I was too good." She felt comforted that he died smiling.

This is the kind of show that should have been treated like gangrene—with surgery—and it was. It is no longer on the air.

"After you had seen one of the episodes," said a viewer, "all you wanted to do was take a three months vacation to Mars—to get away from it all."

Not every Lear show is as degrading as "Hot L Baltimore" (though MH2 with its May Olinsky Sex Survey and its Wanda-Lila-Merle *ménage à trois* could not have been far behind), and probably Lear did not set out to debauch America. Very likely he merely wanted to make his millions quickly and was willing to try anything that looked lucrative, be it good or bad.

On a PBS interview (February 3, 1977) with Jean Wolf he said, when she asked him if any subject was taboo on his shows, that some shows implied that "nothing is more important than a lost skate key or a bent fender." He wanted to portray problems that people really grapple with. He added, "What can be shocking if it comes out of everybody's experience? You can find it in the headlines."

In short, he was saying that he would not necessarily stop at anything, and that his characters were patterned, not after average people, but after those who made headlines with the scandalous and the bizarre.

Then he said that people "love to feel," even if the feeling is indignation, and "98 percent enjoy expressing a point of view," even if it is condemnation of his series.

Since he himself started his TV career as a scripter, he is still interested in the actual writing of his shows and has a hand in it. To be fair, it must be said that he does not always and inevitably act the part of lurid Lear. For instance, earlier episodes of "All in the Family" (an adaptation of a British sitcom) probably had fewer offensive tidbits than some of the current episodes. By introducing the series (says former CBS-TV president Robert Wood) Lear "changed the face of television." He widened the range of controversial subjects allowed on TV. Though "All in the Family" is far less popular today than formerly (and it may be axed by the time this book goes to press), back in 1971, its heyday, about a third of all Americans watched it regularly and it made the *Guinness Book of World Records* for commanding the highest TV advertising rates up until that time.

From "All in the Family" came several spinoffs. Jean Wolf, asking about these, received the answer that they were not planned; rather, they evolved from, as Lear put it, "other people's needs." For example, he said it was to keep director Bob Weiskopf happy and to cut him in on the pie of success that he developed "All's Fair." Lear gave the directors a percentage of the take.

Despite the variety of Lear shows, they have one point in common: rapid-fire dialogue that is funny, even if much is funny at the expense of the sacred—to him nothing *is* sacred. Heartbreak and hilarity too go hand in hand, as we saw on MH2. One critic called Lear the "20th-century Voltaire TV packager."

If he has any fixed philosophy it is ultraliberal. He is president of the Civil Liberties Union of Southern California, and one viewer asked, "Where do his ACLU ideas stop and his comedy begin?" (Incidentally, his wife is national chairperson for a feminist legislation-seeking group called Women's Lobby.)

Former Congressman John Rarick of Louisiana said a few years ago (in the *Congressional Record*) that the ACLU has been "in the forefront of every attack on freedom and decency since its inception." It is the organization that wants the words "In God we trust" removed from coins and bills; the organization that defended the right of Communists to speak on college campuses; the organization that has fought for liberalization of abortion laws; and the first American organization to make the charge "police brutality." According to the Catholic League for Religious and Civil Rights, the ACLU shows a complete disregard for religious liberty. Roger Baldwin, founder of the ACLU, once said, "I seek the social ownership of property, the abolition of the propertied class. . . . Communism is the goal."

Despite this ACLU credo, which Lear, as head of the Southern California branch, apparently supports, his sitcom "All's Fair" contained a few paltry pseudo-conservative ideas. When the script for the pilot (that is, the introductory or test episode)

237

appeared early in 1976, the *Wall Street Journal* wrote that it was easy for its four godfathers (executive producer and packager Lear, plus the three producers, Rod Parker, Bob Schiller, and Bob Weiskopf) to evolve the character of liberal girl photographer Charley, because all of them "share a distinctly antiestablishment, extremely liberal political view." The catch was evolving Richard's character. The same paper said that Lear and his group were "like students examining an anthropological oddity."

The writer of the *Wall Street Journal* article, Benjamin Stein, thought it amusing that Lear mentioned as a rare "sympathetic conservative" one of his (Lear's) favorite fictional characters, Andrew Undershaft of George Bernard Shaw's play, *Major Barbara*. Undershaft's remark that poverty is the worst sin Lear regarded as, believe it or not, a virtual manifesto of conservatism. Undershaft was a munitions maker who gladly sold to either side as long as he was paid. What each was fighting for did not concern him.

Some of us might find that attitude nearer to the liberal's (and to Lear's), for a liberal prides himself on being so tolerant that he can always see both sides of an issue. Stein implied as much; he said of Lear, "He is personally liberal . . . but he will sell laughs to any side."

Lear wants no restrictions. He and his Tandem Productions, along with the Writers Guild of America, pleaded that the Family Hour infringed on the First Amendment. The Family Hour was not particularly effective, so perhaps its abolition is unimportant, but Lear's attitude is interesting. Though he and others spoke grandiosely about freedom of speech, they looked suspiciously like men who were worried about their wallets, or as TV critic Rex Polier put it, they wanted no cutbacks on "Beverly Hills pads, Mercedes Benzes, and the Good Life."

The August 25, 1975, issue of *Time* quoted Lear as saying, "It's like a knee in the groin of social criticism." (His escape trivia and his sick sex are social criticism?)

When the court decision came abolishing the Family Hour, *Variety* (November 10, 1976) quoted Lear as calling it "a victory for all Americans."

"All Americans"? Well, it was a victory for Lear, and it seemed to boost his prestige. Of all the people behind the screen, few are more prestigious. No wonder it is hard to imagine TV executives ordering him around.

Prince of Violence

Another seemingly independent-minded producer is Quinn Martin. If Lear is king of sitcoms, maybe Martin is at least a prince of the action shows.

Some producers have declared that executives want more violence added to shows to hike the ratings. However, Martin was quoted in *TV Guide* as saying, "I've never been asked to insert violence in a show."

Is that because, being so eminent in his field, he is allowed his head? Or because he provides enough violence without prodding? It is probably a combination of both. With the exception of his cop show "Barnaby Jones," most of his productions lack neither mayhem nor gore.

Martin made his reputation back in 1959 with "The Untouchables," the first of the the hype-violent shows. In an interview he said that "it probably played the most important part in my career."

Afterwards, he formed his own company and produced "The Fugitive," which won an Emmy for best dramatic show.

Martin said he looks for "scripts that deal with human emotions, that don't write down to people," and added, "I surround myself with good people—that's another secret."

During the 1976–77 season Martin's hit show was "The Streets of San Francisco." In filming the series, Martin operated from a waterfront building and managed to get in some fine shots of the bay and the city. As one viewer said, "For a cost-free trip to the Golden Gate, watch 'Streets.' "

Within the same season Martin produced "Tales of the Unexpected" and "The City." Then he produced "The Unwanted," which one critic dubbed "The Unbelievables" because the episodes were television at its most unreal and most preposterous.

Still, Martin, like Lear, is a talented man.

Crescendo of Crime

Others have topped him in crime, though not in talent: Sam Peckinpah, David Gerber, and Aaron Spelling.

Peckinpah could have tutored Jack the Ripper. His production "Getaway" is one for Ripley's "Believe It or Not." It featured ten shootings (all but one fatal), five attempted shootings (guns fired but nobody hit), seven threatened shootings (guns pointed at people but not fired), one kidnapping, five assaults (people knocked down, etc.), one elevator murder (protagonist cuts elevator cables while somebody is inside), one hanging, one bank robbery, and plenty of property destruction. To cap it off, there was brutality toward a woman by her husband.

The gory trail began after the wife had seduced a politician on the parole board in order to persuade him to parole her then imprisoned husband. It ended when she and her husband escaped across the Mexican border, rich and free.

Peckinpah also produced "Wild Bunch," which one critic called "a ballet of blood." It had about twice as many killings as "Getaway." Only a trained mathematician could or would have kept count.

David Gerber has produced some dillies too, including episodes of "Police Story," "Quest," "Police Woman," "Medical Center," "Gibbsville," and "Joe Forrester."

Gerber testified before Congress on September 30, 1976, saying, "I think the idea of violence on television upsetting society today is ludicrous in terms of total blame, or even a major share of the blame of what is going on in the world, in our society, and in our country today."

Though he is right up to a point—TV cannot take full or exclusive blame—still he is apparently doing what he can in his milieu to encourage violence.

TV Guide (October 30, 1976) panned Gerber's former production "Quest," saying it "rustled up an Old West . . . where soldiers, Indians, outlaws, and lawmen are merely different kinds of cold-blooded killers, where bandits kill their victims by slowly tearing them apart, and where women are raped and tortured to insanity before their husbands' eyes."

The magazine admitted that brutality was not unknown to the Old West, but said that "generosity, optimism, and sweetness of spirit" also existed, none of which Gerber portrayed.

Producer-supplier Aaron Spelling is another of the Vive-la-Violence boys. He, along with Leonard Goldberg, is responsible for such shows as "The Rookies," "S.W.A.T.," "Charlie's Angels," and "Starsky and Hutch."

240

"Starsky and Hutch" has been called one of the most violent shows on television and "S.W.A.T." isn't far behind. Notwithstanding, Spelling feels virtuous because, he explains, "We don't use blood squibs or electronically triggered clothing jerks" when a bullet hits.

He and Goldberg are experts at chilling, suggestive violence. *TV Guide* (November 27, 1976) described a couple of episodes: "Fade in. Sinister figure . . . lurks in dark, deserted place. Cut to innocent victim approaching. Figure leaps out, maniacally grinning, knife raised to strike. Cut away to expression on victim's face—or to squalling cat whose tail has been stepped on—or to squealing tires . . . leaving the victim's fate to the viewer's imagination."

Another episode: "A stripper . . . is caught making a phone call. . . . The bad guys figure she is informing. At the fadeout, the heavy says to his henchman, 'See that she will never be able to make the same mistake again.'" The viewer, used to TV horrors, wonders if she will have her tongue torn out, her dialing finger chopped off, or just be killed with a nice neat bullet through the head.

Spelling said, "You can't do a show without threats."

He produces so many TV shows that it is probably hard for him to remember his past work; or more likely he figures that the public won't remember. At any rate, he used the same plot in two different shows, "Charlie's Angels" and the now-defunct "Mod Squad." Of course this happens fairly often on TV, and probably Spelling is no more guilty than others.

His greatest success in the 1976–77 season was "Charlie's Angels." In its first week on the air, it found a niche among the top ten of the Nielsen's. What's more, it edged higher as the weeks passed. According to *Time* (November 22, 1976), mail for the Angels runs to at least 18,000 pieces a week. Commercial spots on the show sell for $100,000 a minute.

Describing how the show was created, Goldberg said that the action-adventure shows featured gruff types like Columbo and Baretta. The thought occurred: "Why not inject some really stunning beauty into the genre and see what happens?"

By "stunning beauty" he meant sex, for he added, "We love to get [the Angels] wet, because they look so good in clinging clothes."

241

Tripping Up the Censor

How do producers and scripters get by the no-no men, the censors? (These behind-screen people need a word too.)

Maybe the answer is that although there are still censors employed today in the sense of being on the payroll, they are not employed in the sense of doing any work. Or maybe there is so much work to do that they cannot possibly tackle all of it. The *Village Voice* (October 25, 1976) said that NBC's head censor and his 27 assistants have to read 2,500 scripts and screen 250 movies and 45,000 commercials each year!

Too, scripters find ways to counter the censors. The procedure is like building up an immunity to a germ.

Milt Josefsberg, producer-writer-script consultant on "All in the Family," wrote in *Variety* (January 5, 1977) about the *modus operandi* that scripters used in the bygone and more innocent age of radio and with milder types of salacious action and speech. Surely, today's scripters employ the same or very similar tricks—that is, if any censor is bold enough in the late 1970s to object to material of any kind.

First of all, Josefsberg intimated that some censors are too guileless or too slow to pick up double meanings or suggestive byplay. (Today, especially, it takes an ultra-alert person to catch them *all*.) In one show, Jack Benny was portrayed as a college student. He was to talk about the "campus queen," a shapely lass built with the generous dimensions of a Mae West, and his line was, "Then *she* walked in wearing 17 fraternity pins—no sweater, just pins."

The censor objected to the line because it was suggestive; 17 pins would leave a lot of frontage exposed. To cover her, he opined, she would need 350 pins.

That censor should have listened to NBC censor Herminio Traviesas when he said, "I've gotta think dirty."

Anyway, when Benny used the 350 number, Josefsberg said, "It got the biggest, dirtiest laugh of the year." The audience evidently figured he chose the large number of pins just to call attention to the girl's big bosom.

Josefsberg told of other ways to outwit the censor. He and his confreres would write a suggestive line, which they figured might draw censor fire, and hold it in abeyance; then they would present a still more suggestive line. After the censor had exploded over the latter, and after they had argued for its use, they then trotted out the first line, which was the one they had wanted from the beginning. By comparison it didn't seem so bad, and usually the censor "compromised" and agreed to allow it.

Danny Arnold, creator and producer of "Barney Miller" and its spinoff "Fish," said that in dealing with the Standards and Practices Bureau (which is the networks' designation for their censorship offices) it is largely a matter of "swapping." The censor says, "Take this out, and you can keep this."

A while back Arnold had to fight the censors to be able to put both streetwalkers and gays into "Barney Miller." Today there are few such fights, as Josefsberg would confirm.

Returning to Josefsberg's article, we might mention an experience he had while writing an episode (in collaboration with Mort Lachman) for "All in the Family." In the episode Archie is to have an operation. While he, with wife Edith, is sitting in the hospital lounge waiting to be admitted, Edith chatters away nervously. To shut her up, Archie hands her a magazine from a pile on one of the tables. He doesn't realize, though the camera makes sure that viewers do, that it is a copy of *Playgirl*. The expression on Edith's face leaves no doubt that she opens it to the centerfold and the male nude. She nudges Archie, but thinking she wants more conversation, he mumbles, "Read, read."

She goes back to the nude and examines it carefully from every angle, while the camera takes close-ups, being sure to catch the least change in her expression—and in Archie's, especially when, a few seconds later, he cocks an eye in Edith's direction and does a double take.

The censor?

Today that kind of thing is not censorable. Josefsberg explained that the "only stipulation was that we get permission from *Playgirl*."

So much worse goes onto the tube, but probably there is a point at which censors do step in. The *Village Voice* (October 25, 1976) declared, "You may not copulate on daytime television [though there are exceptions] . . . but you may prattle incessantly of incest, rape, bestiality, or necrophilia."

At night, standards are relaxed somewhat. The bedroom scene in "Dawn: The Portrait of a Teenage Runaway" was shot through gauze so that the scene was blurred and shadowy. That was enough to satisfy the censor.

A censor's lot, like that of the policemen in *The Pirates of*

243

Penzance, "is not a happy one." He has few guidelines to follow. NBC puts out a booklet, "NBC Broadcast Standards for Television," and the National Association of Broadcasters has a booklet called "The Television Code," but the wording is loose. The censor must interpret directives like, "Speech should be consistent with the standards that prevail throughout a substantial portion of the television audience," and, "Obscene, indecent or profane material is banned."

In this day of shifting "standards," and of the belief that whatever you feel is right, *is* right, words have lost their meaning for many people, including censors.

But enough on censors.

The Top Brass

We have not yet focused on those network executives who have the last word. Although many are men and women of outstanding ability, suffice it here to give just one example, the impresario whom *Variety* (January 5, 1977) ranked as "the best programming chief in TV history, a man whose singular dedication to his specialty will make him a hard man to beat for years to come."

That man is Fred Silverman.

The National Association of Television Program Executives gave him the 1977 Person of the Year Award.

His salary, like Barbara Walters', compares favorably with that of the president of the United States. Probably nobody at ABC begrudges him a penny. When that network hired Silverman, it was the weak sister of the trio of commercial networks. Today it is number one in top-ten ratings.

Working for ABC's president, Fred Pierce, Silverman has helped develop such favorites as "The Tony Randall Show" and "Charlie's Angels." He upped the rating of "Happy Days" when he took Fonzie, one of the gang in the show, and gave him a definitely stellar role. He authorized the 1977 eight-part TV film based on Alex Haley's book *Roots.*

Though "Roots" was a sensationalized and incendiary drama with much stomach-turning brutality, Silverman's im-

244

mense promotional campaign (which touted it as authentic history), plus the drama's superb acting and its emotion-charged scenes, won it the largest audience in TV history. No thanks to Silverman, but thanks rather to the common sense of the average black, "Roots" didn't in its initial telecast trigger race riots like those of the 1960s. Now its executive producer, David Wolper, is saying there will be a sequel. Probably Silverman will see to that; he knows how to capitalize on success. Meantime, Silverman has started a trend of running multipart films on consecutive nights.

Because Silverman is so shrewd and so hard-driving, virtually all ABC shows under his aegis do well. Among the current ones (as this book is being written) are much tamer offerings than "Roots," series like "Laverne and Shirley," "Family," and the bionics.

In the past, while Silverman was still with CBS, he had much to do with that network's successes, "Canon," "Maude," "Rhoda," "Sonny and Cher," "Phyllis," and "Tony Orlando and Dawn."

According to *Time* (November 22, 1976), he reads as many as 1,500 series proposals a season, as well as every script and every script rewrite. Furthermore, he approves every ten-second promotional spot and every newspaper ad for ABC programs. He said at the February 1977 Convention of the National Association of Television Program Executives that ABC-TV had then some 55 pilots in the works, but even with that many, he expected to bring only about four or five hours of new shows on in the 1977–78 season.

He is adept at juggling time slots and putting the right show into the right place. A mistake in this area can be costly. As NBC's Paul Klein said, "You look for little edges. It is more important where you put a show than what it is." This was proved to Tony Orlando; his show, "Tony Orlando and Dawn," went off the air, not because of demerits, but because it was slotted opposite the stiff competition of "Happy Days."

Silverman's innovative programming that aired "Roots" on consecutive nights turned out to be a stroke of genius. He has also sustained weak or new, unproven shows by scheduling them between strong long-popular shows.

This TV magnate also has an eye for spotting spinoff possibilities. From "The Six Million Dollar Man" he spun "The Bionic Woman" and "Future Cop," and he's about to follow

245

up these successes with a bionic boy. "Rhoda" he evolved from "The Mary Tyler Moore Show," "Maude" from "All in the Family," "Huggy Bear and Turkey" from "Starsky and Hutch," and there's to be a spinoff from "Welcome Back, Kotter" starring Ron Palillo. He believes that "personality is the key" to success in TV and he saw that the personalities in these spinoffs were strong enough to carry shows of their own.

Sometimes Silverman introduces a new show by using in the cast a popular character from an old show. That gets the debuting show off to a good start. In TV talk, it is known as "stunting."

He has another trick. Silverman had the insight to realize that he could ape legitimate theater, which tries its shows "on the road" before it opens them on Broadway; he gave some of his shows short runs in the regular season (not just in the summer-replacement period) before he scheduled them as continuing series. "Family" was one such show. In March 1976 he said, "Let's make just six episodes, put them on the air this season, and see what happens." By the time the schedule makers were ready for work in April, "Family" was confidently listed for the season beginning in the fall of '76.

Despite his great success, Silverman has made mistakes. "The Bill Cosby Show," "Mr. T and Tina," and "Me and the Chimp" were disasters. Then he made a mistake financially (though not in any other way) about "Mary Hartman." While he was still with CBS, Norman Lear came to him with this idea for a soap-opera farce. Silverman was interested enough to fund two pilot scripts, but when he saw them, he turned thumbs down. He thought MH2 "too weird" to attract viewers.

Aside from "Roots," his big 1976–77 success was (as it was for producer Spelling and script supervisor Wambaugh) "Charlie's Angels." His approach (if that serial is any indication) seems to be: Give the viewers something on the intellectual level of comic books, add sex, and season with violence.

Probably he would (and probably most of the other people mentioned in this chapter would) say: You can't argue with success.

True, you can't. But what is success? Success is a subjective concept, and your idea and mine may not be just money. We may call decent, intelligent, and artistic shows great successes, even if they don't always fill the coffers to overflowing.

We may tend to agree with a cartoon of "The New Neighbors." Husband and wife are watching television and the man says, "The laughter was live, but they should have canned the producer, the director, and the writers."

Chapter 20

You Can Make the Difference

What'll You Have?

Mark Twain said that everybody talks about the weather, but nobody does anything about it. Everybody talks about TV, but nobody . . . no, it is not quite fair to say nobody does anything about it. A few are trying.

Who are they? What are they doing? And what can be done? To most of us it seems that nothing *can* be done.

That is not really true. There are possibilities.

Whenever there is a problem—any problem from a leaky faucet to a nationwide general strike—many people say, "Let the government handle it."

Our Constitution guarantees freedom of speech and of the press, and the courts have ruled that the guarantee gives TV a green light to do pretty much what it wants. But if the government could restrain TV, that might be so much the worse, for it seems to smack of dictatorship.

The second alternative is that the networks censor themselves. During the Family Hour era, network officials talked glibly of "voluntary" censorship and "self-censorship," but did we get better programs?

Frothy foolishness filled a short hiatus between sexy soap operas and gory crime shows, spicy sitcoms, telefilms, etc.

However, some TV self-censorship has been effective—so far as it goes. Sporadically, affiliates in the hinterland have turned down some warped network programs. Then (although this is not censorship in the strict sense of the word) we should mention that some packagers and producers have done something positive for TV by providing substitutes for the warped stuff—decent, clean, nonviolent shows.

We need more of the same. To get it, there is a third alternative, or at least a backup to the second alternative, and that is action by the public.

The public includes you and me, to be sure, but it also includes all sorts of organizations from the churches to the smallest clubs, and it certainly includes business, which sponsors programs.

A few of these have already gotten into the act and have done good work.

Mutiny among the Affiliates

As we said, affiliates throughout the country have occasionally refused to run network products.

WITI-TV, an ABC affiliate in Milwaukee, refused "Revenge for Rape," a telefilm about a man who set out to revenge the rape of his wife and ended up killing the wrong people. The show was full of brutality and bloodletting.

"Death Wish," which had a similar plot and almost as much gore, ran into trouble too; affiliates in Pittsburgh, Hartford, Jacksonville, and San Francisco all turned it down.

CBS's corpse-strewn, blood-soaked "Helter Skelter," the reenactment of the real-life Manson murders, including the slaughter of Sharon Tate and four other people, was blacked out in Pittsburgh; San Francisco; Portland, Maine; Peoria, Illinois; and Monterey, California.

ABC's degrading "Little Ladies of the Night," the teleplay about pimps and teenage prostitutes, was dumped by KATV-TV in Little Rock, Arkansas, by WAST-TV in Albany, New York, and by KTUL-TV in Tulsa, Oklahoma, while KAAL-TV in Austin, Minnesota, delayed the broadcast for 90 minutes.

As far back as 1972 there was a notable example of affiliate mutiny. CBS had scheduled a slightly sanitized version of the X-rated movie *The Damned*. It depicted life under the Nazis and dealt at length with sexual perversion. Thirty of the usual 169 CBS late-show stations turned it down.

Here and there too a series that ordinarily affiliates carry will have one episode that they reject. A surprising number of affiliates vetoed the "Maude" abortion episode. Several affiliates also axed an episode of "Good Times" (a show that supposedly has teenage appeal) in which J.J., the young son, suspected he had contacted a venereal disease. Then, while Boston was seething with racial turmoil, an affiliate station there refused a "Welcome Back, Kotter" episode spotlighting racial tension in the school. Another Boston affiliate delivered an ultimatum: it would not air a "Police Woman" episode unless portions were deleted.

Affiliate stations in Little Rock and Tulsa demurred about the ABC film "Secrets," aired February 20, 1977. Nashville and Jacksonville turned it down cold, and Milwaukee asked permission to push it back from 8:00 to 10:30 P.M. A United Press International writer said of the film that it was "as close to a skin flick as network television ever gets." The protagonist was a nymphomaniac who slept with every willing man she met, including a blind piano tuner, a taxi driver, and a 17-year-old who was her kid sister's boyfriend.

In the fall of 1977 about 20 affiliates refused to run "Soap" while another 40 refused to run it in the scheduled time slot and postponed it until later in the evening. That was probably as close to a mutiny among the affiliates as has ever occurred.

More affiliates would turn down network products if station personnel always had enough lead time to preview a program, come to a decision, and find a suitable substitute for the time slot.

Donald McGannon, president of Westinghouse Broadcasting Co., which owns five outlets in major TV markets, petitioned the FCC to require the networks to allow prescreening of prime-time shows four weeks in advance. The FCC denied the plea.

Certainly, too, more affiliates would turn down network productions if the station managers weren't afraid of their own necks. In 1976 CBS abruptly ended a 23-year-old affiliation with Spokane's KXLY-TV because that station had replaced a number of network programs with syndicated series popular with local viewers.

From the network people's viewpoint, the incident was a good object lesson to hold up to other station managers in the hinterlands. Although the networks lack legal authority to compel affiliates to take specific programs, they have this threat of refusing to renew an affiliate's contract. A contract, by FCC rules, runs for two years, so the threat is always there, a veritable sword of Damocles. In addition, the networks have dozens of more subtle ways to punish recalcitrant affiliates. Pressures to toady to the networks are tremendous.

Naturally, the network people want to keep the affiliates in line. The affiliates may depend on the networks for high-cost shows supplied *gratis*, but the networks depend indirectly on the affiliates for the continuation of their immense revenues. To attract national advertisers, network officials must be able to show that they have so many sure outlets, representing, by Nielsen's reckoning, so many millions of people.

At present the networks are riding high. Despite their huge advertising charges, they have sold every available moment for months to come.

From the viewpoint of those of us who want better TV, it is unfortunate that the networks are so powerful, and our hats are off to those affiliates who have braved network wrath to spare us a few horrors.

In the future, affiliates may have more independence. The non-network-owned stations decided recently to join forces to combat the paucity of first-run programs by underwriting specials of their own. Calling their venture "Operation Prime-Time," they plan to dramatize Taylor Caldwell's book *Testimony of Two Men*.

TV Guide (January 29, 1977) mentioned too that the advertising agency of Ogilvy and Mather has announced plans to form a fourth network, to be called MetroNet. It plans to serialize such classics as *Wuthering Heights* and *Rebecca*. The impetus behind this move is not so much to bring viewers better programs as to secure a medium where advertising can be placed less expensively than on the present Big Three.

At the February 1977 convention of the National Associa-

251

tion of Television Executives Convention in New Orleans, Robert Wussler, president of CBS-TV, told a caucus of CBS affiliates that network dominance would drastically diminish if a fourth network succeeded in producing quality prime-time offerings.

Not Bound to Be Bad

But the present see-scape isn't all bad. Though this book has concentrated on the seamy side of television, there are many good shows—far too many to list here in one segment of one chapter. A word of thanks should be said here to packagers and producers of these shows.

Because TV can be so good, it is frustrating if not infuriating that often it is so bad. There seems to be no reason but media moronity for the inferior stuff, since many shows that do uphold a moral code play leapfrog with other listings to land among the top 20 of the Nielsen's, have tremendous staying power, or both.

Lawrence Welk brought his champagne music to television in 1955. It is still there. "Gunsmoke," the western series, was on television for about 20 years. "What's My Line?" and "Wonderful World of Disney" are hardy perennials too. In the TV industry the Disney show is known as "Death Valley" because any other show in the same time slot has a horrendous time competing with it and getting sufficient Nielsen points to stay on the air.

One of the few shows that have ever rivaled it is "I Love Lucy." That program of *innocent* bedlam lasted from October 1951 through May 1957. Then Lucy hour specials came into being. In 1967 CBS syndicated the program. By this time it had been sold to broadcasters in dozens of foreign countries and was dubbed in Italian, French, and Spanish, to name a few. Today the show is still syndicated to 51 U.S. stations and ten foreign spots.

On November 28, 1976, to celebrate the anniversary of Lucille Ball's television debut 25 years before, CBS put on a special, "CBS Salutes Lucy." But maybe the best proof of Lucy's popularity is one lone statistic: on January 19, 1953, when Lucille Ball, as Lucy, became an on-screen mother, 44 million people viewed the program. The very next day, when Dwight D. Eisenhower, an admired war hero, was inaugurated as president of the United States, 29 million people viewed the event on TV. Although it doesn't speak very well of our public spirit, it does speak well of the popularity of a clean show.

Ironically, however, it must be said the Lucille Ball show bankrolled the violent "Untouchables." It seems as though you can't win.

Of course, all of this is history. A current good show, "The Waltons," while not in a class with Lucy, is doing very nicely, thank you. The actress who mothers the Walton clan through its trials and triumphs, in the role of Olivia, is Michael Learned. She has won an Emmy for best actress in a dramatic series. "The Waltons" is a low-key saga of a rural Virginia family during the Great Depression; it underscores home life, yet it stays up there in its high Nielsen eyrie.

Almost the same can be said about "Little House on the Prairie." Then there are (or were) other popular, though clean, shows. Prominent among them are "LaVerne and Shirley," "The Captain and Tennille," and "The Mary Tyler Moore Show," which in the 1976–77 season was in its seventh year. Although MTM went off the air, it was so successful that one of its stars, Edward Asner, went on being Lou Grant in a new series simply called "Lou Grant." Confident that the untried vehicle would meet with popular approval, CBS, according to one publicity release, did an almost unprecedented thing: it bought the show without even ordering and viewing a pilot.

But to go on with other good shows, there are the "National Geographic" specials, "The Undersea World of Jacques Cousteau," "Grizzly Adams," and "Wild, Wild World of Animals."

Not to be overlooked either are the "highbrows" that rarely draw a mass audience, but whose devotees make up in enthusiasm what they lack in numbers. Who can forget Kenneth Clark's superb "Civilization" or Alistair Cooke's "America"? Then "Masterpiece Theatre" gave us such gems as the "Forsyte Saga," "Upstairs, Downstairs," and "The Pallisers." Praiseworthy too are "Great Performances," "Anyone for Tennyson?" and "The Boston Pops" with Arthur Fiedler. "Of Lands and Seas" pleases travel buffs, though admittedly it is uneven and sometimes poorly presented.

Tops with some viewers are "Firing Line," where urbane and erudite Bill Buckley never fails to hold a lively discussion with his guest; "Wall Street Week," where charming, articulate, and highly knowledgeable Louis Rukeyser leads his confreres in animated and interesting stock-market talk; and "Washington Week in Review," where members of the press provide food for thought even though some of the views they express evince the almost ubiquitous liberal bias on television.

But to return to the shows that are universally popular as well as excellent, there are clean, nonviolent films that have made it big on the ratings. *Gone with the Wind* immediately comes to mind. Though it dealt with warfare, it portrayed no gratuitous violence, no sadism or brutality, no kinky sex—and it was a super-hit. *Variety* (November 17, 1976) said it was "the highest rated" and "the most watched" film ever run on the networks (and so it was until that time). Some 110 million people saw it. The same *Variety* item mentioned the top three previous shows. Two of them were "Bob Hope Christmas Shows," 1970 and 1971. The third was NBC's "The First Fifty Years: The Big Event" (November 21, 1976). The three had one thing in common: they were all decent and delightful. The last-named show lasted not 30 minutes, 60 minutes, or two hours; preempting regular shows, it lasted a history-making four and a half hours. Imagine, four and a half hours of TV without a raunchy moment!

It can happen here. But it doesn't happen often, that's obvious. So we need the third alternative—organizations and individuals must get busy.

Many of them already have.

Onward, Christian Soldiers!

To begin with, churches and churchmen are moving. A United Methodist minister and a Roman Catholic priest in a small Minnesota town protested in late 1976 to a local station, CATV-TV, when *Shampoo* was televised on cable television. Moreover, they warned their parishioners not to see it or to expose their children to it.

In January 1977 the Southern Baptists' Christian Life Commission held regional meetings in Richmond, Virginia, Arlington, Texas, and Montgomery, Alabama, discussing TV. (Another meeting was to be held later in San Francisco.) Meantime, they selected home missionaries to "monitor TV violence and immorality" during the first week of February 1977 and to warn churchgoers about objectionable programs.

In mid-1976 the National Council of Churches asked the 205 affiliates of CBS to boycott "Death Wish" because of its "excessive violence and its antisocial message." The U.S. Catholic Conference and the American Catholic bishops joined in the plea.

As an aside, it is strange that these churchmen should have boycotted this particular violent show rather than some others. "Death Wish" was one of the few shows that have been truly sympathetic to the victim of the crime rather than to the criminal.

It is surprising too that for the most part, the churches seem more concerned about violence and "antisocial behavior" than about kinky sex, materialism, hedonism, and subtle or overt scoffing at all that is sacred and all that bears a religious or patriotic stamp.

However, there are some exceptions, some notable church-related organizations that are concerned with the *whole* mess of TV excesses. For instance, there is Catholic Views Broadcasts, Inc.; it speaks out against TV's downgrading of religion and patriotism. Its director, Fr. Kenneth Baker, has appeared on "Firing Line," "The David Susskind Show," "Lou Gordon," and ABC's "A.M. New York" to explain and uphold the traditional Catholic stands and Americanism.

At least in a few instances CVB and Morality in Media (an organization concerned mainly with obscenity) have worked together. MIM taped an antiobscenity program which CVB has helped to distribute. How widely it can be distributed depends on the funds that the organization can raise to send sample tapes to stations around the country.

Morality in Media was founded about 15 years ago by a minister, a rabbi, and a priest, and it has done yeoman work in fighting filth in *all* the media. Its current president, Rev. Morton Hill, S.J., was appointed in 1968 to the Presidential Commission on Obscenity and Pornography. Out of that appointment came the "Link-Hill Report," a document that was cited five times by the U.S. Supreme Court in the decision about obscenity in 1973.

More recent than the above organizations is Television Awareness Training (TAT). Started by churchmen of the American Lutheran Church, the Church of the Brethren, the United Methodist Church, and the New York–based Media Action Research Center (MARC), TAT takes a new approach. Instead of complaining to sponsors, to the networks, or to local stations, TAT members are turning to us, the viewers, and, in the words of one of their leaders, trying to make us "aware of the discrepancies between TV values and real-life values."

The first workshop was held at Emory University in Atlanta and men and women, mostly from the East Coast and the South, were trained to conduct, in their turn, other training sessions for the public in their home territory.

Ecumenical and Responsible

After "Soap" premiered in the fall of 1977, various religious bodies saw the value of working together. The Milwaukee-based "No Soap" coalition coordinated the work of the National Federation for Decency, the National Union of Christian Schools, Morality in Media, and Catholic and Baptist organizations. According to the November 1977 issue of *Conservative Digest,* "The campaign has been so successful that only one advertiser, Bic, appeared on all of the first three episodes, and ABC had to cut its standard rate of $75,000 per prime time 30-second spot, to $40,000 for "Soap" . . . after Anacin withdrew its sponsorship of an early episode, ABC ran the scheduled Anacin ad free because it couldn't find a replacement."

Furthermore, the efforts of the coalition were successful in forcing a rewrite of the pilot, which featured the seduction in church of a Catholic priest. This abomination was never shown in the homes of America, thanks to the coalition.

Another ecumenical group is the Inter-Faith Committee against Blasphemy. It has two targets, the movies as well as TV. This organization put on a program (which Philadelphia station WPHL-TV ran on January 24, 1977, and station WTAF-TV ran on February 8 and April 20, 1977) discussing in particular two offensive movies. Although these movies have not yet been aired on TV, they, like many other theater movies, may well be shown in the future. One, *The Passover Plot*, is based on a book by Dr. Hugh Shonfield that "proved" Jesus was an agitator, and a fraud who did not die from crucifixion, much less rise from the dead. He took a narcotic drug intending to go through a mock crucifixion to make himself seem a martyr and thus help his cause of expelling the Romans. But he had not counted on the lance thrust into his side. Even that did not kill him, however. He was taken down from the cross and temporarily put into the tomb from which he later emerged. Because of the lance wound, he did not live long (probably about 40 days) and saw few people besides his own intimate friends.

The other movie discussed was *The Many Faces of Christ*, based on a book by Jens Joergen Thorsen, in which Christ was portrayed as a homosexual.

The committee asked the public to boycott the movies and to protest any steps taken to televise them.

Besides protests, there are other means of improving TV. Some organizations have encouraged good scripts.

The Human Family Educational and Cultural Institute offers prizes to TV writers who emphasize humane values and the Judeo-Christian traditions.

This organization came into being because of the vision of three men, Ellwood Kieser, C.S.P., executive producer of a syndicated religious series called "Insight" from Paulist Productions (a company staffed by people of various denominations); James Moser, creator of "Ben Casey," "Medic," and "Slattery's People"; and John Furia, a former president of the Writers Guild of America. They obtained funding from the Lilly Endowment, and in July 1975 Fr. Kieser presented the first Humanitas Prizes on NBC's "Today Show": $25,000, $15,000, and $10,000 to writers in the 90-, 60-, and 30-minute categories.

Hazardous to Health

Many completely secular organizations are also concerned about TV. The American Medical Association declared that televised violence is an environmental hazard threatening the health of American youth.

Dr. Robert Stubblefield, psychiatrist from Connecticut, said at the 1976 AMA Convention that he had treated children who were diagnosed as schizophrenic, but whose real trouble was that they came from homes where there might be five children and seven TV sets. They had almost no interaction with those around them; the figures on the screen peopled their world. In February 1977 the AMA asked ten major corporations to stop sponsoring violent television shows.

The AMA gave a grant of $25,000 to the National Citizens Committee for Broadcasting to support its monitoring activities. This organization, headed by the zealous Nicholas Johnson, formerly of the FCC, is fighting hard for improved TV. It puts out a newsletter, *Media Watch*, giving pertinent information about various aspects of television.

Also doing effective work and publishing TV information is the National Association for Better Broadcasting. It has particularly fought horror telefilms and programs highlighting brutality and violence-just-for-kicks. In its fall 1976 brochure it mentioned having asked 24 advertisers, in its campaign in the Los Angeles area, to withdraw their sponsorship of "degenerate horror movies [shown during the] daytime and early evening hours." Fifteen of the advertisers indicated that they would withdraw their commercials from these programs. Each season the NABB puts out a rating guide for family viewing that costs $1.00.

In Chapter 11 we talked about what Action for Children's Television (ACT) is doing to lessen TV violence in kid-vid, and we mentioned too the good work of the National Parent-Teacher Association.

The Committee on Children's Television in California is promoting quality programming for children.

Unique among organizations concerned about TV is Accuracy in Media (AIM). It points out errors of commission and omission, and challenges the news media to present the facts. Professor Abraham Kalish, executive secretary of AIM, says that members have written hundreds of letters to the newspapers documenting serious errors in TV newscasts, but only a few have been printed. That means having to resort to the costly business of taking out newspaper ads.

Kalish said at a forum held at the American Heritage Center,

Searcy, Arkansas, "Only one TV network has corrected errors we pointed out, and only in one documentary." He added that the organization has therefore been forced to take cases to the FCC.

He might have complained too about the networks' shyness to debate with AIM. The New York Chapter of the Public Relations Society invited CBS News president Richard Salant to debate AIM's chairman, Reed Irvine, on bias in the media. Though Salant accepted, when it came down to the wire, he backed out.

A Bow to Business

There seems no end to organizations that are rousing themselves and questioning current TV entertainment. Business too is stirring. We have mentioned the Lilly Endowment, which funded the Humanitas Prizes for better TV scripts; the funds originally came from business, from the drug firm of Eli Lilly and Company. Other businesses have done as much or more.

Atlantic Richfield, Exxon, Polaroid, Xerox, IBM, Martin Marietta, Travelers Insurance Company, and Sperry Rand have all given money to public educational television. The Prudential Insurance Company helped underwrite the 22-part Victorian drama "The Pallisers"; Gulf Oil underwrites the "National Geographic" specials; and Alcoa underwrites the Pittsburgh Symphony broadcasts with André Previn. The Ford Foundation and the Mellon Trust have each contributed $2,000,000 to WQED-TV, Pittsburgh's community-owned public television station.

Mobil sponsored the BBC production "Ten Who Dared," the excellent series dramatizing the courage and accomplishments of nine men and one woman. Since the networks were forbidden by government regulations to take on the foreign series, the oil company arranged for it to be carried simultaneously across the country.

International Telephone and Telegraph Company provided funds to originate, produce, and distribute the children's series "Big Blue Marble." For this "distinguished service" the National Association for Better Broadcasting presented ITT with a special award, and the citation called "Big Blue Marble," "the most significant program series to be introduced in the field of entertainment for children during the past several years." BBM is aired on 115 commercial and PBS stations.

Besides encouraging good programs, business has protested bad ones. J. Walter Thompson, the world's largest advertising firm, put out a persuasive film with a message to this effect, "Let's cut out the violence. Are we barbarians that we tolerate this 'entertainment'?"

The agency has used the film as a sort of road-show, taking it cross-country and showing it to clients, advertising clubs, and institutions like the Annenberg School of Communications at the University of Pennsylvania.

As a result of the J. Walter Thompson show, Samsonite luggage stipulated that its commercials were not to be run on shows depicting gratuitous violence. Samsonite is only one of many firms that do not want ads for their products sandwiched between bullets and blood. Other companies are Procter & Gamble, Hunt-Wesson, Pfizer, Toyota, Ralston-Purina, Kraft, and General Mills.

Johnson & Johnson has withdrawn ads from as many as 24 shows, including "Kojak" and "Police Story." Bristol-Myers in the course of a year took its commercials from 19 episodes of several shows, including "Police Woman" and "Streets of San Francisco." Gillette Company refused to advertise on shows where knives, daggers, and clubs are wielded, but does not object to guns.

McDonald's, whose commercials used to appear on the gory shows, has, according to the U.S. Catholic Conference's biweekly publication, "donned sackcloth and ashes." No longer are we urged to come to McDonald's for a hamburger just after we have seen three men tortured, two women raped, and one child abused.

More recently, Eastman Kodak, General Motors Chevrolet Division, Schlitz Brewing Company, and Sears, Roebuck have all announced antiviolence advertising policies. A General Foods spokesman remarked, "A blood-and-guts environment is a terrible place to put a Jell-O commercial."

Some network people say that advertisers could be using their stated concern about violence to drive down the prices of commercials.

Besides Violence

Alas, comparatively few corporations object to their commercials appearing on the shows that degrade or exploit sex. Back in 1975, after "Born Innocent" with its perversion and rape first appeared on TV screens (it was rerun in 1977), Miracle Whip canceled $2,000,000 worth of advertising. It now restricts its commercials to news, comedies, and game shows. *Variety* (April 27, 1977) devoted a column to Bristol-Myers' stand; a company spokesman declared it wanted ads only on programs "in good taste."

A dozen major corporations, including General Foods and Colgate-Palmolive, refused to let their commercials air during the MH2 programming time in areas where it appeared in the daytime lineup. They felt that the serial was a moral hazard to children. Palmolive did advertise on MH2 in those areas where it appeared late at night.

Shortsighted Sponsors

Companies that disregard the content of shows that they sponsor are really running a risk of hurting themselves. Even Art Buchwald has joined the chorus of criticism. In one of his syndicated newspaper columns (August 8, 1977) he included three mocking, make-believe letters to sponsors of violent programs. He assured the gentlemen that he would unfailingly buy their products because he and his "entire family" enjoyed seeing: in one instance, a man buried up to his neck in sand while a "villain poured honey on his head so that ants would eat him"; in another, "someone kidnapped, mugged, or killed" every few minutes; and in a third, "blood all over the place."

If many people are as revolted by these shows as Buchwald (and they are), it does not make sense for companies to sponsor them.

Then why should any business firm have wanted to sponsor "Executive Suite," which knocked business in general?

Revlon sponsored that series until its demise in January 1977.

Or why should any business firm want to sponsor "All in the Family," which pokes fun at so many values that have made America great and have provided a climate favorable to business enterprises?

Carnation Little Friskies sponsors that series.

As Yul Brynner said in *The King and I*, "It's a puzzlement" —or it is until we remember two facts. First, the networks are enjoying a seller's market; little time is available, so it is often a matter of firms' grabbing whatever they can get. Second, television is a numbers game; or as they say in the business, advertising sells on a "cost-per-thousand-viewers' basis." To explain: the Nielsen's indicate that 30 million people look at No. 1 show, so it costs X dollars; 31 million look at No. 2 show, so it costs X-plus dollars; 32 million look at No. 3 show, so it costs X-plus-plus dollars.

In short, the advertiser of the past never bought a show; he bought an audience of so many million people. He might hardly have known whether it was a quiz show, a soap opera, a sitcom, a telefilm, or an action-adventure serial, and he could not have cared less.

Only since the deluge of criticism against TV have a few advertisers looked at show content. And since the rates went up in the fall of 1976 these men have begun too to think of the steep cost and to ask themselves: "Should we switch to outside billboards, or magazine ads, or what have you?"

The majority of advertisers still take into account audience numbers only. As in the case of "Executive Suite," the sponsor was paying for rope that could eventually hang him.

How the Ratings Work

At this point it might be a good idea to insert a word about ratings. A.C. Nielsen Co. estimates biweekly, on the basis of a small sampling of the population, the TV tastes of all the rest of us. In about 1,200 homes from coast to coast, meters that register which program is on are attached to TV sets. Each

"Nielsen family" represents about 58,000 other American families, or domiciles.

Another rating company is the ARB (American Rating Bureau), which, besides the meters, often uses random phone calls, asking people throughout the country which program they are watching at the moment.

Do the results point to the conclusion that we, the public, like the violence, the raw sex, the trash? Superficially, it would indeed seem so, and this is the standby argument of the network people. They tell us, "We only give you what you want."

Elsa Goss of the editorial board of the *Philadelphia Inquirer* does not believe that, and she protested (January 9, 1977) that TV "gives us what it wants us to want."

But most of us would probably say, "We watch the stuff only because there is nothing much else to watch." At the end of a hard day, we relax in a favorite chair, shift our minds into neutral, and look at whatever is before us on the screen. If we don't really like what we see, we still go on looking because it is distracting. The junk keeps our minds off our problems about getting out that rush order, or replacing that key employee who quit. It gives our mind a respite from the nagging worry of how to handle Junior's insubordination in using our car without permission, or his sister's infatuation with the marijuana-smoking lad next door.

The soaps are different; since they run during the day, they reach a slightly different type of audience. The networks defend themselves against the excesses in such shows by saying that they only reflect life as it is.

Well, they reflect it and distort it. Everything is larger and blacker and bolder and more immoral than is the average. The soaps reflect real life only in the way that a caricature resembles the real person. Though life may be "just one damned thing after another," the writers of soaps make it one DAMNED THING in capital letters.

"Granted, we exaggerate," say the network people. "The exaggeration helps viewers to face their own troubles." Though misery loves the company of equal misery, it prefers the company of greater misery.

For example, when we find out that our teenage daughter has been sleeping with her boyfriend and is pregnant, we are distressed, but we would be more distressed if we had not seen on TV a number of teenage girls who sleep around and one or two who had not only become pregnant but contracted a venereal disease.

Still, on balance, TV didn't help us, for it may well have been the cause of our daughter so easily consenting to go to bed with her boyfriend.

So it seems that we have gone around in a circle and come back to the point: something must be done about TV. A few TV people have done a little, and so have a few organizations and businesses.

But it isn't enough. So what next?

That question makes you and me feel like the little guy standing in front of one of those old war posters looking up at a bearded gentleman in striped red and white pants, blue jacket, and stovepipe hat. He is looking straight at us and pointing a finger our way while he says, "Uncle Sam needs YOU!"

Most of us have to admit that we have not done much to support organizations that are working for better TV, nor have we done much on our own. What can we do?

Lend a Hand

Bad shows, like bad habits, come in infinite varieties, and it is easier to chide them than to offer solutions or to do something constructive ourselves. We cannot afford to be like the man who sat complacently on the sinking Titanic saying, "Why should I worry? It's not my beat."

We look around vaguely wondering what to do, and we tell ourselves that one person's voice cannot mean much in a medium where an audience of 15 million is considered meager. (To sustain itself on prime time, a show must have at least 20 million viewers.)

That you and I might do anything constructive seems, at first glance, to be as presumptuous as thinking we can stay the sun in the sky.

Yet we are not entirely helpless. We have seen that organizations are already "doing something." (And they are meeting

264

with a little success; for instance, Robert T. Howard, president of NBC, was quoted in *Variety* (February 23, 1977) as saying that he is "taking positive and practical steps to reduce the number" of violent programs on his network.) Organizations would meet with more success if we the people would support them and work with them.*

As Pat Boone said on the program about blasphemy in "entertainment," sometimes we ask, "Why don't 'they' do something?" But, he added " 'They' can't do anything. If anything is to be done, you and I must do it." "They" is the composite of you and me.

The first thing we can do, it would seem, is to donate our services or our cash, or both, to the organizations already at work.

Then we can act, directly. We can write letters or make phone calls to the networks, to the local stations, and to the sponsors.

If many people praise a good show, the TV tycoons are likely to present more of the same genre; if many people object to a bad show, these same TV tycoons are likely to swing the ax.

When MH2 first went on the air, a local station in Richmond, Virginia canceled the series after only six episodes because so many viewers wrote or called the station voicing disgust and indignation. And in Little Rock, Arkansas, thousands of petitions, letters, and phone calls objecting to the show's obscenity and vulgarity ran it off the air.

Virtually the same thing happened with "Hot L Baltimore," which premiered back in 1975. The howls of horror caused the series to be canceled in short order.

When "Born Innocent" appeared, it provoked a rash of letters and phone calls to the networks, and letters to the editor. According to *Time* (August 25, 1975), the furor was an important factor in the networks' agreeing "voluntarily" to police themselves by establishing the Family Hour.

The networks, and even the affiliates, do not always gauge the public's taste correctly. In November 1976 ABC's Milwaukee affiliate refused to air the gory and sexy "Revenge for Rape." Afterward, the station manager expected letters and calls of complaint because cancellation of a show usually

* In the appendix to this book is a list of some of the organizations we can support, or can write to in order to complain about or commend a program.

evoked them. They didn't come. On the contrary, in the first five days after the cancellation 200 letters of commendation arrived.

Taking two aspirin won't make a bad show go away, but two lines per postcard, written by enough people, very well might. In fact, a viewer did write his local station using less than one line. He inelegantly but eloquently said, "Mary Hartman stinks."

And let's not forget that if we write a regular letter to the station manager, we can get extra mileage from it if we make carbon copies to send to the network home office, the sponsor, the local newspapers, and perhaps to the FCC and *TV Guide*.

Remember: the Sunday supplements of metropolitan newspapers carry a TV section and in it is usually a letters column. The local station managers no doubt read these letters carefully.

Who Picks Up the Tab?

Letters to sponsors are probably as important as those to the networks, or to the local station. Sponsors pay the bills.

When in 1927 Philo T. Farnsworth, working in a darkened room to send images without wires, used a dollar sign as a test pattern, he didn't know how appropriate that sign was. TV runs on dollars as a car runs on gas. If sponsors withdrew enough advertising, imagine what would happen. We have noted that some corporations have of late refused to advertise on violent shows. Maybe the day will come when they will turn thumbs down on shows that are antireligious, anti-American, and full of sick sex. In the final analysis the sponsors' word is law to the TV moguls.

An Illinois woman, Ethel Daccardo, has studied the question, What can I do? She declared that if only 25 or 30 people out of the 30 or more million viewers were to write a sponsor, the impact would be tremendous. Since advertisers buy an audience of a certain size, and give no thought to the show itself, they would find letters commenting on the entertainment revealing and probably upsetting.

If the letter writer was a stockholder in the company and said so in the letter, perhaps that would carry a bit more weight. But stockholder or no, Mrs. Daccardo said that such letters would send the president of a company into a huddle with the board of directors. If the letters said the show was disgraceful and disgusting, the sponsor might exclaim, "We can't advertise in a spot where we could lose customers rather than gain them."

When the networks saw a trickle of advertising escaping them for such a reason, they might ask, "What can we do to revamp the show? Or what can we substitute for it?"

If, on the other hand, the sponsor had letters telling him how great the show was, he would go to the networks and make sure that his product continued to be advertised in the same program, while the network official, if he had requests for advertisements in a specific program, would think of extending it, or of finding a similar show for the next season.

Sponsors are on our side. Not that they necessarily like or dislike the same shows that we do, but because they are bound to please us. If we are displeased, we may fail to buy products lauded in their commercials.

Incidentally, there are several ways to get the addresses of sponsors. A call to the local station or to the public library's research department may do it. Or there is a $2.00 booklet that supplies names and addresses of all network advertisers. It is put out by:

> National Television Advertisers
> 3245 Wisconsin Avenue
> Berwyn, Illinois 60402

For $5.95 a more complete book is available, *The Television Sponsors Directory*. It contains names of products cross-referenced with names of manufacturers and subsidiaries. To order it, write:

> Everglades Publishing Co.
> P.O. Drawer Q
> Everglades, Florida 33929

Double Strength

Complaining to a sponsor takes on added strength if it is reinforced with a threat not to buy his merchandise unless he gives assurance that he will find other ways to advertise. Obviously, the threat has to be carried out, so that the sponsor feels pocketbook pain. Dr. F. J. Ingelfinger, editor of the *New England Journal of Medicine,* has asked parents to boycott products associated with violence in kid-vid.

Unfortunately for the protesting viewer, there are often many advertisers for one program, and it would be a persistent person indeed who would write to them all. Most of us are prone to take the course of least persistence.

Unfortunately too, the viewer is not always aware of "hidden" sponsors. For example, when a Philadelphia affiliate ran MH2, commercials appeared for: Cottonelle, Baggies, Ajax, Anacin, Noxzema, Palmolive Cold Power, and others. Yet numerous as these are, they were not the only MH2 advertisers. If on Mary Hartman's kitchen table there were a box of cereal and a can of tomatoes, the manufacturer of the cereal and the canner of the tomatoes had given "consideration" in one form or another (not necessarily money) to the production company to use their product. They knew that millions of viewers would see it and subconsciously register a picture. Then the next time these viewers would go to the supermarket they would spot on the shelves a familiar-looking product and, all things being equal, buy it rather than something they had never seen before, or had seen less often.

If sight plays a part, so does hearing. In one episode Mary Hartman, in her usual way of jumping to confusions, asked if the raisins in the tiny boxes of *Sun Maid* brand had the same vitamin strength as those in the larger boxes. Another time she said to the men at the plant, "Bring in your overalls and I'll *Scotch Guard* them for you." In an episode of "All in the Family" a *Ramada Inn* was mentioned.

Speaking of an inn recalls the section of Chapter 8 of this book that noted how a newscast described an X-rated hotel in the Pocono Mountains. Did money, or any other "consideration," change hands between the hotel owner and the production unit? A legitimate question.

When we were talking about censors, we mentioned the

man who took as his slogan, "You gotta think dirty." To spot all the advertisers, "You gotta think devious," and look for hidden commercials. Like the faces drawn into a puzzle, they may not be immediately perceptible.

Two-Way Street

Protesting objectionable programs is not the only avenue of action. Occasionally we have a chance to ask for a special program. Here's an example: The American Security Council Education Foundation, in cooperation with the AFL–CIO, has produced a documentary for TV on national defense titled "The Price of Peace and Freedom."* Any station may have the documentary *gratis* whether it is run on a sustaining or a sponsored basis. ASCEF has a leaflet about the film, which anybody can obtain by writing to:

> American Security Council
> Education Foundation
> Boston, Virginia 22713

Those of us who believe that the price of peace is preparedness and who realize that the news we get is inadequate will want to take or mail this leaflet to the managers of local stations, requesting that the film be shown in our area.

The Ultimate Weapon

Besides complaints, protests, and offering substitute programs, we can still make the ultimate move: turning off our sets.

What? That's utterly unrealistic!

Maybe it is unrealistic and perhaps undesirable too—on a

---

* CBS's special "Who's Ahead? The Debate over Defense" (April 20, 1977) used several minutes of footage from this documentary.

permanent basis. But if enough people did it sporadically, the network people would get such a bad case of jitters they would gladly supply better fare.

A Methodist minister, Rev. Donald Wildmon of Southaven, Mississippi, twice launched what he called "Turn Off Television Week" with some success. Between February 27 and March 5, 1977, and between July 24 and July 30, 1977, he asked people to turn the dial to Off.

He publicized his suggestion by sending news releases to papers throughout the country, and by radio when time was given to him *gratis* "in the public interest."

When this writer, inspired by an article in the *Chicago Tribune* (March 8, 1977), phoned him, he said, "For the first effort we spent less than $500 altogether, but I had calls from over 200 newspapers and radio stations asking me what was going on. In the Memphis area, the three network affiliates had around 1,400 calls apiece in the first eight hours of the boycott. In San Jose, California about 800 women belonging to an organization called Build the Earth went from door to door asking for cooperation in the Turn Off. I heard from church groups, synagogues, and civic groups in Dallas, Milwaukee, San Francisco, towns in Louisiana and the Carolinas, and . . . well, I heard from some thousands of groups. Conservatively, I'd reckon a couple of million sets went off that week."

Although "a couple of million" is only a handful as the networks count audiences, no movement in the history of the world has started out with tens of millions. Who can say what will happen as time goes on?

Mr. Wildmon declares that he has just begun to fight. He is organizing what he calls the "National Federation for Decency." Because NBC is presently lowest in the ratings and hence the most vulnerable, Wildmon said he gave that network an ultimatum: Tone down the sex and the violence or we'll call for a boycott of one or more of your sponsors. He asked too that between April 4 and 15, 1977, viewers opposed to raw sex and violence join "Let Your Light Shine" and turn on their headlights for daytime driving to signify their feelings.

Surely all this is a beginning, and a great deal can happen if you and I back Mr. Wildmon's ideas and the other ideas discussed here. It would seem that we cannot lose. We are going to get exactly what we want—if we want it enough to do something.

After all, we are not wedded to TV as is, for better or for worse, since we ourselves, not circumstances, can determine the better or the worse.

E. B. White, one of the pioneers of the TV industry, said years ago that television was going to be a test of our modern world. It has, he said, opened up vistas "beyond the range of our ordinary vision," and so we shall discover either a "new and unbearable disturbance" or "a saving radiance in the sky. We shall stand or fall by television—of that I am quite sure."

Appendix

Some Useful Addresses

ABC
1330 Avenue of the Americas
New York, New York 10019

Accuracy in Media Inc.
777 14th Street, N.W.
Washington, D.C. 20005

Action for Children's Television
(ACT)
46 Austin Street
Newtonville, Massachusetts
02160
(Membership $15; quarterly
newsletter $5)

American Council for
BetterBroadcasting
120 East Wilson Street
Madison, Wisconsin 53703

Cable TV Information Center
2100 M Street, N.W.
Washington, D.C.

Catholic League for Religious
and Civil Rights
1100 West Wells Street
Milwaukee, Wisconsin 53233

Catholic Views Broadcasts
86 Riverside Drive
New York, New York 10024

CBS
51 West 52nd Street
New York, New York 10019

Citizens Communications
Center
1914 Suderland Place
Washington, D.C. 20036

Committee on Children's
Television
1511 Masonic Avenue
San Francisco, California 94117

Federal Communications
Commission (FCC)
1919 M Street, N.W.
Washington, D.C. 20554

Firing Line
Post Office Box 5966
Columbia, South Carolina 29250
(Transcripts of broadcasts, $1.00
each)

House Interstate and Foreign
Commerce Committee
Subcommittee on
Communications
House Office Building
Washington, D.C. 20515

Inter-Faith Committee against
Blasphemy
Post Office Box 90
Glendale, California 91209

Marin Motion Picture and
Television Council
Post Office Box 1021
San Rafael, California 94902

Media Watch
1028 Connecticut Avenue, N.W.
Washington, D.C. 20036

Morality in Media
487 Park Avenue
New York, New York 10022

National Association for Better
Broadcasting
Post Office Box 130
Topanga, California 90290
(Publishes *Annual Guide for
Family Viewing*)

National Citizens Committee for
Broadcasting

1346 Connecticut Avenue, N.W.
Washington, D.C. 20036

National Federation for
Decency
Post Office Box 1398
Tupelo, Mississippi 38801

National Television Advertisers
3245 Wisconsin Avenue
Berwyn, Illinois 60402

NBC
RCA Building
30 Rockefeller Plaza
New York, New York 10020

PBS
482 L'Enfant Plaza, S.W.
Washington, D.C. 20024

People for Quality in
Broadcasting
Post Office Box 66
Bellevue, Washington 98009

Pittsburgh Conference on
Children's Television
55 Chapel Ridge Place
Pittsburgh, Pennsylvania 15238

Radio Television Council of
Greater Cleveland
Post Office Box 5254
Cleveland, Ohio 44101

Senate Commerce Committee
Subcommittee on
Communications
Senate Office Building
Washington, D.C. 20510

TV Guide
Triangle Publications Inc.
Post Office Box 400
Radnor, Pennsylvania 19088
(Yearly subscription $12.00;
contains valuable information
about forthcoming programs)

Index

276

277

278